ART IN MODERN BALLET

ART
in modern
Ballet

By George Amberg

PANTHEON

MANUFACTURED IN U.S.A.

TEXT PRINTED BY L. F. WHITE CO., NEW YORK

PLATES BY PHOTOGRAVURE & COLOR CO., NEW YORK

BOUND BY RUSSELL-RUTTER CO., NEW YORK

DESIGNED BY JACQUES SCHIFFRIN

COPYRIGHT 1946 BY PANTHEON BOOKS INC.

41 WASHINGTON SQUARE, NEW YORK

CONTENTS

LIST OF PLATES

52 BRAQUE: Les Fâcheux, 1924
Costume for First Masque (Front)
Courtesy Editions des Quatre Chemins

53 BRAQUE: Les Fâcheux, 1924
Costume for Second Masque
Courtesy Editions des Quatre Chemins

54 BRAQUE: Les Fâcheux, 1924
Costume for L'Elégant
Courtesy Editions des Quatre Chemins

55 BRAQUE: Les Fâcheux, 1924
Design for Setting
Courtesy Editions des Quatre Chemins

56 MATISSE: Le Chant du Rossignol, 1920
Sketch for Curtain
Wadsworth Atheneum

57 DERAIN: Fastes, 1933
Design for Setting
Courtesy "Formes"

58 DERAIN: Fastes, 1933
Sketch for Roman Masks
Courtesy "Formes"

59 DERAIN: La Boutique Fantasque, 1919
Design for Setting
Courtesy Archives Internationales de la Danse

60 BÉRARD: Mozartiana, 1933
Sketch for Setting with Figures
Collection Mrs. Philip R. Claflin

61 BÉRARD: Symphonie Fantastique, 1936
Design for Detail for Setting: Scene I
Collection Museum of Modern Art

62 BÉRARD: Symphonie Fantastique, 1936
Costume for Ghoul
Courtesy Victor Hugo Gallery, New York

63 BÉRARD: Symphonie Fantastique, 1936
Costume for The Beloved
Collection John Carr Doughty

64 BÉRARD: Symphonie Fantastique, 1936
Costume for Young Musician
Collection David Mann

65 BÉRARD: Costume for Harlequin, 1931
Wadsworth Atheneum

66 BÉRARD: Les Elfes, 1924
Design for Costume
Collection Ballet Russe de Monte Carlo

67 BÉRARD: Les Elfes, 1924
Costumes for Stag and Doe
Collection Ballet Russe de Monte Carlo

68 LAURENCIN: Les Biches, 1924
Sketch for Curtain
Courtesy Editions des Quatre Chemins

69 LAURENCIN: Les Biches, 1924
Sketch for Costume
Courtesy Editions des Quatre Chemins

70 LAURENCIN: Les Biches, 1924
Sketch for Costume
Wadsworth Atheneum

71 LAURENCIN: Les Biches, 1924
Design for Curtain
Courtesy Editions des Quatre Chemins

72 VERTÈS: Bluebeard, 1941
Costume for Bluebeard
Collection Madame Karinska

73 VERTÈS: Bluebeard, 1941
Costumes for Gypsies
Owned by the Artist

74 VERTÈS: Brahms Variations, 1944
Costume for Warrior
Collection George Lurcy

75 VERTÈS: Brahms Variations, 1944
Costume for Man
Collection Museum of Modern Art

76 VERTÈS: Bluebeard, 1941
Design for Setting: Scene III
Owned by the Artist

77 BAUCHANT: Apollon Musagète, 1928
Design for Curtain: Birth of Apollo
Courtesy Albright Art Gallery, Buffalo

78 BAUCHANT: Apollon Musagète, 1928
Design for Setting Champs Elysées
Wadsworth Atheneum

79 DE CHIRICO: Le Bal, 1929
Design for Setting
Wadsworth Atheneum

80 DE CHIRICO: Le Bal, 1929
Costume for Man
Wadsworth Atheneum

81 DE CHIRICO: Le Bal, 1929
Costume for Woman
Wadsworth Atheneum

82 DE CHIRICO: Les Bacchantes, 1937
Costume for Apollo
Courtesy Victor Hugo Gallery, New York

83 DE CHIRICO: Prothée, 1938
Design for Costume
Courtesy Victor Hugo Gallery, New York

11

116 BASALDUA: La Boîte à Joujoux, 1936
Design for Setting
Owned by the Artist

117 BASALDUA: Alleluia, 1936
Design for Setting
Owned by the Artist

118 MÉRIDA: Cinco Dancas en Ritmo Bulgaro, 1945
Costume for Women Dancers
Owned by the Artist

119 MÉRIDA: Cinco Dancas en Ritmo Bulgaro, 1945
Costume for Male Dancers
Owned by the Artist

120 MÉRIDA: Cinco Dancas en Ritmo Bulgaro, 1945
Design for Setting
Owned by the Artist

121 MÉRIDA: Circo Orrin, 1945
Costume for Artiste
Owned by the Artist

122 MÉRIDA: Circo Orrin, 1945
Costume for Dog
Owned by the Artist

123 MÉRIDA: Circo Orrin, 1945
Design for Setting
Owned by the Artist

124 RIVERA: H.P., 1932
Costume for Banana
Collection Museum of Modern Art

125 RIVERA: H.P., 1932
Costume for Tobacco
Collection Museum of Modern Art

126 RIVERA: H.P., 1932
Costume for Man
Collection Museum of Modern Art

127 OROZCO: Pausa, 1945
Design for Curtain
Owned by the Artist

128 OROZCO: Umbral, 1943
Design for Costumes
Owned by the Artist

129 OROZCO: Pausa, 1945
Design for Setting
Owned by the Artist

130 OROZCO: Umbral, 1943
Design for Costumes
Owned by the Artist

131 DE DIEGO: Sonatas Españolas, 1945
Costume for Man
Courtesy Ballet Waldeen

132 DE DIEGO: Sonatas Españolas, 1945
Costume for Woman
Courtesy Ballet Waldeen

133 DE DIEGO: Sonatas Españolas, 1945
Sketch for Three-Dimensional Setting
Courtesy Ballet Waldeen

134 JUNYER: La Nuit de la St. Jean, 1939
Costumes for Satyrs and Centaurs
Owned by the Artist

135 JUNYER: The Cuckold's Fair, 1943
Design for Setting
Owned by the Artist

136 JUNYER: La Nuit de la St. Jean, 1939
Costumes for Devils
Owned by the Artist

137 JUNYER: The Cuckold's Fair, 1943
Costumes for Boy and Girl
Owned by the Artist

138 DALI: Mad Tristan, 1944
Painting for Front Curtain
Courtesy Bignou Gallery, New York

139 DALI: Mad Tristan, 1944
Costume for Boat
Collection Countess Pecci-Blunt

140 DALI: Romeo and Juliet, 1942
Painting for Setting: Act I
Collection Marquis George de Cuevas

141 DALI: Romeo and Juliet, 1942
Painting for Setting: Act II
Collection Marquis George de Cuevas

142 DALI: Cafè de Chinitas, 1943
Painting for Front Curtain
Collection Marquis George de Cuevas

143 DALI: Cafè de Chinitas, 1943
Painting for Backdrop
Collection Marquis George de Cuevas

144 DALI: Sentimental Colloquy, 1944
Painting for Backdrop
Courtesy Bignou Gallery, New York

145 DALI: Sentimental Colloquy, 1944
Design for Costume
Courtesy Victor Hugo Gallery, New York

146 DALI: Sentimental Colloquy, 1944
Design for Costume
Courtesy Victor Hugo Gallery, New York

147 DALI: Mysteria, 1942
Transformation Costumes for Angel and Demon
Collection Dr. Harry Lepman

148 DALI: Mysteria, 1942
Drawings for Costumes
Collection Mr. and Mrs. Julius Fleischmann

149 DALI: Mysteria, 1942
Preliminary Study
Collection Mr. and Mrs. Julius Fleischmann

150 SCHLEMMER: The Triadic Ballet, 1922
Costume Projects
Courtesy Walter G. Hendrich

151 HEYTHUM: Bal des Mannequins, 1933
Design for Setting and Costumes
Owned by the Artist

152 SELIGMANN: The Golden Fleece, 1941
Costume for Wind
Owned by the Artist

153 SELIGMANN: The Golden Fleece, 1941
Costume for Phenix
Owned by the Artist

154 AYRTON: Le Festin de l'Araignée, 1944
Costume for Praying Mantis
Collection John Carr Doughty

155 AYRTON: Le Festin de l'Araignée, 1944
Costume for Spider
Collection John Carr Doughty

156 HECKROTH: Pandora, 1944
Costumes for Monsters
Courtesy Jooss Ballet

157 HECKROTH: Pandora, 1944
Costume for Monster
Courtesy Jooss Ballet

158 HECKROTH: A Spring Tale, 1939
Costume for Storm Witch
Courtesy Jooss Ballet

159 HECKROTH: A Spring Tale, 1939
Costume for The Wondrous Hermit
Courtesy Jooss Ballet

160 HURRY: Hamlet, 1942
Design for Setting
Collection Robert Helpmann

161 HURRY: Hamlet, 1942
Costume for Ophelia
Collection Robert Helpmann

162 HURRY: Hamlet, 1942
Costume for Hamlet
Collection Robert Helpmann

163 HURRY: Le Lac des Cygnes, 1943
Costumes for the Mazurka
Courtesy Sadler's Wells Ballet

164 HURRY: Le Lac des Cygnes, 1943
Costumes for Czardas
Courtesy Sadler's Wells Ballet

165 PIPER: The Quest, 1943
Costume for Avarice
Courtesy Sadler's Wells Ballet

166 PIPER: The Quest, 1943
Costume for Envy
Courtesy Sadler's Wells Ballet

167 PIPER: The Quest, 1943
Design for Setting: Scene V
Courtesy Sadler's Wells Ballet

168 PIPER: The Quest, 1943
Design for Setting: Scene III
Courtesy Sadler's Wells Ballet

169 FURSE: The Prospect Before Us, 1940
Design for Setting: The Stage of the Pantheon
Collection John Carr Doughty

170 FURSE: The Prospect Before Us, 1940
Design for Setting: The Stage of the King's Theatre
Collection John Carr Doughty

171 FURSE: The Prospect Before Us, 1940
Costume for M. Didelot
Collection John Carr Doughty

172 FURSE: The Prospect Before Us, 1940
Costume for A Dancer
Collection John Carr Doughty

173 BOUCHÊNE: L'Enfant Prodigue, 1931
Costume for the Son as the King
Courtesy Jooss Ballet

174 BOUCHÊNE: L'Enfant Prodigue, 1931
Costume for the Son
Courtesy Jooss Ballet

175 BURRA: Miracle in the Gorbals, 1944
Design for Curtain
Owned by the Artist

176 BURRA: Miracle in the Gorbals, 1944
Design for Setting: The Gorbals
Owned by the Artist

177 WILSON: Un Songe, 1945
Design for Setting
Courtesy Jooss Ballet

178 WHISTLER: The Rake's Progress, 1935
Design for Front Curtain (1942)
Courtesy Sadler's Wells Ballet

179 NASH: The Truth about the Russian Dancers, 1920
Costume for Madame Karsavina
Collection John Carr Doughty

180 NASH: The Truth about the Russian Dancers, 1920
Costume for Golfer
Collection John Carr Doughty

181 BENOIS, NADIA: Lady into Fox, 1939
Costume for Silvia as Fox
Collection John Carr Doughty

182 BENOIS, NADIA: Lady into Fox, 1939
Costume for Silvia
Collection John Carr Doughty

183 HOWARD: Carnival of Animals, 1943
Costume for Cuckoo
Owned by the Artist

184 HOWARD: Carnival of Animals, 1943
Costume for Aquarium
Owned by the Artist

185 FEDOROVITCH: Dante Sonata, 1940
Costume for Children of Darkness (Man)
Collection John Carr Doughty

186 FEDOROVITCH: Dante Sonata, 1940
Costume for Children of Darkness (Woman)
Collection John Carr Doughty

187 JONES: Skyscrapers, 1920
Design for Setting
Collection Benjamin Webster

188 JONES: Til Eulenspiegel, 1916
Costume Sketch for Professors
Owned by the Artist

189 BREININ: Undertow, 1945
Design for Backdrop: Act II
Courtesy Downtown Gallery, New York

190 BREININ: Undertow, 1945
Design for Backdrop: Act I
Courtesy Downtown Gallery, New York

191 MIELZINER: Pillar of Fire, 1942
Design for Setting
Owned by the Artist

192 WATKINS: Transcendence, 1934
Costumes for Sylphides
Collection Museum of Modern Art

193 WATKINS: Transcendence, 1934
Costume for Blind Girl
Collection Museum of Modern Art

194 DE MOLAS: Gala Performance, 1941
Costume for Man
Courtesy Captain Richard Pleasant

195 DE MOLAS: Gala Performance, 1941
Costume for Girl
Courtesy Captain Richard Pleasant

196 DE MOLAS: Capriccioso, 1940
Design for Setting
Courtesy Captain Richard Pleasant

197 DE MOLAS: Black Ritual, 1940
Design for Setting: Act II
Courtesy Captain Richard Pleasant

198 SMITH: Fancy Free, 1944
Design for Three-Dimensional Setting
Courtesy Bonestell Gallery, New York

199 SMITH: Saratoga, 1941
Design for Setting
Owned by the Artist

200 SMITH: Rodeo, 1942
Design for Three-Dimensional Setting: Act II
Collection Ballet Russe de Monte Carlo

201 SMITH: Rodeo, 1942
Design for Backdrop: Act II
Collection Ballet Russe de Monte Carlo

202 SMITH: Rodeo, 1942
Design for Backdrop: Act I
Collection Ballet Russe de Monte Carlo

INTRODUCTION

I

IN 1909, Serge de Diaghilev organized the Ballet Russe in Paris. This may be considered a key sentence for our investigation. The year marks accurately the beginning of modern design for the ballet. At this time Paris afforded the artistic climate, the potential talent and the receptive audience for the development of so daring a venture as a modern ballet. For since its inception the Ballet Russe has been a symbol of art in progress, increasingly so when it turned from imported Russian designers to the foremost easel painters of the School of Paris. Eventually the term *Ballet Russe* became both fashionable and explicit, until it was identified with classic theatrical dancing par excellence. Diaghilev, an inspired and inspiring man, though not a creative artist himself, set definite standards for ballet in Western Europe and henceforth dominated the ballet stage with absolute authority until his early death in 1929. In those two decades ballet design had become firmly and definitely established as a legitimate category of the arts, and since it attracted many artists of stature, it assumed a lasting significance.

The scenic practice thus brilliantly demonstrated was sound in essence and intentions, though dubious in its ultimate consequences. Originally Diaghilev conceived the coincident performance of dance, music, and painting, which is ballet, not as the chance sum of separate unequal parts, but as an indivisible, *collective whole*. This interpretation, for all its apparent novelty, was not a true innovation nor a radical reform. If removed from specific indications of style and taste, which date the visual evidence as a product of our century's first quarter, Diaghilev's basic conception emerges as the classic formula of choreographic, musical and plastic integration. Throughout several centuries this very principle had been an esthetic demand of the foremost ballet theorists and reformers. It is a timeless ideal. Diaghilev resumed and perfected the sound principle and broke with the anemic tradition of mediocrity as preserved and practiced in the contemporary ballet scene. For this, precisely, was the situation of the international ballet theatre at the time the Ballet Russe began to perform: The conservative Imperial Russian Ballet contributed a highly perfected dance practice which was, however, unknown outside Moscow and St. Petersburg. The customary ballet music had hardly more specific relevance or artistic value than the accompaniment of the silent films. Settings and costumes were lacking entirely in imagination and distinction; indeed no example illustrates the change between "before and after" more conclusively than a comparison between the Ballet Russe designers and their immediate predecessors.

At the time of Diaghilev's arrival, ballet had degenerated from the prodigal spectacles of royal and aristocratic sovereigns into a bourgeois institution which subsisted merely on the strength of thoughtless tolerance. There was neither need nor room for the inspired images of genuine artists; not even in Paris, the capital of the arts. The Paris Opera, owing to its distinguished record of two-and-one-half centuries of prominence in the lyric theatre and the dance, was still the European center of what was left of ballet in 1909. As the official company of the famous "Académie de Musique et de Danse" it was sadly representative, indeed, of the generally lamentable state of the ballet. Surrounded by a Chinese wall of conventions it had lost all contact with the art, the music and the social developments of its time. No regenerative spirit was left within and no forceful criticism or support was offered from without to overcome the inertia of habit. This situation accounts for the fact that Bakst's "Scheherazade" and its now faded oriental trimmings once scandalized one half of the public and wildly excited the other. Twenty-five years thence it is easy to realize that this impact on the audience was largely due to an effect of contrast and surprise. Such unprecedented color, splendor and daring were a new experience for a whole generation of spectators and precipitated a reaction against the wonted monotony of scenic clichés and the poverty of visual imagination. The painter's sudden rise to prominence and fame in the Ballet Russe was by no means an historically unique occurrence; it was in keeping with the noblest theatrical tradition. For ballet is theatre, "frankly, blatantly, and insistently" (Antheil).

II

THE popularity of the ballet throughout several centuries of brilliant history derives essentially from the same set of sensual, emotional, social and esthetic responses to which, in a more inclusive definition, the theatre owes its permanent validity. Theatre arises from primitive ritual. This moment marks man's most significant attempt at formal expression in direct response to the unfathomable, fear- and awe-inspiring mysteries of nature. At all times and with all peoples ritual performances assume spontaneously the form of dance, thus giving suggestive evidence of universality. Isadora Duncan condensed it in the formula: *Dance is exaltation.* Even in its very early stages, dance requires and produces rhythmical motion, physical pattern and spatial organization, i. e., structural principles for the realization of artistic form. The simultaneously dawning knowledge that emotions, urges and desires, thoughts and feelings, and even abstractions are communicable — in terms of symbol and representation — must be deemed a revelation of immeasurable consequence. Martha Graham condensed it in the formula: *Dance is communication.* The fundamental identity of all categories of theatrical art should never be forgotten. Only on so broad a basis can it be understood that theatre and ballet represent but two different conceptions of the same fundamental problem of self-realization. And this problem cannot be considered apart from qualities inherent or implied in the original experience of the dance. As media of expression, dance and speech are equally adequate. But as opposed to the complex idiom of the literary theatre, the ballet's pre-eminently visual language is nearer the primitive origins and almost universally intelligible. This accounts for the ballet's easy geographical spread and the international familiarity with its foremost representations and representatives.

The history of the ballet demonstrates a constant shift of emphasis and interest. Beginning in the late 16th century with the royal court ballets in France, it passed through every conceivable form of presentation: through mainly decorative phases, through operatic stages, through times of drama and pantomime, through periods of acrobatic virtuosity. But at all times it manifested an obvious tendency toward the spectacular, toward challenging and stimulating visual elaboration. Even the conventional and inept scenic display of the average twentieth-century opera ballet reveals traces of some anonymous painter's futile efforts to live up to the memory of a glorious past. Hence the persistence of Italian Renaissance and French Baroque motifs: vanishing-point perspective, symmetrical vistas, rows of Ionic columns, convulsive architecture, heavy folded draperies, cumbersome, anachronistic costumes; and hence the complete disregard of modern stage techniques and lighting facilities. This situation had lasted too long to be defined as a crisis which would call for radical decisions. The arrival of Diaghilev and the birth of modern ballet occurred at a random moment, without warning or preparation. Although Diaghilev made history, he had not come with the intention of reforming the Western ballet, in fact he was quite unconcerned with its state. Lacking the opportunity to realize his plans in Russia, tired of wasting his time and energies in hopeless struggles, and unwilling to compromise, he simply chose the traditional place of refuge for fugitives from reaction. The organization was complete in Diaghilev's mind; it was ready to function because he brought with him his friends and long-time collaborators and imported the company whole. Director, choreographer, composers, dancers and designers were all Russians. *European ballet became Russian ballet.*

III

THE artistic evolution of the Ballet Russe demonstrates two distinctly different phases — roughly Russian and Gallic — clearly separated by the First World War. Until the war it had been almost exclusively Russian, with dancers from the Imperial Ballet, with Fokine as choreographer, with composers like Borodin, Tcherepnine, Tchaikowsky, Rimsky-Korsakoff and Strawinsky, with designers like Bakst and Benois, Golovine, Korovine and Roerich, Soudeikine and Dobujinsky, Gontcharova and Larionow. Diaghilev showed an uncanny capacity for maintaining authority and directing this colorful group of varied and high-strung artistic temperaments toward concerted efforts and complete integration in work.

During its first active years the ensemble was, moreover, united by a force stronger yet than the personality of its director or the cooperative spirit of its members:

it formed so compact an ethnic and cultural organism that it was practically self-sufficient. The company was both compelled and determined to live on its own artistic resources, and there was ample talent within the producing group to supply the entire ambitious repertoire. The rather abrupt change of policy was not solely due to deliberate purpose and resolution. Several determining circumstances coincided with the war: Fokine's departure as leading choreographer, the break with Nijinsky as both outstanding choreographer and dancer, and the sudden end of Russian importation, the source of a fresh supply of reliable performers. Thus Diaghilev's experimentation with new art and new artists was as much a matter of necessity as of choice. In the meantime, he had been exposed to the atmospheric and spiritual climate of Paris for several consecutive years. Here, fresh in everyone's memory, the masters of impressionism had recently won the victory of modern painting over literal realism, and younger generations of talented artists had set out determinedly to explore still more unusual realms of the creative spirit. Diaghilev was deeply affected by the tumultuous surroundings of insatiable artistic curiosity, boundless energy, and daring experimentation. However, there was no indication of an esthetic or moral dilemma, no sign of hesitation among several possible courses. Diaghilev comprehended and adopted every style with the same ease. His preoccupation with esthetic issues was thoroughly practical and was directed solely by his personal conviction. But "any practical activity will, provided that it is integrated and moves by its own urge to fulfillment, have esthetic quality" (Dewey).

In those years of steady artistic development the Ballet Russe had been performing with rapidly growing success. With its spreading sphere of influence its director had become at the same time the promoter and the exponent of signal changes in the world of art. Each new ballet performance carried the weight of an authoritative statement in the name of progress. The Ballet Russe had become *the first modern company in our century*. It was modern in the double sense of being fashionable as well as progressive. There was an unmistakable tendency toward modishness, exclusiveness and sophistication, which became sometimes an end in itself and therefore did not survive the passing moment of contemporaneousness. The total accomplishment, however, transcended the limited duration of fashion, sensation and mere novelty. If not always for lasting intrinsic value, many of the some seventy ballets of the repertoire remain valid as significant statements of a period of artistic transition and gradual consolidation. The ambiguities and contradictions regarding the style of the later performances imply indeed the very same esthetic confusion and complexity which characterizes the formative process of contemporary art in general. In our present esthetic estimation the notoriety of the ballet's experimental period, ostensibly inaugurated with the Cocteau-Massine-Picasso-Satie "Parade," overshadows the theatrical import of the prewar, Russian phase. In strict analysis, however, Bakst's discovery of the scenic image as a theatrically integrated visual concept, and his mastery of its application, were of greater importance for the modern ballet scene than the décors and costumes of Matisse, Derain, Braque and de Chirico. Once Diaghilev had started to experiment with the controversial contributions of the School of Paris, he never again fully achieved the integrity and purity of his original intentions. Inevitably, with the declining standard of dance technique, the postwar performances became "anti-theatrical and anti-choreographic" (Kirstein).

Benois was right in calling Diaghilev a "magician." He achieved veritable miracles of conversion with his faithful audience. The very same spectators who had been brought up on the obvious pictures of the conventional ballet stage now readily believed in the abstract images of a Miro and Picasso, with the unqualified faith and confidence which form public opinion. This unusual accomplishment merits analysis. With regard to esthetic experience, the chief characteristic of public opinion may be thus defined: that the level of appreciation of the total aggregate is infinitely lower, the rate of reaction infinitely slower than that of its individual members. The broader and faster the public response, the greater the temptation to press the rare advantage. Hence the tendency to overstatement and exaggeration in the promotion of advanced ideas. It is a commonplace that the lasting contributions to the cultural possessions of our time are not the exclusive gift of a single individual or of a limited group, but "the work of the collective consciousness of the whole epoch" (Friedell). Posterity's time-tested standards of valuation are not necessarily different in essence from the spontaneous assertions of contemporaries. But as a common rule the popular acceptance of progress in any form of achievement is predicated upon its ulterior results and consequences, i.e., upon the *questionable test of success*.

IV

DIAGHILEV was fully aware of the esthetic responsibility which went with his successes, and he was ready to assume it. It was his strength as well as his limitation that he never doubted the validity of his own judgment and therefore never hesitated to affirm it publicly in a presentation which was accessible to every chance purchaser of a ballet ticket. And although he stated emphatically that he considered it "blasphemous to force ideas," he ignored the fact that the powerful appeal of the new, the fashionable and the sensational had just this effect. It would be quite unjust, though, to doubt the sincerity of Diaghilev's patrons merely on account of certain snobbish tendencies. Progressive ideas are frequently carried and promoted by a small group of confirmed believers and a large one of snobs. Indeed modern art owes a debt of gratitude to the contagious enthusiasm and the staunch support of the minority, which is willing to take the risk of an immediate commitment, as against the delayed approval of the majority. This is a deliberate argument in defense of the typical clan of balletomanes which used to crowd Diaghilev's *premières* and which is just as familiar a sight at every first night of the ballet today. This craving for the new and the sensational, which is so obviously open to scorn, ridicule and serious criticism, is also a powerful driving force which prevents the unorthodox from settling down into habit, comfort, and convention. There seems to be a general assumption, based on an idealized legend, that Diaghilev was widely popular like film and radio stars, or even choreographers and ballerinas. But Diaghilev was not a performer himself; he was modest like a true grand-seigneur; he was the mysteriously unknown moving force behind the mechanism of his company; there exist only a few amateur photographs of him. Actually the average contemporaries of the Ballet Russe knew it merely from the striking posters in the streets of a few European capitals. In our ballet-conscious time it is hard to realize that the Diaghilev company, during the whole twenty-year period of its activity, performed almost exclusively before a few thousand select connoisseurs.

With the limitation of possible financial returns on one side and the extravagance of expenditures on the other, the Ballet Russe was an enterprise of evident luxury. His preoccupation with an all-absorbing task may have been the basic cause for Diaghilev's unconcern with commercial considerations; it may also suggest that his company, as a collective entity, was but loosely fitted into the general cultural and economic pattern of the society of his time. Whatever high artistic purposes Diaghilev may have served, whatever productive impulses his initiative may have imparted to the development of our modern ballet, there was a quality of preciousness and artificiality in his later work which precluded a natural social spread. As a matter of sober fact the company's precarious material existence depended substantially upon the generosity of benefactors, a condition reminiscent of the remote past when royal patrons had supported the ballet as a noble, though exorbitant, private entertainment. Certainly nobody realized then that a personal and rather esoteric amusement for the few held all the potentialities of becoming a popular entertainment for the millions. In the meantime, the vital need for this sort of spectacle has been confirmed in telling figures, and certain symptoms promise an eventual breakaway from a principle which had been set up as a rigid model and respected like a monument. But although many of our more recent ballets answer different, timelier, and more complex needs, the usual "Russian" repertoire is still animated, if not dominated, by the spirit of Diaghilev. Fokine, Massine, Ninette de Valois, Lifar, Balanchine, the very personalities who shaped the modern ballet in France, England and America, relate it inevitably to the original Ballet Russe whence they all come. And many of the foremost painters of today have first been known, outside studios and private galleries, for having designed the magnificent settings and costumes of Diaghilev's productions.

Inspired by the high ideal that "this form of art does not admit of mediocrity" (Noverre), Diaghilev called upon the best artists then in Paris, persuading and inspiring them to invent scenic spectacles of unforgettable excitement and beauty. Every experimental attempt, every controversial movement, every revolutionary discovery in the world of art contributed striking effects to each new ballet performance. The imposing list of expressionist, cubist, constructivist, and other progressive scene and costume designers who worked for Diaghilev, reads like a representative summary of modern painting, proving his unfailing flair for genuine creative quality. While the performances thus gained immensely in pictorial interest and visual appeal, they lost proportionately the essential justification for their existence: for "the ballet must remain tightly connected with its natural base — the dance" (Lifar). It is a matter of conjecture whether Diaghilev had fulfilled his task and destination when he died. His romanticized death in Venice and the somewhat sentimental transfiguration of his enigmatic personality seem strangely removed from our atomic age. To the coterie of balletomanes, esthetes, artists and critics who had formed the majority of Diaghilev's audience, theatrical dancing was so entirely identified with the initiator and director of the Ballet Russe that his end signified to them the end of ballet in general. Since then innumerable living witnesses of the active company have kept vouching in good faith for the accuracy of their nostalgic recollections, each one unwittingly contributing another bit of doubtful evidence toward the growing legend of Diaghilev. In our modern appreciation of the ballet we should be concerned with issues of greater consequence, involving new ways of seeing and visualizing, a new realization of our esthetic demands and duties, and indeed the very foundation of our social concepts. Consequently we should no longer be satisfied with the simple affirmation of past experiences in beauty, even though they may have been our own.

Upon close examination all the evidence seems to indicate that the original Ballet Russe, or what was left of it, was approaching a point when it would have exhausted the creative substance on which it had started out. The exemplary synthesis of the initial productions, the unique cohesion of the original ensemble were in a process of slow disintegration. Totally dependent and relying on dictatorial leadership, the organization continued to function with a semblance of vitality which was borrowed to an ever-increasing degree from the contributing composers and painters. It became obvious that the body of the company would not survive the spirit of its animator by a day, and there was indeed sad truth in the fear that with Diaghilev his ballet would pass away. Barely three years later René Blum and de Basil found only fragments and debris scattered on French soil when they decided to revive the Ballet Russe. During two full decades of residence in foreign territory the Diaghilev company had remained an alien group which was neither socially nor nationally integrated in the country of its choice. It was international and cosmopolitan for want of a more specific association, Russian in stock, with French superimpositions, not more at home in Monte Carlo than any *habitué* of the Casino, as ephemeral an art event in Paris as the yearly Salon. *Russian Ballet had become international ballet.* When Diaghilev's company disbanded, the vacant place was taken automatically by a reorganized "Ballet Russe"; not even an attempt was made to lay the foundations for a national ballet. "Russian" was a synonym for classic theatrical dancing, and several companies claim proudly their descent from the Original Ballet Russe de Monte Carlo. Each one of those several organizations has legal, moral and artistic titles to ballets from the original repertoire which they continue to revive. The merit of this practice is doubtful; its consequences, however, are obvious. An undiscriminating public is led to believe that those second- and third-time revivals represent absolute standards of excellence.

The dry artificiality of those revivals is the more conspicuous because in most instances they are not freely recreated in a congenial spirit, but rather academically restored from inaccurate memories with a pretense at authenticity. In the most flagrant cases this practice amounts to "spectral blackmail" (Kirstein), i.e., deliberate or careless misinformation, trading on the publicity value of past successes, on the emotional leniency of sentiment, or, worse yet, on the credulity of the public. Nothing could do more serious harm to the rational ideal of Diaghilev's true intentions and achievements (or to our appreciation of his scenic images) than the indiscriminate repetition of his once successful ballets. One may say, paradoxically, that they would not be dead but for those revivals. This is not so much a sweeping condemnation of the principle as a caution against the usual practice. It should be realized that many of the most famous ballets remain valid only in our memory, on the comparative level of equivalent and simultaneous data, like a phrase which derives its full meaning from its relative position in the context. In our present repertoire there are, for instance, regular performances of "Le Spectre de la Rose" (1910), "Scheherazade" (1910), "Les Sylphides" (1910), "L'Après-Midi d'un Faune" (1912), "Petrouchka" (1912), to mention but a few favorites. The dates are suggestive. All these revivals reach far back behind two world wars, conjuring the pale ghosts of a regretted past which offered comfort and security. It has been conveniently forgotten that it took fighting spirit and considerable courage to assert artistic convictions against bourgeois lethargy, moral outrage and outright hostility. It has been forgotten because it is hard to discover the cause for scandal, sensation and provocation in the dated statements of the "Spectre" or "Scheherazade." Surely those ballets are danced splendidly, and they are executed with perfect sincerity. But ballet is not merely a pretext for the display of technical mastery and professional devotion. There should be a deeper motivation, one which a modern audience could accept without concessions or embarrassment. It is time to gauge our true assets and to protest against the one-sided, sentimental presentation of Diaghilev's lifework. It is time to acknowledge a change in our vision, our world and our *Weltanschauung.*

V

THROUGHOUT all the years of his activity the rich source, from which Diaghilev drew the substance he worked with, was the Russian Academy; he had in no way revolutionized the *danse d'école,* but rather amplified or specified its use as a medium of modern art expression. A brief recapitulation will help to clarify the situation. First of all, Marius Petipa, of late ungratefully forgotten, would seem to deserve fair rehabilitation. For all the dated taste and faded splendor of his ballets, he was a master of choreography and well-integrated ensemble composition. Through consistent and conscientious work he perfected the ultimate ballet formula which now seems empty and mechanical, but which remains nonetheless the foundation of modern theatrical dancing. Thus ballet in the early twentieth century signified the artificial glory of a formal tradition; a fine potential instrument of little artistic use; perfect, yet inert. The signal for a departure in new directions was given by a dancer of the New World: Isadora Duncan. She performed and lectured in Russia, attacking the rigidity of the ballet code and the physical restrictions of the traditional costume, and promoting instead a "natural" dance, i.e., a free interpretation of antique Greece in plastic poses, floating movements, loose costumes and bare feet. It is impossible to evaluate in this limited space the power and fascination of this priestess of beauty who swept the world with a message of sublime freedom. A declared enemy of the ballet, she denied its every tradition. Emotional rather than methodical in her criticism, she could not and would not conceive of a possible synthesis. The typical reproach of the "artificiality" of the *danse d'école* is based on a romantic idealization of "nature" as the paradigm of perfection, and not on a realization of artistic principles. Duncan expressed in her violent and intolerant language an opinion which was, and still is, widely shared by balletomanes and balletophobes alike, namely that ballet is virtually the abstraction of an art which can materialize at will in many different ways and forms of dancing. That is not so. The ballerina's rise on the toes is a symbol, not a stunt. Ballet cannot be understood, appreciated, and considered *in abstracto,* i.e., apart from the specific technique called "classic" with reference to a traditional code of posture and movement. This approved kinetic system, based on five absolute positions of the feet, assures functional and mechanical perfection of a compelling logic. Matured during many centuries, it contains the cumulative efforts, experiences and accomplishments of prominent dancers, dancing masters, choreographers and theorists, and has gradually reached a degree of purity which comes close to being absolute. It is, therefore, a fundamental mistake to reform the ballet by an attempt either to improve upon or to abolish its technique.

Fokine realized, as acutely as Duncan, the inadequacy of the academic style and system, as practiced at the Marinsky Theatre; as an active dancer and choreographer he also recognized the potentialities of the traditional idiom. To him, Isadora may have been a symbol, a promise and a force, but definitely not an example to be followed. Ballet without the basis of the *danse d'école* would simply cease to exist. Fokine stated his intended reforms in an official and now historical document, and his rational principles succeeded where Duncan's attempted revolution was bound to fail. He never attacked the formal technique as such, but its conventional mechanicalness. Thoroughly and methodically he developed both principles and practice for the staging of interpretative ballets. Each ballet presented a definite story which determined the style of the interpretation and in turn demanded a specific expression in body movement and gesture. It was *style* rather than creative originality which elevated Fokine's best works to the rank of art, and which explains why they survived the dullness of antiquated subject matter and the dilution of countless revivals. For the sake of style Fokine advocated unity of conception and harmonious blending of the three elements: music, painting and dancing. This proved to be an immensely fruitful conception, giving access to the ballet to composers and painters who had hitherto no solid ground for creative contributions. Thus it was Fokine who prepared the ground for Diaghilev and who was the natural choreographer for his ballets. It took the possessed genius of Nijinsky to complete eventually Fokine's precedent, and to reveal the tremendous potential energies contained in the accumulated stock of theatrical dancing. Modern ballet had become a reality, and for one brief moment Diaghilev's grandiose vision had passed over the ballet stage. "As Isadora had in her amateur way made every possibility an ideal if unrealized standard, he (Nijinsky) as professional creator in tradition, made it an absolute, methodical realization" (Kirstein).

VI

The outstanding characteristic of the first Ballet Russe was the forceful concentration of all the divergent creative talents and tendencies in one steady point of focus. Diaghilev's death caused deep confusion. He had not planned for future and posterity; he had not provided for succession and successors; he had left neither school, nor disciples, nor an articulate statement of theories, rules and principles for the continuation of his work. Without coherent style and direction, without an adequate ensemble of dancers, without funds or assured support, Diaghilev's Ballet Russe represented a poor legacy indeed. The reorganization of this disintegrated and disillusioned company seems almost a miracle. It was due to the cold, sober, businesslike determination of de Basil, who deserves decidedly more credit than he is usually given, and who has done more for the international promotion of the ballet than the competing companies care to admit. De Basil's prospects seemed fairly promising because he started with the help and cooperation of René Blum as co-director, Balanchine as ballet master, Massine as choreographer, and Grigorieff as stage manager. The new cooperative venture was not to last long, though. For various reasons, too involved to be investigated here, one associate after the other split with de Basil. Balanchine went first to Paris and then to America, where he stayed. Disagreements with Blum deprived the company of a man of exquisite taste and valuable experience and, incidentally, of the Monte Carlo theatre. Finally Massine parted with the director, and with him went the hope for the systematic building of a new, modern repertoire. In passing, as it were, Fokine and Nijinska contributed each a few new ballets. Surprisingly enough, de Basil's company has survived a turbulent time of constant crises and pioneered successfully in Latin-America; it is still in existence, though at present without active ensemble and without a home. This forced inactivity is symptomatic of an unsound general situation.

Diaghilev had held a unique and privileged position because his company had been unequalled, unrivalled and uncontested for the whole period of its existence. His death was followed by a troubled and suggestive interregnum during which not a single new choreographer, no new dancer, no hitherto unknown composer or designer appeared on the ballet scene. Fokine produced ballets for Anna Pavlova, Ida Rubinstein, for his own "Fokine Ballet" and for Russia, Italy, England and America. Lifar was appointed *premier danseur* and *maître de ballet* at the *Opéra* in Paris. Balanchine organized "Les Ballets 1933" for one brilliant season in Paris and later "The American Ballet" in America. Ninette de Valois had gone to England, preparing the ground for the "Sadler's Wells Ballet." Massine traveled, choreographed and danced for several years in various countries until he was made *maître de ballet* of the first "Ballet Russe" in America. Nijinska was *maître de ballet* in Buenos Aires, choreographer for the "Ida Rubinstein Ballet" and founder of her own "Théâtre de Danse." Thus in superficial appearance the foremost ballet professionals showed every sign of confidence, optimism and initiative. Their productions were competent, beautiful, stimulating and effective enough to cover temporarily the shortage of first-rate soloists and well-trained *corps de ballet*. In reality all this enterprising activity was lacking in leadership and sustained, consistent policy. Everything evolved around the same few Diaghilev veterans. However, the amazing productivity of those few modern choreographers filled the immediate needs of the repertoire, and hid the ominous fact that they perpetuated an empty formula. The ballet had absorbed and used everything that a cosmopolitan art in Paris had to offer it. The finest composers and the greatest painters had carried Diaghilev's final formula of musical and decorative sophistication to the extreme. For theatrical dancing it was a time of latent crisis; for ballet design it was decidedly a most profitable development. The artists, for the most part distinguished easel painters, created with an unrestrained disregard of stage mechanics and dance requirements never before permitted them in the modern theatre. They established the supremacy of the scenic image as an uncontested principle before anybody became aware of its basic fallacy.

At this critical moment European ballet owed to Russia, for the second time in the same century, the restoration of its waning vital forces. Several great ballerinas from the former Imperial Marinsky Theatre, refugees from the revolution, had opened modest ballet schools in Paris and had begun to train the children of the conservative Russian colony in the conservative manner, the exacting technique and rigid discipline of the traditional *danse d'école*. Three prodigious dancers in their early teens, Toumanova, Baronova and Riabujinska, emerged as genuine ballerinas, demonstrating to a whole generation of awakening children the unrealized dance potentialities of their physiques and their artistic aspirations. The changes since the early thirties are profound and significant; they reveal a negative as well as a positive aspect. With de Basil, in point of time, began a practice of keen competition, artistic instability and dubious ballet politics which gradually developed to truly alarming proportions. Today there exists, for instance, a confusing abundance of "Russian Ballets" with equally legitimate claims for recognition, making equally justified efforts to secure the services of the few specialized choreographers who are able to revive from memory the "Russian" repertoire. The physical data are still available: the original scores remain, settings and costumes are in warehouses or may be copied easily, and the choreography can be reconstructed with just so much style as to appear genuine to an unsuspecting audience. However, despite the careful preservation of time-tested appearances, it becomes glaringly obvious that the classic tradition is not automatically contained in a retrospective repertoire. We may soon be given an opportunity of seeing the contemporary Soviet-Russian ballet. It will be "Russian" and "traditional" and "genuine" beyond any possible doubt. But it has never felt the impact of Diaghilev's subtle assault on our taste which we take for granted, and from which it seems so hard to recover.

Many symptoms foreshadow the end of the stereotyped, pseudo-Russian predominance, and the definitive affirmation of a mature, self-confident native ballet in every country. For Russia's most important contribution to the Western ballet since Diaghilev has been a host of outstanding teachers, i.e., the only means for an independent growth. In France, in England and America they directed academies and companies in which they trained not only new performers, but also new pedagogues and perfect technicians of the *danse d'école*. The vogue of ballet which is now surging over the world receives its strongest incentive from the youthful enthusiasm and the splendid technique of *new generations of dancers*. There are now excellent academies in England and America, in Italy and France, and the continuity of classic theatrical dancing is assured — as it should be — in the daily accomplishments of countless young ballet performers. England's "National Ballet" gives highest promise. Catherine Littlefield in Philadelphia, Ruth Page in Chicago, William Christensen in San Francisco have worked consistently for many years toward a truly American ballet. Lincoln Kirstein's "Ballet Caravan" and "American Ballet" built an exemplary repertoire relying primarily on American subjects, authors, composers, designers and dancers. Mexico has a native ballet company composed exclusively of Mexican artists and performers. In France, a newly founded company presents an ensemble of French dancers, although in the customary setup. With the inexhaustible resources of sound national stock, supplying fine native-born and trained dancers, composers, choreographers and designers, the ideal of a representative *national ballet* is well on its way to realization.

This sketchy outline of the modern ballet may seem inequitably balanced, which indeed it is. Without thereby indicating critical emphasis, a few names have been cited, whereas many important personalities, many noteworthy experiments, many fine companies have not been mentioned at all. However, while the complete history of the contemporary ballet has been dealt with in an extensive literature, no attempt seems to have been made before to define the esthetic position of ballet design as a specific phenomenon of modern art. Hence the task consisted primarily in an effort to supply, in brief, specific information which would help to clarify the issue.

VII

THE ballet theatre is not an art museum. The fact that Diaghilev's legacy of beautiful ballet designs is sufficiently important to warrant appreciation and preservation for its own sake and to enter our art museums and collections, has confused the esthetic issue. In accepting the premises of a spectacle which presents mute characters conveying moods, emotions and dramatic events in strictly stylized body movement, we renounce the claim for an objectively valid environment. Even the most rational intelligence agrees willingly to take angels and devils for granted for the duration of a performance. Actually, as well as esthetically, the ballet owes its very existence to the spectator's spontaneous or deliberate acceptance of its specific validity, regardless of the factual or imaginative tendencies prevailing in the artistic intention. This process may be visualized as an exchange of "incoming and outgoing energies" (Dewey). In any scenic presentation the magic power to carry conviction depends on the degree of genuine theatrical perfection, not on the exactitude, truthfulness or probability obtained in one direction, nor on the quantitative effort of imagination expended in the other. The legitimate, though not the usual standard of evaluation of scenic and costume designs is their theatrical relevance, i.e., the validity of any latent or patent qualities requires confirmation in the specific terms of scenic function, usefulness and applicability. It must be admitted, however, that the remarkable success of modern design for the ballet is primarily due to chance contributions by easel painters of distinction. Many of the most valued treasures have been created and appreciated on questionable premises, owing their particular charm to the artists' flagrant unconcern with function and execution. As a category, ballet design lives still on borrowed fame, rather than on its own theatrical resources. For the stature of its foremost representatives imposes artistic standards and principles which are essentially alien to the stage. Hence the conspicuous absence of professional designers, whose sober, workman-like projects and blueprints compare unfavorably with the unrestrained renderings of the ballet painters.

Scenic designs may be defined as authentic documents of artistic intention in a state of yet unachieved purpose. The graphic execution on paper and canvas, regardless of its possible excellence, is but one phase in a total creative process, a transitional recording of the artist's vision before it becomes involved in the mechanics of the stage realization. Whatever objective artistic quality the designs may reveal is an incidental, or even an accidental circumstance. Familiarity with the artist's idiom accounts, however, for their immediate appeal to the theatrically untrained beholder, who is naturally unconcerned with scenic implications. In an art exhibition what may subsequently occur on the stage may be irrelevant for our esthetic judgment or enjoyment, i.e., once the designs are properly translated in actual settings and costumes, light and movement. The curious fact is that ballet design owes its artistic significance to the very circumstance which tends to make it esthetically suspect: namely that it has been conceived to serve a purpose. It is disconcerting to find creative imagination conditioned upon objective contents and concrete requirements. There is, indeed, an element of realism even in the most radically abstract theatrical work, due to its eventual execution in three-dimensional stage reality. Although both project and realization may hold identical qualities of magic and fascination, this physical condition becomes the ultimate test for the artist's achievement. If the painter's two-dimensional rendition be considered as absolutely self-sufficient and definitive, it does not permit of any further form of elaboration, transformation or reinterpretation in whatever other esthetic media. Its very state of finality and perfection condemns its use for the stage.

A ballet production may be defined summarily as the creation of a valid reality in scenic terms, i.e., "the creation of that mysterious place called ballet to be inhabited by young dancers" (Kochno) refers as much to an actual space-time reality as to the vision of the mind's eye. The artist appears as mediator between pure imagination and specialized utility. In physical as well as esthetic appreciation, the spatial and functional development of the stage image transcends the plane and static surface of painting or drawing. The three-dimensional actuality of the stage and the performer determines specific relations and tensions in space, and specific problems of scale and proportion, with which a painter is not ordinarily concerned, nor even familiar. But the same sureness and authority which conveys character, style and distinction to a design may also benefit the scenic realization, provided it be determined by the same central idea as libretto, music, choreography and dance. This problem cannot be solved by a mechanical agreement between several contributing arts or artists. The principle involved concerns the essential integration, the "coherence of imagination" (Venturi) which makes a work of art intelligible and acceptable *in terms of its own medium*. All the properties and elements of the medium contribute in varying degrees toward the unified artistic whole which we call ballet. And they cannot do this unless they subordinate portions of their specific integrity. But ballet is primarily dance; costumes and settings are accessories, not essentials. This does not suggest at all that the designer's work implies necessarily a compromise. Quite the contrary: his achievement is the greater the better he succeeds in asserting the totality of his intentions and capacities in a partial statement. Then, and only then, may he be identified with his work.

ACKNOWLEDGEMENTS

THE accumulated treasures of modern ballet design are staggering in number. While so vast and varied a subject calls ideally for comprehensive treatment, physical limitations and wartime restrictions compelled a severe selection, and the scope, variety, and inequality of the material suggested the necessity for condensation. The very process of elimination implies selective principles and inevitable disagreements between conflicting views and opinions. Rather than compromise in a hopeless attempt to please everybody the editor endeavored to offer a truly *representative* survey of contemporary trends and achievements. It is also doubtful whether further amplification or an alternative choice would have yielded information of a greater or different relevance.

The editor owes a debt of gratitude to many people who cooperated graciously in a task of extensive, painstaking, and difficult research, for the material used in the preparation of this book was not easily available. Considered and treated primarily as working sketches, many fine drawings have been handled with carelessness, damaged beyond repair, or thrown away with the workshop's waste; many others are scattered all over the world in private collections unknown or inaccessible to the public; and still others could be obtained in reproductions only. At present there exist only a few important collections specifically devoted to ballet design: *Les Archives Internationales de la Danse* in Paris, founded by Rolf de Maré; the former collection of Serge Lifar, now in the *Wadsworth Atheneum* in Hartford, Connecticut; the former Lincoln Kirstein Dance Archives, now a section of *The Museum of Modern Art* in New York; the collection of the *Ballet Russe de Monte Carlo* in New York, organized by Serge J. Denham. All four collections were prime sources of important works.

Space prevents extending individual thanks to the innumerable people who have helped with the preparation of this book, giving generously of their valuable time, knowledge, and experience. All lenders are accurately listed with their respective loans; to all of them editor and publisher wish to extend their sincere gratitude and appreciation. The editor also wishes to thank in particular the many artists, residing in this country, who supplied information on their own works, and to Mr. W. H. Allner, Representative of "Graphis" in Paris; Mr. Francisco Borrell, New York; Mr. Gabor Cossa of the "Ballet Jooss" in London; Mr. Max Erlanger de Rosen in Paris; Mr. Michel Florisoone, Conservateur, Musée du Louvre, Paris; Mr. Baird Hastings in Paris; Mr. Arnold L. Haskell in London; Mr. Alexandre Iolas in New York; Mr. Ladislas Medgyes in New York; Miss Helen Pep in New York; The *Sadler's Wells Ballet* in London; Dr. Pierre Tugal, Conservateur, Archives Internationales de la Danse in Paris; the *Wadsworth Atheneum* in Hartford, Connecticut (Mr. C. C. Cummings, Director, Mrs. Florence Paull Berger, General Curator, Miss Marjorie L. Ellis, Assistant); and Mr. W. Walter in Paris. Special thanks are due to Mr. de Brunoff for authorization to use the Bakst drawing for "La Belle au Bois Dormant," to "The Encyclopedia Americana" for permission granted to the author to quote from his contribution on Ballet; to "Graphis" in Zurich for authorization to reproduce three Cassandre illustrations; to Mr. Paul Rosenberg for permission to reproduce drawings from the Picasso portfolio of "Tricorne."

31

It is my particular wish to express my deep gratitude to my immediate assistants who helped with never-failing patience, devotion, and competence: Mrs. Sara Yancey Belknap who devoted many months of careful professional research to the Ballet Index; Colette Keiffer who was my untiring assistant during the long period of preparation; Helen Ward whose experience benefits the literary execution and the accuracy of proofreading; Soichi Sunami who again proved his exceptional capacities as a photographer of works of art. Finally a special word of appreciation is due to Mrs. Janet Leeper in London whose reliable and finely discriminating cooperation is responsible for the excellence of the English section.

GEORGE AMBERG

INDEX

THE index lists 833 titles with full data. (Nrs. 820-833 are listed as supplement at the end of the list, as this material became available too late for inclusion in the main body of the index.) It is condensed from many times this figure because reliability rather than completeness determined the ultimate inclusion. This selection, consequently, represents but a fraction of the international ballet repertoire since 1909. Its usefulness resides primarily in the fact that it offers a convenient reference tool and a sizable contribution toward an eventual comprehensive ballet catalogue. However, a task of such all-inclusive scope can be successfully achieved only if conceived and organized as a collective work. Hence the editor extends to every reader the express invitation to cooperate actively in checking data, rectifying possible mistakes, supplying missing information, and contributing source material.

Although no effort has been spared to check each entry carefully against every source available in this country, the causes for errors are still manifold. They are specifically mentioned here in the hope that students, collectors, artists, and producers will learn from past experience, and in the future preserve original records. Mistakes are usually due to:

Rarity or inaccessibility of original sources, particularly concerning smaller or short-lived companies or unique performances.

Inaccuracy and contradictions in secondary sources due to lack of scholarship and conscientiousness in average ballet literature.

Perpetuation of misinformation in ballet history owing to the use and reprint of unreliable source material.

Unrecorded change of originally scheduled dates, places, titles, artists or cancellation of the performance, after printed information has been released.

Revival of the same ballet with a different title or with different settings and costumes, revised choreography, newly arranged music.

Use of identical titles for different ballets or for condensed or fragmentary versions of the original work.

Constant changing and regrouping of ballet companies with partly identical repertoires, simultaneously performing the same ballet in a similar version with identical title, music, choreography, and décor.

Frequent change of place and touring of whole companies or individual artists and subsequent scattering of records.

Free translation or complete change of titles in different languages.

Chronological conflict between the time the scenic artist dated his designs and the date of the actual performance.

The index closes as of December 31, 1945. Whenever possible, titles are listed in the language of the country in which the ballet was first performed. Data which lack confirming documentation or are merely inferred are inserted in square brackets.

The editor gratefully acknowledges the invaluable cooperation and assistance of Mrs. Sara Yancey Belknap, who devoted infinite care and patience to painstaking and often tedious research. Correspondence may be addressed to the editor, Department of Dance and Theatre Design, The Museum of Modern Art, 11 West 53rd Street, New York 19, N. Y.

BALLET INDEX

1909 – 1945

1 AENEAS, *Ballet in One Act with Chorus*
BOOK: J. Westerings
MUSIC: Albert Roussel
CHOREOGRAPHY: Leonide Katchourowsky
SETTINGS: Helen Scherbatov
COSTUMES: Helen Scherbatov
PREMIÈRE: Brussels, 1935

AFTERNOON OF A FAUN
see L'APRÈS-MIDI D'UN FAUNE

2 AIR AND VARIATIONS, *Classic Ballet in One Act*
MUSIC: Johann Sebastian Bach; arr. Trude Rittmann
CHOREOGRAPHY: William Dollar
SETTING: Walter Gifford
COSTUMES: Walter Gifford
COMPANY: The American Ballet Caravan
PREMIÈRE: Wellesley, Massachusetts, 1938

3 ALAMEDA – 1900
BOOK: Martin Luis Guzmán
MUSIC: Mexican Themes
CHOREOGRAPHY: Gloria Campobello
SETTING: Julio Castellanos
MEN'S COSTUMES: Julio Castellanos
WOMEN'S COSTUMES: Nellie Campobello
COMPANY: Ballet of the City of Mexico
PREMIÈRE: México, D. F., 1944

4 ALCINA SUITE
MUSIC: George Frederic Handel
CHOREOGRAPHY: Andrée Howard
SCENERY: Andrée Howard
COSTUMES: Andrée Howard
COMPANY: Marie Rambert Company
PREMIÈRE: London, 1934

5 ALEKO, *Ballet in Four Acts*
BOOK: Leonide Massine and Marc Chagall, after Pushkin
CHOREOGRAPHY: Leonide Massine
ARTISTIC COLLABORATOR: Henry Clifford
MUSIC: Peter Tchaikowsky, arr. Erno Rapee
SETTINGS: Marc Chagall
COSTUMES: Marc Chagall
COMPANY: Ballet Theatre
PREMIÈRE: México, D. F. and New York, 1942

6 ALEXANDRE LE GRAND, *Choreographic Epic in Three Scenes with Prologue and Epilogue*
BOOK: Serge Lifar
MUSIC: Philippe Gaubert
CHOREOGRAPHY: Serge Lifar
SETTING: Paul-René Larthe
COSTUMES: Paul-René Larthe
COMPANY: Théâtre National de L'Opéra
PREMIÈRE: Paris, 1937

7 ALLELUIA
BOOK: Jan Cieplinsky
MUSIC: Philippe Pedrell
CHOREOGRAPHY: Jan Cieplinsky
SETTING: Hector Basaldua
COSTUMES: Hector Basaldua
COMPANY: Teatro Colon
PREMIÈRE: Buenos Aires, 1936

8 ALMA MATER
BOOK: Edward M. M. Warburg
MUSIC: Kay Swift; orch. Morton Gould
CHOREOGRAPHY: George Balanchine
COSTUMES: John Held, Jr.
COMPANY: The American Ballet
PREMIÈRE: Hartford, Connecticut, 1934

9 ALT WIEN
MUSIC: Ludwig van Beethoven
CHOREOGRAPHY: Adolph Bolm
SETTING: Nicolai Remisoff
COSTUMES: Nicolai Remisoff
COMPANY: Chamber Music Society
PREMIÈRE: Washington, D. C., 1928

10 AMARILLA, *Ballet in One Act*
BOOK: Alexander Glazounov and Riccardo Drigo
MUSIC: Alexander Glazounov and Riccardo Drigo
CHOREOGRAPHY: Ivan Clustine
SETTING: Georges Barbier
COSTUMES: Georges Barbier
COMPANY: Pavlova Company
PREMIÈRE: London, 1912

11 AN AMERICAN PATTERN
BOOK: Ruth Page and Nicolai Remisoff
MUSIC: Jerome Moross

CHOREOGRAPHY: Ruth Page and Bentley Stone
SETTING: Nicolai Remisoff
COSTUMES: John Pratt
MASKS: Viola Clark
COMPANY: Page-Stone Ballet
PREMIÈRE: Chicago, Illinois, 1935

12 AMERICANS IN PARIS
BOOK: Nicolai Remisoff
MUSIC: George Gershwin
CHOREOGRAPHY: Ruth Page
SETTING: Nicolai Remisoff
COSTUMES: Nicolai Remisoff
COMPANY: Page-Stone Ballet
PREMIÈRE: Cincinnati, Ohio, 1936

13 AMORAS
MUSIC: Edward Elgar; orch. Julian Clifford
CHOREOGRAPHY: Mona Inglesby
SETTING: William Chappell
COSTUMES: William Chappell
COMPANY: The International Ballet
PREMIÈRE: London, 1938

14 EL AMOR BRUJO
MUSIC: Manuel de Falla
CHOREOGRAPHY: Adolph Bolm
SETTING: Rollo Peters
COSTUMES: Rollo Peters
COMPANY: Chicago Allied Arts
PREMIÈRE: Chicago, Illinois, [1925]

15 EL AMOR BRUJO, *Ballet in One Act*
BOOK: G. Martinez Sierra
MUSIC: Manuel de Falla
CHOREOGRAPHY: Argentinita
SETTING: Oscar Weidhaas
COSTUMES: Freddie Wittop
COMPANY: Argentinita Company
PREMIÈRE: New York

EL AMOR BRUJO
see also L'AMOUR SORCIER

16 UN AMOUR DU MOYEN AGE
BOOK: Pia Mlakar
MUSIC: Vivaldi, Handel, Bach; arr. Drago M.
Sijanec
CHOREOGRAPHY: Pino Mlakar
COSTUMES: Wilhelm Reinking
COMPANY: Les Archives Internationales de la
Danse
PREMIÈRE: Paris, 1932

17 L'AMOUR SORCIER, *Ballet in One Scene*
MUSIC: Manuel de Falla
CHOREOGRAPHY: Leon Wojcikowski
SETTING: Michel Kedziora

COSTUMES: Michel Kedziora
COMPANY: The Polish Ballet
PREMIÈRE: [Paris], 1938-39

18 L'AMOUR SORCIER
BOOK: G. Martinez Sierra
MUSIC: Manuel de Falla
CHOREOGRAPHY: Serge Lifar
SCENERY: Yves Brayer
COSTUMES: Yves Brayer
COMPANY: Théâtre National de L'Opéra
PREMIÈRE: Paris, 1943

19 AMPHION
BOOK: After Paul Valéry
MUSIC: Arthur Honegger
CHOREOGRAPHY: Aurel M. Milloss
SETTING: Georges de Chirico
COSTUMES: Georges de Chirico
COMPANY: Scala Opera Ballet
PREMIÈRE: Milan, 1944

20 AMPHION
BOOK: After Paul Valéry
MUSIC: Arthur Honegger
CHOREOGRAPHY: Leonide Massine
SETTING: Alexandre Benois
COSTUMES: Alexandre Benois
COMPANY: Ida Rubinstein Ballet
PREMIÈRE: Paris, 1931

21 ANCIENT RUSSIA, *Ballet in One Act and
Three Scenes*
BOOK: Bronislava Nijinska
MUSIC: Peter Tchaikowsky
CHOREOGRAPHY: Bronislava Nijinska
SETTING: Nathalie Gontcharova
COSTUMES: Nathalie Gontcharova
COMPANY: Ballet Russe (Denham)
PREMIÈRE: Cleveland, Ohio, 1943

22 ANDALUSIANA
MUSIC: Georges Bizet
CHOREOGRAPHY: Boris Romanoff
SETTING: Boberman and Hosianson
COSTUMES: Boberman and Hosianson
COMPANY: Russian Romantic Theatre
PREMIÈRE: Berlin, 1922

23 LES ANIMAUX MODÈLES
BOOK: After La Fontaine
MUSIC: Francis Poulenc
CHOREOGRAPHY: Serge Lifar
SETTING: Maurice Brianchon
COSTUMES: Maurice Brianchon
COMPANY: Théâtre National de L'Opéra
PREMIÈRE: Paris, 1942

24 ANNA ANNA, or THE SEVEN CAPITAL
SINS
BOOK: After Bert Brecht
MUSIC: Kurt Weill
CHOREOGRAPHY: Harald Lander
SETTING: Svend Johannsen
COSTUMES: Svend Johannsen
COMPANY: Royal Theatre
PREMIÈRE: Copenhagen

25 APOLLON ET DAPHNÉ
BOOK: Hubert Landau and Caird Leslie
MUSIC: Jean-Philippe Rameau; orch. I. Szelenyi
CHOREOGRAPHY: Caird Leslie
COSTUMES: Hubert Landau
COMPANY: Les Archives Internationales de la
Danse
PREMIÈRE: Paris, 1932

26 APOLLON ET LA BELLE, *Ballet in Six Scenes*
BOOK: Bronislava Nijinska
MUSIC: Ludomir Rozycki
CHOREOGRAPHY: Bronislava Nijinska
SETTING: Wladyslaw Daszewski
CURTAIN: Wladyslaw Daszewski
COSTUMES: Wladyslaw Daszewski
COMPANY: The Polish Ballet
PREMIÈRE: Paris, 1937

27 APOLLON MUSAGÈTE
BOOK: Adolph Bolm
MUSIC: Igor Strawinsky
CHOREOGRAPHY: Adolph Bolm
SETTING: Nicolai Remisoff
COSTUMES: Nicolai Remisoff
COMPANY: Chamber Music Society
PREMIÈRE: Washington, D. C., 1928

28 APOLLON MUSAGÈTE
BOOK: George Balanchine
MUSIC: Igor Strawinsky
CHOREOGRAPHY: George Balanchine
SETTINGS: André Bauchant
COSTUMES: André Bauchant
COMPANY: Ballet Russe (Diaghilev)
PREMIÈRE: Paris, 1928

29 APOLLON MUSAGÈTE
BOOK: George Balanchine
MUSIC: Igor Strawinsky
CHOREOGRAPHY: George Balanchine
SETTING: Stewart Chaney
COSTUMES: Stewart Chaney
COMPANY: The American Ballet
PREMIÈRE: New York, 1937

30 APOLLON MUSAGÈTE
BOOK: George Balanchine
MUSIC: Igor Strawinsky
CHOREOGRAPHY: George Balanchine
SETTING: Pavel Tchelitchew
COSTUMES: Pavel Tchelitchew
COMPANY: Teatro Colon
PREMIÈRE: Buenos Aires, 1942

31 APPARITIONS
BOOK: Constant Lambert
MUSIC: Franz Liszt; arr. Constant Lambert
CHOREOGRAPHY: Frederick Ashton
SETTINGS: Cecil Beaton
COSTUMES: Cecil Beaton
COMPANY: Sadler's Wells Ballet
PREMIÈRE: London, 1936

32 L'APPEL DE LA MONTAGNE
BOOK: Fauré Le Bret
MUSIC: Arthur Honegger
CHOREOGRAPHY: Jean Peretti
SETTING: Roger Wild
COSTUMES: Roger Wild
COMPANY: Théâtre National de L'Opéra
PREMIÈRE: Paris, 1945

33 L'APRÈS-MIDI D'UN FAUNE, *Ballet in One
Act*
BOOK: Vaslav Nijinsky
MUSIC: Claude Debussy
CHOREOGRAPHY: Vaslav Nijinsky
SETTINGS: Léon Bakst
COSTUMES: Léon Bakst
COMPANY: Ballet Russe (Diaghilev)
PREMIÈRE: Paris, 1912

34 L'APRÈS-MIDI D'UN FAUNE
BOOK: Vaslav Nijinsky
MUSIC: Claude Debussy
CHOREOGRAPHY: Serge Lifar
SETTING: Hector Basaldua
COSTUMES: Hector Basaldua
COMPANY: Teatro Colon
PREMIÈRE: Buenos Aires, 1934

35 L'APRÈS-MIDI D'UN JOUR D'ÉTÉ
BOOK: Jarmila Kroshlova
MUSIC: Vaclav Smetack
CHOREOGRAPHY: Jarmila Kroshlova
COSTUMES: Barka Nevole-Ova
COMPANY: Les Archives Internationales de La
Danse
PREMIÈRE: Paris, 1932

ARAGONESA
see JOTA ARAGONESA

36 ARLEQUINADE
Music: Riccardo Drigo
Choreography: Nicholas Zverev and Oboukov
Setting: Mstislav Dobujinsky
Costumes: Mstislav Dobujinsky
Company: Lithuanian State Ballet
Première: Kaunas, Lithuania, 1934

37 ARLECCHINATA
Music: [Jean Joseph] Mondonville
Choreography: Adolph Bolm
Setting: Nicolai Remisoff
Costumes: Nicolai Remisoff
Company: Society of Chamber Music
Première: Washington, D. C., 1928

Astuces Féminines
see Cimarosiana

Astuzie Femminili
see Cimarosiana

38 AUBADE, *Choreographic Concerto*
Music: Francis Poulenc
Choreography: George Balanchine
Setting: Angeles Ortiz
Costumes: Angeles Ortiz
Company: Nemchinova Company
Première: Paris, 1930

39 AUBADE, *Choreographic Concerto*
Music: Francis Poulenc
Choreography: George Balanchine
Setting: Dimitri Bouchêne
Costumes: Dimitri Bouchêne
Company: Nemchinova Company
Première: Monte Carlo, 1934

40 AUBADE
Music: Francis Poulenc
Choreography: Catherine Littlefield
Setting: R. Deshays
Costumes: J. Pascal
Company: Philadelphia Opera Ballet
Première: Philadelphia, Pennsylvania, 1936

41 AUBADE
Music: Francis Poulenc
Choreography: George Balanchine
Setting: A.-M. Cassandre
Costumes: A.-M. Cassandre
Company: Ballet Russe (Blum)
Première: London, 1936

42 AUBADE
Music: Francis Poulenc
Choreography: Margarete Wallmann
Setting: Hector Basaldua
Costumes: Hector Basaldua

Company: Teatro Colon
Première: Buenos Aires, 1942

43 AUCASSIN AND NICOLETTE
Book: Wendy Toye
Music: Joseph Holbrook
Choreography: Wendy Toye
Setting: Motley
Costumes: Motley
Company: Markova-Dolin Company
Première: London, 1936

44 AURORA'S WEDDING
Book: Marius Petipa
Music: Peter Tchaikowsky
Choreography: After Marius Petipa
Setting: Mstislav Dobujinsky
Costumes: Léon Bakst
Company: Ballet Russe (Diaghilev)
Première: Brussels, 1928

45 AURORA'S WEDDING
Book: Marius Petipa
Music: Peter Tchaikowsky
Choreography: Katchurovsky, after Petipa
Setting: Mstislav Dobujinsky
Costumes: Mstislav Dobujinsky
Company: Théâtre Royal de la Monnaie
Première: Brussels, 1937

Aurora's Wedding
See also Princess Aurora
The Sleeping Princess
The Sleeping Beauty
Le Mariage d'Aurore

46 BABA-YAGA
Music: Anatol Liadov
Choreography: Leonide Massine
Costumes: Michael Larionow
Decors: Michael Larionow
Company: Ballet Russe (Diaghilev)
Première: Paris, 1917

47 BACCHANALE, *Ballet in One Act*
Book: Salvador Dali
Music: Richard Wagner
Choreography: Leonide Massine
Setting: Salvador Dali
Costumes: Salvador Dali
Company: Ballet Theatre
Première: New York, 1939

48 BACCHANALE, *Ballet in One Scene*
Book: Igor Schwezoff
Music: Richard Wagner
Choreography: Igor Schwezoff
Scenery: Mario Conde

40

COSTUMES: Igor Schwezoff
COMPANY: Teatro Municipal
PREMIÈRE: Rio de Janeiro, 1945

49 LES BACCHANTES
BOOK: After Euripides
MUSIC: Vittorio Rieti
CHOREOGRAPHY: Alexandre Iolas
SETTING: Georges de Chirico
COSTUMES: Georges de Chirico
COMPANY: Greek Government
PREMIÈRE: Athens, 1937

BACH CONCERTO
see CONCERTO BAROCCO

BACH CYCLE
see CONSECRATION
DANSE NOBLE
THE LAMENT

50 A BACH SUITE
MUSIC: Johann Sebastian Bach
CHOREOGRAPHY: William Christensen
SETTING: Armando Agnini
COSTUMES: Armando Agnini
COMPANY: [San Francisco Opera]
PREMIÈRE: San Francisco, 1938

51 LE BAISER DE LA FÉE, *Ballet-Allegory in
Four Scenes*
BOOK: Igor Strawinsky, after Hans Christian
Andersen
MUSIC: Igor Strawinsky
CHOREOGRAPHY: Bronislava Nijinska
SETTING: Alexandre Benois
COSTUMES: Alexandre Benois
COMPANY: Ida Rubinstein Ballet
PREMIÈRE: Paris, 1928

52 LE BAISER DE LA FÉE, *Ballet-Allegory in
Four Scenes*
BOOK: Igor Strawinsky, after Hans Christian
Andersen
MUSIC: Igor Strawinsky
CHOREOGRAPHY: Bronislava Nijinska
SETTING: Hector Basaldua
COSTUMES: Hector Basaldua
COMPANY: Teatro Colon
PREMIÈRE: Buenos Aires, 1933

53 LE BAISER DE LA FÉE, *Ballet-Allegory in
Four Scenes*
BOOK: Igor Strawinsky, after Hans Christian
Andersen
MUSIC: Igor Strawinsky
CHOREOGRAPHY: Frederick Ashton
SETTING: Sophie Fedorovitch

COSTUMES: Sophie Fedorovitch
COMPANY: Sadler's Wells Ballet
PREMIÈRE: London, 1935

54 LE BAISER DE LA FÉE, *Ballet-Allegory in
Four Scenes*
BOOK: Igor Strawinsky, after Hans Christian
Andersen
MUSIC: Igor Strawinsky
CHOREOGRAPHY: George Balanchine
SETTING: Alice Halicka
COSTUMES: Alice Halicka
COMPANY: The American Ballet
PREMIÈRE: New York, 1937

55 LE BAL, *Ballet in One Act*
BOOK: Boris Kochno
MUSIC: Vittorio Rieti
CHOREOGRAPHY: George Balanchine
SETTING: Georges de Chirico
COSTUMES: Georges de Chirico
COMPANY: Ballet Russe (Diaghilev)
PREMIÈRE: Paris, 1929

56 LE BAL
BOOK: Kurt Jooss, after Boris Kochno
MUSIC: Vittorio Rieti
CHOREOGRAPHY: Kurt Jooss
SETTING: Hein Heckroth
COSTUMES: Hein Heckroth
COMPANY: Jooss Ballet
PREMIÈRE: Essen, Germany, 1930

57 BAL DES MANNEQUINS
MUSIC: Bruno Jasienski
CHOREOGRAPHY: E. F. Burian
SETTING: Antonin Heythum
COSTUMES: Antonin Heythum
COMPANY: Theatre D 34
PREMIÈRE: Prague, 1933

58 BAL DES MARIONNETTES
MUSIC: Erik Satie
CHOREOGRAPHY: Adolph Bolm
SETTING: Nicolai Remisoff
COSTUMES: Nicolai Remisoff
COMPANY: Chicago Allied Arts
PREMIÈRE: Chicago, Illinois, 1925

59 BALILLA
BOOK: Giuseppe Adami
MUSIC: Carmine Guarino
CHOREOGRAPHY: Boris Romanoff
SETTING: Mario Pompei
COSTUMES: Mario Pompei
COMPANY: Teatro Reale
PREMIÈRE: Rome, 1935

41

60 BALLADE
Book: After French Folk Song
Music: John Colman
Choreography: Kurt Jooss
Costumes: Hein Heckroth
Company: Jooss Ballet
Première: London, 1935

61 BALLET IMPÉRIAL, *Ballet in Three Movements*
Music: Peter Tchaikowsky
Choreography: George Balanchine
Setting: Mstislav Doboujinsky
Costumes: Mstislav Doboujinsky
Company: The American Ballet Caravan
Première: Rio de Janeiro, 1941

62 BALLET MÉCANIQUE, *Ballet in One Act*
Book: Adolph Bolm
Music: Alexander Mossolov
Choreography: Adolph Bolm
Costumes: Adolph Bolm and Nicolai Remisoff
Company: The American Ballet
Première: Los Angeles, 1932

Le Ballet Mécanique
see also Mechanical Ballet

63 A BALL IN OLD VIENNA
Music: Joseph Lanner; arr. Frederic Cohen
Choreography: Kurt Jooss
Costumes: Aino Siiomola
Company: Jooss Ballet
Première: Cologne, Germany, 1932

64 BALUSTRADE, *Ballet in One Act and Four Movements*
Music: Igor Strawinsky
Choreography: George Balanchine
Setting: Pavel Tchelitchew
Costumes: Pavel Tchelitchew
Company: Ballet Russe (de Basil)
Première: New York, 1941

65 BARABAU, *Ballet with Choirs*
Book: Vittorio Rieti
Music: Vittorio Rieti
Choreography: George Balanchine
Setting: Maurice Utrillo
Costumes: Maurice Utrillo
Company: Ballet Russe (Diaghilev)
Première: London, 1925

66 BARABAU
Book: Vittorio Rieti
Music: Vittorio Rieti
Choreography: Ninette de Valois
Setting: Edward Burra

Costumes: Edward Burra
Company: Sadler's Wells Ballet
Première: London, 1936

67 BAR AUX FOLIES-BERGÈRE, *Ballet in One Act*
Book: Ninette de Valois
Music: Emmanuel Chabrier
Choreography: Ninette de Valois
Setting: William Chappell
Costumes: William Chappell
Company: Marie Rambert Company
Première: London, 1934

68 BARN DANCE, *Ballet in One Act*
Book: Catherine Littlefield
Music: Folk Tunes; arr. David Guion, John Powell, L. M. Gottschalk
Choreography: Catherine Littlefield
Setting: Angelo Pinto
Costumes: Salvatore Pinto
Company: Philadelphia Opera Ballet
Première: Philadelphia, Pennsylvania, 1937

69 THE BARTERED BRIDE, *Three Dances*
Music: Bedrich Smetana
Choreography: William Christensen
Setting: J. C. Taylor
Costumes: J. C. Taylor
Company: Portland Rose Festival
Première: [Portland, Oregon], 1936

70 BARTLEMAS DANCES or BARTLEMAS FAIR
Music: Gustav Holst
Choreography: Walter Gore
Costumes: William Chappell
Company: Marie Rambert Company
Première: Oxford, England, 1941

71 THE BAT
Book: Lincoln Kirstein
Music: Johann Strauss
Choreography: George Balanchine
Costumes: Keith Martin
Company: The American Ballet
Première: New York, 1935

Beach
see Plages

72 LE BEAU DANUBE
Book: Leonide Massine
Music: Johann Strauss
Choreography: Leonide Massine
Setting: V. and E. Polunin
Costumes: Etienne de Beaumont

COMPANY: Les Soirées de Paris
PREMIÈRE: Paris, 1924

73 LE BEAU DANUBE, *Ballet in One Act*
BOOK: Leonide Massine
MUSIC: Johann Strauss; arr. and orch. Roger Desormières
CHOREOGRAPHY: Leonide Massine
SETTING: V. and E. Polunin
COSTUMES: Etienne de Beaumont
COMPANY: Ballet Russe (de Basil)
PREMIÈRE: Monte Carlo, 1933

BEETHOVEN VARIATIONS
see VARIATIONS

74 BEHIND THIS MASK, *Ballet in Four Scenes*
MUSIC: David Sheinfield
CHOREOGRAPHY: Kurt Graff
SETTING: Spencer Davies
COSTUMES: John Pratt
COMPANY: Kurt Graff Ballet
PREMIÈRE: Chicago, Illinois, 1938

75 BELKIS, QUEEN OF SHEBA
MUSIC: Ottorino Respighi
CHOREOGRAPHY: Leonide Massine
SETTING: Nicholas Benois
COSTUMES: Nicholas Benois
COMPANY: Scala Opera Ballet
PREMIÈRE: Milan, 1932-33

76 LA BELLE AU BOIS DORMANT, *Ballet in Five Scenes*
BOOK: Marius Petipa
MUSIC: Peter Tchaikowsky; orch. Igor Strawinsky
CHOREOGRAPHY: Marius Petipa, with additions by Bronislava Nijinska
SETTING: Léon Bakst
COSTUMES: Léon Bakst
COMPANY: Ballet Russe (Diaghilev)
PREMIÈRE: London, 1921

77 BELOVED, *Ballet in One Act*
BOOK: Bronislava Nijinska
MUSIC: Schubert-Liszt; arr. Darius Milhaud
CHOREOGRAPHY: Bronislava Nijinska
SETTING: Nicolas de Molas
COSTUMES: Nicolas de Molas
COMPANY: Ballet Theatre
PREMIÈRE: New York, 1941

BELOVED
see LA BIEN-AIMÉE

78 BERCEUSE
MUSIC: Riccardo Pick-Mangiagalli
CHOREOGRAPHY: Cia Fornaroli

SETTING: Achille Broggi
COSTUMES: Titina Rota
COMPANY: Italian Chamber Ballet
PREMIÈRE: San Remo, Italy, 1933

79 THE BETROTHAL
MUSIC: Coleridge-Taylor
CHOREOGRAPHY: Joan Innes
SETTING: Elizabeth Agombar
COSTUMES: Elizabeth Agombar
COMPANY: Ballet Trois Arts
PREMIÈRE: London, 1939

80 LES BICHES, *Ballet with Chorus in One Act*
BOOK: Bronislava Nijinska
MUSIC: Francis Poulenc
CHOREOGRAPHY: Bronislava Nijinska
SETTING: Marie Laurencin
CURTAIN: Marie Laurencin
COSTUMES: Marie Laurencin
COMPANY: Ballet Russe (Diaghilev)
PREMIÈRE: Monte Carlo, 1924

81 LA BIEN-AIMÉE, *Ballet in One Act*
BOOK: Alexandre Benois
MUSIC: Schubert and Liszt; arr. Darius Milhaud
CHOREOGRAPHY: Bronislava Nijinska
SETTING: Alexandre Benois
COSTUMES: Alexandre Benois
COMPANY: Ida Rubinstein Ballet
PREMIÈRE: Paris, 1928

82 LA BIEN-AIMÉE, *Ballet in One Act*
BOOK: Alexandre Benois
MUSIC: Schubert and Liszt; arr. Darius Milhaud
CHOREOGRAPHY: Bronislava Nijinska
SETTING: George Kirsta
COSTUMES: George Kirsta
COMPANY: Markova-Dolin Company
PREMIÈRE: London, 1937

THE BIG CITY
see IMPRESSIONS OF A BIG CITY

83 BILLY THE KID, *Character Ballet in One Act*
BOOK: Lincoln Kirstein
MUSIC: Aaron Copland
CHOREOGRAPHY: Eugene Loring
COSTUMES: Jared French
COMPANY: The American Ballet Caravan
PREMIÈRE: Chicago, Illinois, 1938

84 THE BIRDS
MUSIC: Ottorino Respighi
CHOREOGRAPHY: Cia Fornaroli
SCENERY: M. Vellani-Marchi
COSTUMES: Titina Rota
COMPANY: Italian Chamber Ballet
PREMIÈRE: San Remo, Italy, 1933

43

85 THE BIRDS
Music: Ottorino Respighi
Choreography: Margarete Wallmann
Setting: M. Zampini
Costumes: M. Zampini
Company: Scala Opera Ballet
Première: Milan, 1937

86 THE BIRDS
Book: Robert Helpmann
Music: Ottorino Respighi
Choreography: Robert Helpmann
Setting: Chiang-Yee
Costumes: Chiang-Yee
Company: Sadler's Wells Ballet
Première: London, 1942

87 THE BIRTHDAY OF THE INFANTA
Book: John Alden Carpenter, after Oscar Wilde
Music: John Alden Carpenter
Choreography: Adolph Bolm
Setting: Robert Edmond Jones
Costumes: Robert Edmond Jones
Company: Chicago Opera Company
Première: Chicago, Illinois, 1920

88 THE BIRTHDAY OF OBERON
Music: Henry Purcell; arr. Constant Lambert
Choreography: Ninette de Valois
Setting: John Armstrong
Costumes: John Armstrong
Company: Sadler's Wells Ballet
Première: London, 1933

89 BLACK RITUAL, OBEAH, *Ritual Scene in Two Parts*
Music: Darius Milhaud
Choreography: Agnes De Mille
Setting: Nicolas de Molas
Costumes: Nicolas de Molas
Company: Ballet Theatre
Première: New York, 1940

90 BLUEBEARD, *Ballet in Four Acts, Three Scenes, and Two Prologues*
Book: Michel Fokine, after Meilhac and Halévy
Music: Jacques Offenbach; arr. Antal Dorati
Choreography: Michel Fokine
Setting: Marcel Vertès
Costumes: Marcel Vertès
Company: Ballet Theatre
Première: México, D. F., 1941

91 BOGATYRI, *Ballet in Prologue and Three Scenes*
Book: Leonide Massine
Music: Alexander Borodin
Choreography: Leonide Massine
Setting: Nathalie Gontcharova
Costumes: Nathalie Gontcharova
Company: Ballet Russe (Massine)
Première: New York, 1938

92 LA BOÎTE À JOUJOUX
Book: André Hellé
Music: Claude Debussy; orch. André Caplet
Choreography: Jean Borlin
Setting: André Hellé
Costumes: André Hellé
Company: Les Ballets Suédois
Première: Paris, 1921

93 LA BOÎTE À JOUJOUX
Music: Claude Debussy
Choreography: Jan Cieplinsky
Setting: Hector Basaldua
Costumes: Hector Basaldua
Company: Teatro Colon
Première: Buenos Aires, 1936

94 BOLERO
Music: Maurice Ravel
Choreography: Bronislava Nijinska
Setting: Alexandre Benois
Costumes: Alexandre Benois
Company: Ida Rubinstein Ballet
Première: Paris, 1928

95 BOLERO
Music: Maurice Ravel
Choreography: Michel Fokine
Setting: Alexandre Benois
Costumes: Alexandre Benois
Company: Ida Rubinstein Ballet
Première: Paris, 1928

96 BOLERO
Music: Maurice Ravel
Choreography: Boris Romanoff
Setting: Hector Basaldua
Costumes: Hector Basaldua
Company: Teatro Colon
Première: Buenos Aires, 1932

97 BOLERO
Music: Maurice Ravel
Choreography: Harald Lander
Setting: Svend Johannsen
Costumes: Svend Johannsen
Company: Royal Theatre
Première: Copenhagen, 1934

98 BOLERO
Music: Maurice Ravel
Choreography: Catherine Littlefield

SETTING: Lee Gainsborough
COSTUMES: Lee Gainsborough
COMPANY: Philadelphia Opera Ballet
PREMIÈRE: Philadelphia, Pennsylvania, 1936

99 BOLERO
MUSIC: Maurice Ravel
CHOREOGRAPHY: Sven Age Larsen
SETTING: Jon Aud
COSTUMES: Jon Aud
COMPANY: Royal Opera House
PREMIÈRE: Stockholm, 193?

100 BOLERO
BOOK: Serge Lifar
MUSIC: Maurice Ravel
CHOREOGRAPHY: Serge Lifar
SETTING: Léon Leyritz
COSTUMES: Léon Leyritz
COMPANY: Théâtre National de L'Opéra
PREMIÈRE: Paris, 1941

101 BOLERO
MUSIC: Maurice Ravel
CHOREOGRAPHY: Bronislava Nijinska
SETTING: Enrico Donati
COSTUMES: Alexander Ignatieff
COMPANY: Ballet International
PREMIÈRE: New York, 1944

102 BORODIN SECOND, *A Russian Epic*
MUSIC: Alexander Borodin
CHOREOGRAPHY: Leonide Massine
SETTING: Nathalie Gontcharova
COSTUMES: Nathalie Gontcharova
COMPANY: Ballet Russe (Massine)
PREMIÈRE: New York, 1939

103 LE BOSQUET
BOOK: After French Court Ballet
MUSIC: Jean-Philippe Rameau; arr. Martin
    Penny
CHOREOGRAPHY: Hans Zullig
SETTING: Doris Zinkeisen
COMPANY: Jooss Ballet
PREMIÈRE: Cambridge, England, 1945

104 LE BOURGEOIS GENTILHOMME, *Ballet in
    Two Scenes*
BOOK: George Balanchine
MUSIC: Richard Strauss
CHOREOGRAPHY: George Balanchine
SETTINGS: Eugene Berman
COSTUMES: Eugene Berman
COMPANY: Ballet Russe (Denham)
PREMIÈRE: New York, 1944

105 LE BOURGEOIS GENTILHOMME, *Comic
    Ballet in Two Scenes*
BOOK: Sobeka (Boris Kochno), after Molière
MUSIC: Richard Strauss
CHOREOGRAPHY: George Balanchine
CURTAIN: Alexandre Benois
SETTINGS: Alexandre Benois
COSTUMES: Alexandre Benois
COMPANY: Ballet Russe (de Basil)
PREMIÈRE: Monte Carlo, 1932

106 LA BOUTIQUE FANTASQUE, *Ballet in One
    Act*
MUSIC: Gioachino Rossini; arr. and orch. Otto-
    rino Respighi
CHOREOGRAPHY: Leonide Massine
SETTING: André Derain
CURTAIN: André Derain
COSTUMES: André Derain
COMPANY: Ballet Russe (Diaghilev)
PREMIÈRE: London, 1919

107 BRAHMS VARIATIONS, *A Ballet in Two
    Scenes*
BOOK: Bronislava Nijinska
MUSIC: Johannes Brahms; orch. Ivan Boutnikoff
CHOREOGRAPHY: Bronislava Nijinska
SETTING: Marcel Vertès
COSTUMES: Marcel Vertès
COMPANY: Ballet International
PREMIÈRE: New York, 1944

108 BRAUTFAHRT, *Tanzmaerchen*
BOOK: Kurt Jooss
MUSIC: 18th Century Music, arr. by Frederic
    Waldman
CHOREOGRAPHY: Kurt Jooss
SETTING: Hein Heckroth
COSTUMES: Kaethe Luening
COMPANY: Neue Tanzbuehne
PREMIÈRE: Muenster, Germany, 1925

109 THE BRIGHT STREAM
BOOK: F. V. Lopukov and Andrey Pyotrovsky
MUSIC: Dimitri Shostakovich
CHOREOGRAPHY: F. V. Lopukov
SETTING: M. P. Bobyshov
COSTUMES: M. P. Bobyshov
COMPANY: Bolshoy Theatre
PREMIÈRE: Leningrad, 1935

110 EL CAFÉ DE CHINITAS, *A Cuadro Flamenco*
BOOK: Argentinita
MUSIC: Spanish Folk; arr. Federico Garcia-
    Lorca
CHOREOGRAPHY: Argentinita
CURTAIN: Salvador Dali

SETTING: Salvador Dali
COSTUMES: Salvador Dali
COMPANY: Ballet Theatre
PREMIÈRE: Detroit, Michigan, 1944

111 CAFÉ SOCIETY, *Ballet in One Act*
BOOK: Catherine Littlefield
MUSIC: Ferde Grofé
CHOREOGRAPHY: Catherine Littlefield
SETTING: Carl Shaffer
COSTUMES: Carl Shaffer
COMPANY: Philadelphia Opera Ballet
PREMIÈRE: Chicago, Illinois, 1938

112 CANCION
BOOK: After Federico Garcia-Lorca
MUSIC: Joaquin Turina
CHOREOGRAPHY: Celia Franca
COSTUMES: Edwin Kersley
COMPANY: The Ballet Guild
PREMIÈRE: London, 1942

113 LE CANTIQUE DES CANTIQUES
BOOK: Serge Lifar
MUSIC: Arthur Honegger
CHOREOGRAPHY: Serge Lifar
SETTING: Paul Colin
COSTUMES: Paul Colin
COMPANY: Théâtre National de l'Opéra
PREMIÈRE: Paris, 1938

114 CAP OVER MILL
MUSIC: Stanley Bate
CHOREOGRAPHY: Walter Gore
SETTING: Nadia Benois
COSTUMES: Nadia Benois
COMPANY: Marie Rambert Company
PREMIÈRE: London, 1940

115 CAPRICCIO ESPAGNOL
MUSIC: Nicholas Rimsky-Korsakov
CHOREOGRAPHY: William Christensen
SETTING: Harriette Meyers
COSTUMES: Harriette Meyers
COMPANY: Portland Symphony Orchestra
PREMIÈRE: Portland, Oregon, 1936

CAPRICCIO ESPAGNOL
see also SPANISH CAPRICCIO

116 CAPRICCIOSO
MUSIC: Domenico Cimarosa; orch. Paul Bowles
CHOREOGRAPHY: Anton Dolin
SETTING: Nicolas de Molas
COSTUMES: Nicolas de Molas
COMPANY: Ballet Theatre
PREMIÈRE: Chicago, Illinois, 1940

117 CAPRIOL SUITE
BOOK: Frederick Ashton
MUSIC: Peter Warlock
CHOREOGRAPHY: Frederick Ashton
SETTING: William Chappell
COSTUMES: William Chappell
COMPANY: Marie Rambert Company
PREMIÈRE: London, 1930

118 THE CARD PARTY, *Ballet in Three Deals*
BOOK: Igor Strawinsky and M. Malieff
MUSIC: Igor Strawinsky
CHOREOGRAPHY: George Balanchine
SETTING: Irene Sharaff
COSTUMES: Irene Sharaff
COMPANY: The American Ballet
PREMIÈRE: New York, 1937

CARD PARTY
see also JEU DE CARTES

119 LE CARNAVAL, *Ballet in One Act*
BOOK: Michel Fokine
MUSIC: Robert Schumann; orch. Rimsky-Korsakov, Glazounov, Liadov and Tcherepnine
CHOREOGRAPHY: Michel Fokine
SETTING: Léon Bakst
COSTUME: Léon Bakst
COMPANY: Ballet Russe (Diaghilev)
PREMIÈRE: Paris, 1910

120 CARNAVAL
MUSIC: Robert Schumann
CHOREOGRAPHY: Michel Fokine
SETTING: Alexandre Benois
COSTUMES: Alexandre Benois
COMPANY: Sadler's Wells Ballet
PREMIÈRE: London, 1933

121 CARNIVAL AT PEST, *Ballet in One Act*
BOOK: Ede Brada
MUSIC: Franz Liszt
CHOREOGRAPHY: Ede Brada
SETTING: Gustáv Oláh
COSTUMES: Gustáv Oláh
COMPANY: Hungarian Opera Ballet
PREMIÈRE: Budapest, 1930

122 CARNIVAL OF ANIMALS, *Ballet in One Scene*
MUSIC: Camille Saint-Saëns
CHOREOGRAPHY: Andrée Howard
SETTING: Andrée Howard
COSTUMES: Andrée Howard
COMPANY: Marie Rambert Company
PREMIÈRE: London, 1943

123 CASSE-NOISETTE, *Ballet in One Act*
MUSIC: Peter Tchaikowsky
CHOREOGRAPHY: Nicholas Sergueff
SETTING: William Chappell
COSTUMES: William Chappell
COMPANY: Markova-Dolin Ballet
PREMIÈRE: Newcastle, England, 1935

124 CASSE-NOISETTE (*Act II*)
MUSIC: Peter Tchaikowsky
CHOREOGRAPHY: Nicholas Sergueff
SETTING: Hedley Briggs
COSTUMES: Hedley Briggs
COMPANY: Sadler's Wells Ballet
PREMIÈRE: London, 1934

125 CASSE-NOISETTE
MUSIC: Peter Tchaikowsky
CHOREOGRAPHY: Ninette de Valois
SETTING: Mstislav Dobujinsky
COSTUMES: Mstislav Dobujinsky
COMPANY: Sadler's Wells Ballet
PREMIÈRE: London, 1936

THE CAT
see LA CHATTE

126 THE CAVE OF SLEEP, *Romantic Ballet in Five Scenes*
BOOK: Pavel Tchelitchew
MUSIC: Paul Hindemith
CHOREOGRAPHY: George Balanchine
SETTING: Pavel Tchelitchew
COSTUMES: Pavel Tchelitchew
COMMISSIONED by Lincoln Kirstein and George Balanchine
PROJECT: 1941

CENDRILLON
see CINDERELLA

127 LES CENT BAISERS, *Ballet in One Act*
BOOK: Boris Kochno, after Hans Christian Andersen
MUSIC: Frédéric d'Erlanger
CHOREOGRAPHY: Bronislava Nijinska
SETTING: Jean Hugo
COSTUMES: Jean Hugo
COMPANY: Ballet Russe (de Basil)
PREMIÈRE: Monte Carlo, 1935

128 CEPHALUS AND PROCRIS
MUSIC: André Grétry
CHOREOGRAPHY: Ninette de Valois
SETTING: William Chappell
COSTUMES: William Chappell
COMPANY: Sadler's Wells Ballet
PREMIÈRE: London, 1931

129 CHANSON CHORÉOGRAPHIQUE
MUSIC: Robert Schumann
CHOREOGRAPHY: John Regan
SETTING: del Renzio
COSTUMES: del Renzio
COMPANY: Ballet Trois Arts
PREMIÈRE: London, 1939

130 LE CHANT DE LA TERRE, *Ballet in Three Scenes*
BOOK: From Polish Folklore
MUSIC: Roman Palester
CHOREOGRAPHY: Bronislava Nijinska
SETTING: Waclaw Borowski
COSTUMES: Waclaw Borowski
COMPANY: The Polish Ballet
PREMIÈRE: Paris, 1937

131 LE CHANT DU ROSSIGNOL, *Choreographic Poem in One Act*
BOOK: Igor Strawinsky and Leonide Massine, after Hans Christian Andersen
MUSIC: Igor Strawinsky
CHOREOGRAPHY: Leonide Massine
CURTAIN: Henri Matisse
SETTING: Henri Matisse
COSTUMES: Henri Matisse
COMPANY: Ballet Russe (Diaghilev)
PREMIÈRE: Paris, 1920

LE CHAPEAU TRICORNE
see LE TRICORNE

132 CHARADE OR THE DEBUTANTE, *Ballet Romance in One Act*
BOOK: Lincoln Kirstein
MUSIC: After American Dance Tunes; arr. Trude Rittmann
CHOREOGRAPHY: Lew Christensen
COSTUMES: Alvin Colt
COMPANY: The American Ballet Caravan
PREMIÈRE: New York, 1939

133 LA CHASSE DE DIANE, *Mythological Ballet*
MUSIC: Michel Levine
CHOREOGRAPHY: Boris Romanoff
SETTING: Leon Zack
COSTUMES: Leon Zack
COMPANY: Russian Romantic Theatre
PREMIÈRE: Berlin, 1922

134 LA CHATTE, *Ballet in One Act*
BOOK: Boris Kochno
MUSIC: Henri Sauguet
CHOREOGRAPHY: George Balanchine
CONSTRUCTIVIST SETTING: Naum Gabo and Anton Pevsner

COSTUMES: Naum Gabo and Anton Pevsner
COMPANY: Ballet Russe (Diaghilev)
PREMIÈRE: Monte Carlo, 1927

135 CHECKMATE, *Ballet in One Scene with Pro-
logue*
BOOK: Arthur Bliss
MUSIC: Arthur Bliss
CHOREOGRAPHY: Ninette de Valois
SETTING: Edward McKnight-Kauffer
COSTUMES: Edward McKnight-Kauffer
COMPANY: Sadler's Wells Ballet
PREMIÈRE: Paris, 1937

136 LE CHEVALIER ET LA DAMOISELLE,
Ballet in Two Acts
BOOK: Serge Lifar and Philippe Gaubert
MUSIC: Philippe Gaubert
CHOREOGRAPHY: Serge Lifar
SETTING: A.-M. Cassandre
COSTUMES: A.-M. Cassandre
COMPANY: Théâtre National de l'Opéra
PREMIÈRE: Paris, 1941

CHILDREN'S TALES
see CONTES RUSSES

137 CHOPIN CONCERTO, *Choreographic Con-
certo in Three Movements*
MUSIC: Frederic Chopin
CHOREOGRAPHY: Bronislava Nijinska
SETTING: Alexander Ignatieff
COSTUMES: Alexander Ignatieff
COMPANY: The Polish Ballet
PREMIÈRE: Paris, 1937

138 CHOPIN CONCERTO, *Ballet in Three Move-
ments*
MUSIC: Frederic Chopin
CHOREOGRAPHY: Bronislava Nijinska
SETTING: Waclaw Borowski
COSTUMES: Waclaw Borowski
COMPANY: Ballet Russe (Denham)
PREMIÈRE: New York, 1942

139 CHOPINADE
MUSIC: Frederic Chopin
CHOREOGRAPHY: William Christensen
SETTING: J. C. Taylor
COSTUMES: J. C. Taylor
PREMIÈRE: Seattle, Washington, 1935

CHOPINIANA
see LES SYLPHIDES

140 CHOPIN IN OUR TIME
MUSIC: Frederic Chopin; arr. Owen Haynes;
Lyrics by John McGee
CHOREOGRAPHY: Ruth Page

COSTUMES: John Pratt
COMPANY: Page-Stone Ballet
PREMIÈRE: Chicago, Illinois, 1941

141 CHOREARTIUM, *Choreographic Symphony in
Four Parts*
MUSIC: Johannes Brahms
CHOREOGRAPHY: Leonide Massine
CURTAIN: George Annenkov
SETTING: Constantin Terechkovitch and Eugène
Lourié
COSTUMES: Constantin Terechkovitch and Eu-
gène Lourié
COMPANY: Ballet Russe (de Basil)
PREMIÈRE: London, 1933

142 CHOUT (LE BOUFFON), *Ballet in Six Scenes*
BOOK: A Russian Fable
MUSIC: Serge Prokofieff
CHOREOGRAPHY: Michel Larionow and Taddie
Slawinsky
CURTAIN: Michel Larionow
SETTING: Michel Larionow
COSTUMES: Michel Larionow
COMPANY: Ballet Russe (Diaghilev)
PREMIÈRE: Paris, 1921

143 CHRISTMAS CAROL
MUSIC: Vaughan Williams
CHOREOGRAPHY: Adolph Bolm
SETTING: Nicolai Remisoff
COSTUMES: Nicolai Remisoff
COMPANY: Chicago Allied Arts
PREMIÈRE: Chicago, Illinois, 1925

144 CHRISTMAS EVE, *Ballet in Three Acts and
Seven Scenes*
BOOK: U. E. Slonimsky, after Nicolas Gogol
MUSIC: B. V. Asafiev
CHOREOGRAPHY: V. A. Varkovitsky
SETTING: A. A. Kolomoytsev
COSTUMES: A. A. Kolomoytsev
COMPANY: [Soviet State Theatre]
PREMIÈRE: Moscow, 1939

145 CHRONICA, *Dance-Drama in Three Acts and
a Prelude*
BOOK: Kurt Jooss
MUSIC: Berthold Goldschmidt
CHOREOGRAPHY: Kurt Jooss
COSTUMES: Dimitri Bouchêne
COMPANY: Jooss Ballet
PREMIÈRE: Cambridge, England, 1939

146 CIMAROSIANA, *Opera Ballet in Three Scenes*
BOOK: Leonide Massine
MUSIC: Domenico Cimarosa; arr. and orch.
Ottorino Respighi

CHOREOGRAPHY: Leonide Massine
CURTAIN: José-Maria Sert
SETTINGS: José-Maria Sert
COSTUMES: José-Maria Sert
COMPANY: Ballet Russe (Diaghilev)
PREMIÈRE: Paris, 1920

147 CINDERELLA
MUSIC: Marcel Delannoy
CHOREOGRAPHY: Ruth Page
SETTING: Nicolai Remisoff
COSTUMES: Nicolai Remisoff
COMPANY: Ravinia Opera Co.
PREMIÈRE: Ravinia, Illinois, 1929

148 CINDERELLA
MUSIC: Maurice Ravel
CHOREOGRAPHY: Frederick Ashton
SETTING: Sophie Fedorovitch
COSTUMES: Sophie Fedorovitch
COMPANY: Marie Rambert Company
PREMIÈRE: London, 1935

149 CINDERELLA, *Ballet in One Act and Three Scenes*
BOOK: After Perrault
MUSIC: Frédéric d'Erlanger
CHOREOGRAPHY: Michel Fokine
SETTING: Nathalie Gontcharova
COSTUMES: Nathalie Gontcharova
COMPANY: Ballet Russe (de Basil)
PREMIÈRE: London, 1938

150 CINDERELLA
BOOK: Nicolai Volkoff
MUSIC: Serge Prokofieff
CHOREOGRAPHY: Rostislav Zakharov
SETTING: Peter Williams
COSTUMES: Peter Williams
COMPANY: Moscow Bolshoi Theatre Ballet
PREMIÈRE: Moscow, 1945

151 CITY PORTRAIT, *Ballet-document in One Act*
BOOK: Eugene Loring
MUSIC: Henry Brant
CHOREOGRAPHY: Eugene Loring
COSTUMES: Forrest Thayr, Jr.
COMPANY: The American Ballet Caravan
PREMIÈRE: New York, 1939

152 CLAIR DE LUNE, *Ballet in Three Movements*
BOOK: Igor Schwezoff
MUSIC: Ludwig van Beethoven; orch. Francisco Mignone
CHOREOGRAPHY: Igor Schwezoff
SETTING: Enrico Bianco

COSTUMES: Enrico Bianco
COMPANY: Teatro Municipal
PREMIÈRE: Rio de Janeiro, [1945]

153 CLASSICAL SUITE
MUSIC: Johann Sebastian Bach
CHOREOGRAPHY: Catherine Littlefield
SETTING: R. Deshays
COSTUMES: P. T. Champs
COMPANY: Philadelphia Opera Ballet
PREMIÈRE: Princeton, New Jersey, 1937

154 CLÉOPATRE, *Ballet in One Act*
BOOK: Michel Fokine
MUSIC: Arensky, Taneyev, Rimsky-Korsakov, Glinka, Glazounov
CHOREOGRAPHY: Michel Fokine
SETTING: Léon Bakst
COSTUMES: Léon Bakst
COMPANY: Ballet Russe (Diaghilev)
PREMIÈRE: Paris, 1909

155 CLÉOPATRE, *Ballet in One Act*
BOOK: Michel Fokine
MUSIC: Arensky, Rimsky-Korsakov, Glinka, Glazounov
CHOREOGRAPHY: Michel Fokine
SETTING: Robert Delauney
COSTUMES: Sonia Delauney
COMPANY: Ballet Russe (Diaghilev)
PREMIÈRE: London, 1918

156 CŒUR DE GLACE
MUSIC: Wolfgang Amadeus Mozart
CHOREOGRAPHY: William Christensen
SETTING: J. C. Taylor
COSTUMES: J. C. Taylor
COMPANY: Portland Symphony Orchestra
PREMIÈRE: Portland, Oregon, 1936

157 LA COLOMBE, *Ballet in One Act*
BOOK: Jules Barbier and M. Carré
MUSIC: Charles Gounod
SETTING: Juan Gris
COSTUMES: Juan Gris
COMPANY: Ballet Russe (Diaghilev)
PREMIÈRE: Monte Carlo, 1924

158 LE COMBAT DES DÉESSES, *Ballet in Two Acts*
BOOK: Viggo Cavling
MUSIC: Emil Reesen
CHOREOGRAPHY: Harald Lander
SETTING: O. Charles Petersen
COSTUMES: O. Charles Petersen
COMPANY: Royal Theatre
PREMIÈRE: Copenhagen, 1933

159 COMMEDIA BALLETICA, *Ballet in Eight Movements*
Music: Igor Strawinsky, after Pergolesi
Choreography: Todd Bolender
Setting: Robert Davison
Costumes: Robert Davison
Company: Ballet Russe (Denham)
Première: New York, 1945

160 LES COMÉDIENS JALOUX
Book: After Molière
Choreography: Bronislava Nijinska
Setting: George Annenkov
Costumes: George Annenkov
Company: Théâtre de la Danse (Nijinska)
Première: Paris, 1932

161 COMPANY AT THE MANOR
Book: Kurt Jooss
Music: Ludwig van Beethoven; orch. Dent
Choreography: Kurt Jooss
Setting: Doris Zinkeisen
Costumes: Doris Zinkeisen
Company: Jooss Ballet
Première: Cambridge, England, 1943

162 COMUS, *Masque in One Act and Two Scenes*
Book: John Milton; arr. Robert Helpmann
Music: Henry Purcell; arr. Constant Lambert
Choreography: Robert Helpmann
Setting: Oliver Messel
Costumes: Oliver Messel
Masks: Oliver Messel
Company: Sadler's Wells Ballet
Première: London, 1942

163 CONCERTO
Music: Wolfgang Amadeus Mozart
Choreography: Keith Lester
Setting: Sophie Fedorovitch
Costumes: Sophie Fedorovitch
Company: Arts Theatre Ballet
Première: London, 1940

164 CONCERTO
Music: Frederic Chopin
Choreography: J. Dolotine
Setting: Boloslav Leitgeber
Costumes: Boloslav Leitgeber
Company: Allied Ballets
Première: London, 1942

165 CONCERTO
Music: Wolfgang Amadeus Mozart
Choreography: George Balanchine
Setting: Pavel Tchelitchew
Costumes: Pavel Tchelitchew

Company: Teatro Colon
Première: Buenos Aires, 1942

166 CONCERTO BAROCCO, *Classic Ballet in One Act and Three Movements*
Music: Johann Sebastian Bach
Choreography: George Balanchine
Setting: Eugene Berman
Costumes: Eugene Berman
Company: The American Ballet
Première: Hartford, Connecticut, 1941

167 CONCERT DANSANT, *Ballet in Three Movements*
Music: Camille Saint-Saëns
Choreography: Igor Schwezoff
Setting: Castelo Bianco
Costumes: Castelo Bianco
Company: Teatro Municipal
Première: Rio de Janeiro, 1945

168 CONCERTO DE CHOPIN
Book: Bronislava Nijinska
Music: Frederic Chopin
Choreography: Bronislava Nijinska
Setting: Waclaw Borowski
Costumes: Waclaw Borowski
Company: The Polish Ballet
Première: Paris, 1937

169 LA CONCURRENCE
Book: André Derain
Music: Georges Auric
Choreography: George Balanchine
Curtain: André Derain
Setting: André Derain
Costumes: André Derain
Company: Ballet Russe (de Basil)
Première: Monte Carlo, 1932

170 CONFESSIONAL
Book: Robert Browning
Music: Jan Sibelius and others
Choreography: Walter Gore
Costumes: Andrée Howard
Company: Marie Rambert Company
Première: Oxford, England, 1941

171 CONFESSIONAL
Music: Camille Saint-Saëns
Choreography: Andrée Howard
Setting: Andrée Howard
Costumes: Andrée Howard
Company: Marie Rambert Company
Première: London, 1943

172 CONSECRATION
Music: Johann Sebastian Bach

CHOREOGRAPHY: Adolph Bolm
SETTING: Benjamino Bufano
COSTUMES: Benjamino Bufano
COMPANY: Hollywood Bowl
PREMIÈRE: Hollywood, California, 1935

173 CONSTANTIA, *Classic Ballet in One Act*
MUSIC: Frederic Chopin; orch. Adolf Schmid
CHOREOGRAPHY: William Dollar
SETTING: Horace Armistead
COSTUMES: Grace Houston
COMPANY: Ballet International
PREMIÈRE: New York, 1944

174 UN CONTE, *Fantasy Ballet in One Scene*
MUSIC: Stanislas Moniuszko
CHOREOGRAPHY: Jan Cieplinski
SETTING: Michel Kedziora
COSTUMES: Michel Kedziora
COMPANY: The Polish Ballet
PREMIÈRE: [Paris], 1938-39

175 LE CONTE DE LA MÈRE L'OYE
MUSIC: Maurice Ravel
CHOREOGRAPHY: Louis de Bercher
SETTING: Hector Basaldua
COSTUMES: Hector Basaldua
COMPANY: Teatro Colon
PREMIÈRE: Buenos Aires, 1945

176 LES CONTES DU BOUFFON, *Ballet in One Scene, Prologue and Epilogue*
BOOK: Igor Schwezoff
MUSIC: Russian Folk Songs; orch. Francisco Mignone
CHOREOGRAPHY: Igor Schwezoff
SETTING: Serge Soudeikine
COSTUMES: Serge Soudeikine
COMPANY: Teatro Municipal
PREMIÈRE: Rio de Janeiro, 1945

177 CONTES RUSSES, *Ballet in One Act and Four Scenes*
BOOK: From Russian Folk Tales
MUSIC: Anatol Liadov
CHOREOGRAPHY: Leonide Massine
CURTAIN: Michel Larionow
DECORS: Michel Larionow
COSTUMES: Michel Larionow
COMPANY: Ballet Russe (Diaghilev)
PREMIÈRE: Paris, 1917

178 COPPELIA, *Ballet in Two Acts*
BOOK: C. H. Nuitter and Saint-Léon
MUSIC: Léo Delibes
CHOREOGRAPHY: Ivan Clustine
SETTING: Joseph Urban
COSTUMES: Joseph Urban

COMPANY: Pavlova Company
PREMIÈRE: [United States, 1915]

179 COPPELIA
BOOK: C. H. Nuitter and Saint-Léon
MUSIC: Léo Delibes
CHOREOGRAPHY: Boris Novikoff
SETTING: Serge Soudeikine
COSTUMES: Serge Soudeikine
COMPANY: Pavlova Company
PREMIÈRE: Paris, 1923

180 COPPELIA
BOOK: C. H. Nuitter and Saint-Léon
MUSIC: Léo Delibes; arr. Frederic Cohen
CHOREOGRAPHY: Kurt Jooss
SETTING: Hein Heckroth
COSTUMES: Hein Heckroth
COMPANY: Jooss Ballet
PREMIÈRE: Essen, Germany, 1931

181 COPPELIA, *Ballet in Two Acts*
BOOK: C. H. Nuitter and Saint-Léon
MUSIC: Léo Delibes
CHOREOGRAPHY: Nicholas Sergueeff
SETTING: Edward Calligan
COSTUMES: Edward Calligan
COMPANY: Sadler's Wells Ballet
PREMIÈRE: London, 1933

182 COPPELIA
BOOK: C. H. Nuitter and Saint-Léon
MUSIC: Léo Delibes
CHOREOGRAPHY: Nicholas Zverev
SETTING: Mstislav Dobujinsky
COSTUMES: Mstislav Dobujinsky
COMPANY: Lithuanian Ballet
PREMIÈRE: Kaunas, Lithuania, 1933

183 COPPELIA
BOOK: C. H. Nuitter and Saint-Léon
MUSIC: Léo Delibes
CHOREOGRAPHY: Nicholas Zverev
SETTING: Mstislav Dobujinsky
COSTUMES: Mstislav Dobujinsky
COMPANY: Ballet Russe (Blum)
PREMIÈRE: London, 1935

184 COPPELIA
BOOK: C. H. Nuitter and Saint-Léon
MUSIC: Léo Delibes
CHOREOGRAPHY: Yvonne Georgi
SETTING: Gerard Hordijk
COSTUMES: Gerard Hordijk
COMPANY: Wagner Vereeniging
PREMIÈRE: Amsterdam, 1937

185 COPPELIA, *Ballet in Three Acts*
BOOK: C. H. Nuitter and Saint-Léon

MUSIC: Léo Delibes
CHOREOGRAPHY: Nicholas Sergueff, after Petipa
SETTING: Pierre Roy
COSTUMES: Pierre Roy
COMPANY: Ballet Russe (Massine)
PREMIÈRE: New York, 1938

186 COPPELIA
BOOK: C. H. Nuitter and Saint-Léon
MUSIC: Léo Delibes
CHOREOGRAPHY: Nicholas Sergueff, after Petipa
SETTING: William Chappell
COSTUMES: William Chappell
COMPANY: Sadler's Wells Ballet
PREMIÈRE: London, 1940

187 COPPELIA, *Ballet in One Act and Three Scenes*
BOOK: C. H. Nuitter and Saint-Léon
MUSIC: Léo Delibes
CHOREOGRAPHY: Simon Semenoff, after Louis Mérante
CURTAIN: Roberto Montenegro
SETTING: Roberto Montenegro
COSTUMES: Roberto Montenegro
COMPANY: Ballet Theatre
PREMIÈRE: New York, 1942

188 COPPELIA
BOOK: C. H. Nuitter and Saint-Léon
MUSIC: Léo Delibes
CHOREOGRAPHY: Nicholas Sergueff
SETTING: Hein Heckroth
COSTUMES: Hein Heckroth
COMPANY: The International Ballet
PREMIÈRE: [London, 1941]

189 LE COQ D'OR, *Ballet in Three Acts, Prologue and Epilogue*
BOOK: V. Bielsky, after Pushkin; revised by Alexandre Benois
MUSIC: Nicholas Rimsky-Korsakov; arr. Nicolas Tcherepnine
CHOREOGRAPHY: Michel Fokine
CURTAIN: Nathalie Gontcharova
SETTING: Nathalie Gontcharova
COSTUMES: Nathalie Gontcharova
COMPANY: Ballet Russe (Diaghilev)
PREMIÈRE: Paris, 1914

190 LE COQ D'OR
MUSIC: Nicholas Rimsky-Korsakov
CHOREOGRAPHY: Adolph Bolm
CURTAIN: Nicolai Remisoff
SETTING: Nicolai Remisoff
COSTUMES: Nicolai Remisoff
COMPANY: San Francisco Opera Company
PREMIÈRE: San Francisco, California, 1933

191 LA CORONELA, *Ballet in Four Episodes*
BOOK: Waldeen, Ledesma, Seki Sano
MUSIC: Silvestre Revueltas
CHOREOGRAPHY: Waldeen
SETTING: Gabriel Fernandez Ledesma
COSTUMES: Gabriel Fernandez Ledesma
COMPANY: Ballet Waldeen
PREMIÈRE: México, D. F., 1940

192 LE CORSAIRE
BOOK: Saint-George and Mazilier
MUSIC: Adolphe Adam
CHOREOGRAPHY: Mazilier
SETTING: Anatol Petritsky
COSTUMES: Anatol Petritsky
COMPANY: Soviet State Ballet
PREMIÈRE: Karkov, 1925

193 COTILLON, *Ballet in One Act*
BOOK: Boris Kochno
MUSIC: Emmanuel Chabrier
CHOREOGRAPHY: George Balanchine
SETTING: Christian Bérard
COSTUMES: Christian Bérard
COMPANY: Ballet Russe (de Basil)
PREMIÈRE: Monte Carlo, 1932

194 LA CRÉATION DU MONDE, *Ballet in One Act*
BOOK: Blaise Cendrars
MUSIC: Darius Milhaud
CHOREOGRAPHY: Jean Borlin
CURTAIN: Fernand Léger
SETTING: Fernand Léger
COSTUMES: Fernand Léger
COMPANY: Les Ballets Suédois
PREMIÈRE: Paris, 1923

195 LA CRÉATION DU MONDE
MUSIC: Darius Milhaud
CHOREOGRAPHY: Ninette de Valois
SETTING: Edward Wolfe
COSTUMES: Edward Wolfe
COMPANY: Sadler's Wells Ballet
PREMIÈRE: London, 1932

196 LES CRÉATURES DE PROMÉTHÉE
BOOK: Serge Lifar
MUSIC: Ludwig van Beethoven
CHOREOGRAPHY: Serge Lifar
SETTING: François Quelvée
COSTUMES: François Quelvée
COMPANY: Théâtre National de l'Opéra
PREMIÈRE: Paris, 1930

197 CROQUIS DE MERCURE
MUSIC: Erik Satie

CHOREOGRAPHY: Andrée Howard
COSTUMES: Andrée Howard
COMPANY: Marie Rambert Company
PREMIÈRE: London, 1938

198 CROSS-GARTERED
BOOK: Episode from Twelfth Night
MUSIC: Girolamo Frescobaldi
CHOREOGRAPHY: Antony Tudor
SETTING: Pamela Boquet
COSTUMES: Pamela Boquet
COMPANY: Marie Rambert Company
PREMIÈRE: London, 1937

199 CSÁRDAJELENET
BOOK: Viktor Lányi
MUSIC: Jenö Hubay
CHOREOGRAPHY: Gyula Harangozó
SETTING: Zoltán Fülöp
COSTUMES: Zoltán Fülöp
COMPANY: Hungarian State Ballet
PREMIÈRE: Budapest, 1936

200 CSONGOR ÉS TÜNDE
BOOK: L. Márkus
MUSIC: L. Weiner
CHOREOGRAPHY: Jan Cieplinsky
SETTING: Gustáv Oláh
COSTUMES: Gustáv Oláh
COMPANY: Hungarian State Ballet
PREMIÈRE: Budapest, 1930

201 CUADRO FLAMENCO, *Suite of Andalusian Dances*
MUSIC: Spanish Folk music; arr. Manuel de Falla
CHOREOGRAPHY: Folk dances
CURTAIN: Pablo Picasso
SETTING: Pablo Picasso
COSTUMES: Pablo Picasso
COMPANY: Ballet Russe (Diaghilev)
PREMIÈRE: Paris, 1921

202 THE CUCKOLD'S FAIR, *Ballet in One Act*
BOOK: Federico Garcia-Lorca and Cipriano Rivas-Cherif
MUSIC: Gustavo Pittaluga
CHOREOGRAPHY: Pilar Lopez
SETTING: Joan Junyer
COMPANY: Ballet Russe (Denham)
PREMIÈRE: Cleveland, Ohio, 1943

203 CUPID AND PSYCHE
BOOK: Gerald Hugh Berners
MUSIC: Gerald Hugh Berners
CHOREOGRAPHY: Frederick Ashton
SETTING: Francis Rose

COSTUMES: Francis Rose
COMPANY: Sadler's Wells Ballet
PREMIÈRE: London, 1939

204 CZERNYANA
MUSIC: Carl Czerny
CHOREOGRAPHY: Frank Staff
SETTING: Eve Swinstead-Smith
COSTUMES: Eve Swinstead-Smith
COMPANY: Marie Rambert Company
PREMIÈRE: London, 1939

DANCE CONCERTO
see DANSES CONCERTANTES

205 DANSE NOBLE
MUSIC: Johann Sebastian Bach
CHOREOGRAPHY: Adolph Bolm
SETTING: Jeanne Berlandina
COSTUMES: Jeanne Berlandina
PREMIÈRE: [Hollywood], 1935

206 LES DANSES
MUSIC: John Field
CHOREOGRAPHY: John Regan
SETTING: Elizabeth Agombar
COSTUMES: Elizabeth Agombar
COMPANY: Ballet Trois Arts
PREMIÈRE: London, 1940

207 DANSES CONCERTANTES, *Ballet in One Act*
MUSIC: Igor Strawinsky
CHOREOGRAPHY: George Balanchine
CURTAIN: Eugene Berman
SETTING: Eugene Berman
COSTUMES: Eugene Berman
COMPANY: Ballet Russe (Denham)
PREMIÈRE: New York, 1944

208 LES DANSES D'AUTREFOIS, *Italian Suite in Six Scenes*
MUSIC: Ottorino Respighi
CHOREOGRAPHY: Jean Cieplinski
SETTING: Michel Kedziora
COSTUMES: Michel Kedziora
COMPANY: The Polish Ballet
PREMIÈRE: [Paris], 1938-39

209 DANSES ESPAGNOLES
MUSIC: Mautis, Albeniz, Espert, Castillo, Turina, de Falla; orch. Ernest Irving
CHOREOGRAPHY: Angelo Andes
SETTING: Hein Heckroth
COSTUMES: Hein Heckroth and Honoria Plesch
COMPANY: The International Ballet
PREMIÈRE: Oxford, England, 1943

210 DANSES PERSANES
BOOK: Igor Schwezoff
MUSIC: Modeste Moussorgsky
CHOREOGRAPHY: Igor Schwezoff
SETTING: David Grey
COSTUMES: David Grey
COMPANY: Ballet Schwezoff
PREMIÈRE: The Hague, Holland, 1934

211 DANSES POLOVTSIENNES
MUSIC: Alexander Borodin
CHOREOGRAPHY: Kurt Jooss
SETTING: Hein Heckroth
COSTUMES: Hein Heckroth
COMPANY: Jooss Ballet
PREMIÈRE: Essen, Germany, 1930

212 DANSES POLOVTSIENNES, *Ballet in One Act*
MUSIC: Alexander Borodin
CHOREOGRAPHY: Michel Fokine
SETTING: Nicholas Roerich
COSTUMES: Nicholas Roerich
COMPANY: Ballet Russe (Diaghilev)
PREMIÈRE: Paris, 1909

DANSES POLOVTSIENNES
see also PRINCE IGOR

213 DANSES SLAVES ET TZIGANES, *in One Act*
MUSIC: Alexander Dargomijsky
CHOREOGRAPHY: Bronislava Nijinska
SETTING: Constantin Korovine
COSTUMES: Constantin Korovine
COMPANY: Ballet Russe (de Basil)
PREMIÈRE: New York, 1936

214 DANSES SLAVES ET TZIGANES
MUSIC: Alexander Dargomijsky
CHOREOGRAPHY: Bronislava Nijinska
SETTING: A. Golovine
COSTUMES: Constantin Korovine
COMPANY: Ballet Russe (de Basil)
PREMIÈRE: [London, 1939]

215 DANSES VILLAGEOISES
MUSIC: André E. M. Grétry
CHOREOGRAPHY: Pratesi
SETTING: Mario Cito Filomarino
COSTUMES: Mario Cito Filomarino
COMPANY: Scala Opera Ballet
PREMIÈRE: Milan, 1933

216 LA DANSEUSE ET LA LARRONNE
MUSIC: Wolfgang Amadeus Mozart
CHOREOGRAPHY: Boris Romanoff
SETTING: Leon Zack
COSTUMES: Leon Zack

COMPANY: Russian Romantic Theatre
PREMIÈRE: Berlin, 1922

217 DANSGILLE
MUSIC: Swedish Folk music
CHOREOGRAPHY: Jean Borlin
SETTING: After old prints
COSTUMES: Native Costumes
COMPANY: Les Ballets Suédois
PREMIÈRE: Paris, 1921

218 DANS LA RUE
BOOK: Tony Gregory
MUSIC: Lennox Berkeley
CHOREOGRAPHY: Tony Gregory
SETTING: Raymond Gid
MASKS: Raymond Gid
COSTUMES: Madeleine Schwab
COMPANY: Les Archives Internationales de la Danse
PREMIÈRE: Paris, 1932

219 DANTE SONATA, *Ballet in One Act*
MUSIC: Franz Liszt; orch. Constant Lambert
CHOREOGRAPHY: Frederick Ashton
SETTING: Sophie Fedorovitch
COSTUMES: Sophie Fedorovitch
COMPANY: Sadler's Wells Ballet
PREMIÈRE: London, 1940

220 DAPHNIS AND CHLOE, *Pastoral Poem in Three Scenes*
BOOK: Michel Fokine
MUSIC: Maurice Ravel
CHOREOGRAPHY: Michel Fokine
SETTING: Léon Bakst
COSTUMES: Léon Bakst
COMPANY: Ballet Russe (Diaghilev)
PREMIÈRE: Paris, 1912

221 DAPHNIS AND CHLOE, *Ballet in Three Scenes*
MUSIC: Maurice Ravel
CHOREOGRAPHY: Catherine Littlefield
SETTING: A. Jarin
COSTUMES: J. Pascal
COMPANY: Philadelphia Opera Ballet
PREMIÈRE: Philadelphia, Pennsylvania, 1936

222 DARK ELEGIES
BOOK: Antony Tudor
MUSIC: Gustav Mahler
CHOREOGRAPHY: Antony Tudor
SETTING: Nadia Benois
COSTUMES: Nadia Benois
COMPANY: Marie Rambert Company
PREMIÈRE: London, 1937

223 DARK ELEGIES
Book: Antony Tudor
Music: Gustav Mahler
Choreography: Antony Tudor
Setting: Raymond Sovey
Costumes: Raymond Sovey
Company: Ballet Theatre
Première: New York, 1940

224 DAVID, *Ballet in Six Episodes*
Book: Poppæa Vanda
Music: Maurice Jacobson
Choreography: Keith Lester
Curtain: Jacob Epstein
Setting: Bernard Meninsky
Costumes: Bernard Meninsky
Company: Markova-Dolin Company
Première: Newcastle-on-Tyne, 1935

225 DAVID TRIOMPHANT, *Ballet in Two Acts and Three Scenes*
Book: Serge Lifar
Music: Claude Debussy and Modeste Mussorgsky
Choreography: Serge Lifar
Setting: Fernand Léger
Costumes: Fernand Léger
Company: [Théâtre National de l'Opéra]
Première: Paris, 1936

Day in a South Part
see Rio Grande

226 DEATH AND THE MAIDEN
Music: Franz Schubert
Choreography: Andrée Howard
Costumes: Andrée Howard
Company: Marie Rambert Company
Première: London, 1937

227 LE DÉJEUNER SUR L'HERBE
Book: Irène Lidova
Music: Joseph Lanner; orch. Alexandre Tcherepnine
Choreography: Roland Petit
Setting: Marie Laurencin
Costumes: Marie Laurencin
Company: Les Ballets des Champs Elysées
Première: Paris, 1945

228 THE DEMON
Music: Paul Hindemith
Choreographer: Kurt Jooss
Setting: Hein Heckroth
Costumes: Hein Heckroth
Company: Neue Tanzbuehne
Première: Muenster, Germany, 1925

229 THE DEN
Book: Kurt Jooss
Music: Frederic Cohen
Choreography: Kurt Jooss
Setting: Hein Heckroth
Costumes: Kaethe Luening
Company: Neue Tanzbuehne
Première: Muenster, Germany, 1926

230 DE PROFUNDIS
Music: Frederic Chopin
Choreographer: Keith Lester
Costumes: Joseph Carl
Setting: Joseph Carl
Company: Arts Theatre Ballet
Première: London, 1940

231 DERVISHES
Book: Jean Borlin
Music: Alexander Glazounov
Choreography: Jean Borlin
Setting: Mouveau
Costumes: Jean Borlin
Company: Les Ballets Suédois
Première: Paris, 1920

232 THE DESCENT OF HEBE
Book: Antony Tudor
Music: Ernest Bloch
Choreography: Antony Tudor
Setting: Nadia Benois
Costumes: Nadia Benois
Company: Marie Rambert Company
Première: London, 1935

Destiny
see Les Présages

233 LES DEUX PIGEONS
Book: H. Régnier and L. Mérante
Music: André Messager
Choreography: Albert Aveline
Setting: Paul-René Larthe
Costume: Paul-René Larthe
Company: Théâtre National de l'Opéra
Première: Paris, 1941

234 DEVIL'S HOLIDAY, *Comic Ballet in Three Scenes and a Prologue*
Book: Frederick Ashton
Music: Vincenzo Tommasini, after Paganini
Choreography: Frederick Ashton
Setting: Eugene Berman
Costumes: Eugene Berman
Company: Sadler's Wells Ballet
Première: London, 1938

235 DEVIL'S HOLIDAY, *Comic Ballet in Three Scenes and a Prologue*
Book: Vincenzo Tommasini
Music: Vincenzo Tommasini, after Paganini
Choreography: Frederick Ashton
Setting: Eugene Berman
Costumes: Eugene Berman
Company: Ballet Russe (Massine)
Première: Monte Carlo, 1939

Le Diable s'amuse
see Devil's Holiday

236 DIANA
Music: Alexander Voormolen
Choreography: Yvonne Georgi
Settings: Gerard Hordijk
Costumes: Gerard Hordijk
Company: Wagner Vereeniging
Première: Amsterdam, 1937

237 LE DIEU BLEU, *A Hindu Legend in One Act*
Book: Jean Cocteau and F. de Madrazo
Music: Reynaldo Hahn
Choreography: Michel Fokine
Setting: Léon Bakst
Costumes: Léon Bakst
Company: Ballet Russe (Diaghilev)
Première: Paris, 1912

238 LES DIEUX MENDIANTS, *Ballet in One Act*
Book: Sobeka (Boris Kochno)
Music: George Frederic Handel; arr. Thomas Beecham
Choreography: George Balanchine
Setting: (for Daphnis and Chloe) Léon Bakst
Costumes: (for Tentations de la Bergère) Juan Gris
Company: Ballet Russe (Diaghilev)
Première: London, 1928

Les Dieux Mendiants
see also The Gods Go A-Begging

239 DIM LUSTRE, *Ballet in One Act*
Music: Richard Strauss
Choreography: Antony Tudor
Settings: Motley
Costumes: Motley
Company: Ballet Theatre
Première: New York, 1943

240 DIONÉ, *Symphonic Legend in One Act and Two Scenes*
Book: Georges Milenoff
Music: Eduardo Sánchez de Fuentes
Choreography: Georges Milenoff
Setting: Frederico Villalba

Company: Pro-Arte Musical
Première: Havana, Cuba, 193?

241 DIONYSIUS
Music: Nicolas Tcherepnine
Choreography: Ivan Clustine
Setting: O. Allegri
Costumes: O. Allegri
Company: Pavlova Company
Première: [Paris, 1923]

242 DIONYSIUS
Book: Mikhail Mordkin
Music: Alexander Glazounov
Choreography: Mikhail Mordkin
Setting: Serge Soudeikine
Costumes: Serge Soudeikine
Company: Mordkin Ballet Company
Première: New York, 1938

243 DON DOMINGO
Book: Alfonso Reyes, after Alarcon
Music: Silvestre Revueltas
Choreography: Leonide Massine
Setting: Julio Castellanos
Masks: Frederico Canessi
Costumes: Julio Castellanos
Company: Ballet Theatre
Première: México, D. F., 1942

244 DON JUAN, *Choreographic Tragi-Comedy in Three Tableaux*
Book: Eric Allatini and Michel Fokine
Music: Christoph Willibald Gluck
Choreography: Michel Fokine
Settings: Mariano Andreù
Costumes: Mariano Andreù
Company: Ballet Russe (Blum)
Première: London, 1936

245 DON QUIXOTE
Music: Minkus
Choreography: Boris Novikoff
Settings: Constantin Korovine
Costumes: Constantin Korovine
Company: Pavlova Company
Première: London, 1927

246 DOUANES
Music: Geoffrey Toye
Choreography: Ninette de Valois
Setting: Hedley Briggs
Costumes: Hedley Briggs
Company: Sadler's Wells Ballet
Première: London, 1932

247 DRAMA BURQUES, *Ballet in One Scene*
Book: Igor Schwezoff

MUSIC: Franz Liszt
CHOREOGRAPHY: Igor Schwezoff
SETTINGS: Enrico Bianco
COSTUMES: Carla Conda Caputa Modes
COMPANY: Teatro Municipal
PREMIÈRE: Rio de Janeiro, 1945

DREAMS
see SONGES

248 DROSSELBART, *Dance Drama in Four Acts*
BOOK: After Grimm by Kurt Jooss
MUSIC: Wolfgang Amadeus Mozart; arr. Frederic Cohen
CHOREOGRAPHY: Kurt Jooss
SETTING: Hein Heckroth
COSTUMES: Kaethe Luening
COMPANY: Folkwang Tanzbuehne
PREMIÈRE: Essen, Germany, 1929

249 DRUMS SOUND IN HACKENSACK
BOOK: Agnes De Mille
MUSIC: Frederic Cohen
CHOREOGRAPHY: Agnes De Mille
COSTUMES: Joep Nicolas
COMPANY: Jooss Ballet
PREMIÈRE: New York, 1941

LE DUC DE BURLEIGH
see MY LORD OF BURLEIGH

250 THE DUKE OF SACRAMENTO (also HOBO OF THE HILLS)
BOOK: Eugene Loring
MUSIC: Norman Dello Joio
CHOREOGRAPHY: Eugene Loring
SETTING: George Bockman
COSTUMES: George Bockman
COMPANY: The Dance Players
PREMIÈRE: Newhope, Pennsylvania, 1942

251 THE DWARF GRENADIER
BOOK: H. Preston
MUSIC: H. Preston
CHOREOGRAPHY: Nicholas Zverev
SETTING: Mstislav Dobujinsky
COSTUMES: Mstislav Dobujinsky
COMPANY: Lithuanian State Ballet
PREMIÈRE: London, 1935

252 UNE ÉDUCATION MANQUÉE
MUSIC: Emmanuel Chabrier
CHOREOGRAPHY: George Balanchine
SETTING: Juan Gris
COSTUMES: Juan Gris
COMPANY: Ballet Russe (Diaghilev)
PREMIÈRE: Monte Carlo, 1924

253 LES ÉLÉMENTS
MUSIC: Johann Sebastian Bach
CHOREOGRAPHY: Michel Fokine
SETTING: Dimitri Bouchêne
COSTUMES: Dimitri Bouchêne
COMPANY: Ballet Russe (Blum)
PREMIÈRE: London, 1937

254 LES ELFES, *Romantic Ballet in One Act*
BOOK: Michel Fokine
MUSIC: Felix Mendelssohn
CHOREOGRAPHY: Michel Fokine
COSTUMES: Christian Bérard
COMPANY: The Fokine Ballet
PREMIÈRE: New York, 1924

255 EL GRECO, *Ballet in One Act*
BOOK: Jean Borlin
MUSIC: D. E. Inghelbrecht
CHOREOGRAPHY: Jean Borlin
SETTING: Mouveau
COSTUMES: After El Greco
COMPANY: Les Ballets Suédois
PREMIÈRE: Paris, 1920

256 ELIZABETHAN SUITE
MUSIC: William Byrd; Giles Farnaby; Henry Lawes
CHOREOGRAPHY: John Regan
SETTING: Rosa Groom
COSTUMES: Rosa Groom
COMPANY: Ballet Trois Arts
PREMIÈRE: London, 1940

257 ELOPEMENT
MUSIC: Wolfgang Amadeus Mozart
CHOREOGRAPHY: Adolph Bolm
SETTING: Nicolai Remisoff
COSTUMES: Nicolai Remisoff
COMPANY: Chicago Allied Arts
PREMIÈRE: Chicago, Illinois, 1924

258 ENCHANTED GROVE
BOOK: Rupert Doone
MUSIC: Maurice Ravel and Claude Debussy
CHOREOGRAPHY: Rupert Doone
SETTING: Duncan Grant
COSTUMES: Duncan Grant
COMPANY: Sadler's Wells Ballet
PREMIÈRE: London, 1932

259 ENCOUNTER, *Classic Ballet in One Act*
MUSIC: Wolfgang Amadeus Mozart
CHOREOGRAPHY: Lew Christensen
COSTUMES: Forrest Thayr, Jr.
COMPANY: The American Ballet Caravan
PREMIÈRE: Bennington, Vermont, 1936

260 ENDYMION
MUSIC: Moritz Moszkowski
CHOREOGRAPHY: Mona Inglesby
SETTING: Sophie Fedorovitch
COSTUMES: Sophie Fedorovitch
COMPANY: International Ballet
PREMIÈRE: London, 1938

261 L'ENFANT ET LES SORTILÈGES, *Lyrical Fantasy in Two Parts*
BOOK: After Colette
MUSIC: Maurice Ravel
CHOREOGRAPHY: Serge Lifar
SETTING: Paul Colin
COSTUMES: Paul Colin
COMPANY: Théâtre National de l'Opéra
PREMIÈRE: Paris, [1939]

262 L'ENFANT PRODIGUE
BOOK: Kurt Jooss, after Boris Kochno
MUSIC: Serge Prokofieff
CHOREOGRAPHY: Kurt Jooss
SETTING: Hein Heckroth
COSTUMES: Hein Heckroth
COMPANY: Jooss Ballet
PREMIÈRE: Essen, Germany, 1931

L'ENFANT PRODIGUE
see also LE FILS PRODIGUE
THE PRODIGAL SON

263 ENIGMA VARIATIONS, *Abstract Ballet in One Act*
MUSIC: Edward Elgar
CHOREOGRAPHY: Frank Staff
SETTING: Guy Sheppard
COSTUMES: Guy Sheppard
COMPANY: Marie Rambert Company
PREMIÈRE: Cambridge, England, 1940

L'ENLÈVEMENT
see ELOPEMENT

264 ENTRE DEUX RONDES
MUSIC: After Jean-Jacques Rousseau
CHOREOGRAPHY: Serge Lifar
SETTING: Nadine Landowska
COSTUMES: Nadine Landowska
COMPANY: Théâtre National de l'Opéra
PREMIÈRE: Paris, 1940

265 L'ÉPREUVE D'AMOUR or CHUNG-YANG AND THE MANDARIN, *Ballet in One Act*
MUSIC: Wolfgang Amadeus Mozart
CHOREOGRAPHY: Michel Fokine
SETTING: André Derain
COSTUMES: André Derain

COMPANY: Ballet Russe (Blum)
PREMIÈRE: Monte Carlo, 1936

266 EPSOM
BOOK: René Kerdyck
MUSIC: Marcel Delannoy
CHOREOGRAPHY [Leonide Massine]
SETTING: Raoul Dufy
COSTUMES: Raoul Dufy
COMPANY: Ballet Russe (Massine)
PREMIÈRE: Monte Carlo, 1938

267 ERRANTE, *Choreographic Fantasy in One Act*
BOOK: George Balanchine and Pavel Tchelitchew
MUSIC: Franz Schubert; orch. Charles Koechlin
CHOREOGRAPHY: George Balanchine
SETTING: Pavel Tchelitchew
COSTUMES: Pavel Tchelitchew
COMPANY: Les Ballets 1933
PREMIÈRE: Paris, 1933

268 ESTANCIA
BOOK: M. Fierro
MUSIC: Alberto E. Ginastera
CHOREOGRAPHY: George Balanchine
SETTING: Horacio Butler
COSTUMES: Horacio Butler
COMPANY: The American Ballet Caravan
PREMIÈRE: Buenos Aires, 1941

269 THE ETERNAL PRODIGAL
BOOK: After Biblical Story
MUSIC: Herbert Kingsley
CHOREOGRAPHY: Gluck-Sandor
SETTING: Nat Karson
COSTUMES: Nat Karson
COMPANY: W. P. A. Federal Theatre
PREMIÈRE: New York, 1936

270 ETERNAL STRUGGLE, *Ballet in One Scene*
BOOK: Igor Schwezoff
MUSIC: Robert Schumann
CHOREOGRAPHY: Igor Schwezoff
SETTING: Kathleen Martin and Florence Martin
COSTUMES: Kathleen Martin and Florence Martin
COMPANY: Ballet Russe (de Basil)
PREMIÈRE: Sydney, Australia, 1940

271 ETERNITY
MUSIC: Gustav Holst
CHOREOGRAPHY: Aida Barona
SETTING: Benno Prival
COSTUMES: Helen Rose
COMPANY: The Hollywood Ballet
PREMIÈRE: Hollywood, California, 194?

L'ÉTRANGE FARANDOLE
see ROUGE ET NOIR

272 ÉTUDE, *Classic Ballet in Three Movements*
BOOK: Bronislava Nijinska
MUSIC: Johann Sebastian Bach
CHOREOGRAPHY: Bronislava Nijinska
SETTING: Bilinsky
COSTUMES: Bilinsky
COMPANY: Ballet Russe (Massine)
PREMIÈRE: Cleveland, Ohio, 1943

ÉTUDE
see also QUEST

273 L'ÉVENTAIL DE JEANNE
MUSIC: Milhaud, Roussel, Ravel, Poulenc,
   Schmitt
CHOREOGRAPHY: Serge Lifar
SETTING: [Marie Laurencin]
COSTUMES: Marie Laurencin
COMPANY: Théâtre National de l'Opéra
PREMIÈRE: Paris, 1937

274 EVERYMAN
BOOK: Morality Play as Ballet with Speech
MUSIC: Richard Strauss; arr. Ernest Irving
CHOREOGRAPHY: Mona Inglesby; produced by
   Leslie French
SETTING: Rex Whistler
COSTUMES: William Chappell
COMPANY: The International Ballet
PREMIÈRE: London, 1943

275 FAÇADE, *Ballet in One Act*
BOOK: After Edith Sitwell
MUSIC: William Turner Walton
CHOREOGRAPHY: Frederick Ashton
SETTING: John Armstrong
COSTUMES: John Armstrong
COMPANY: Camargo Society
PREMIÈRE: London, 1931

276 LES FÂCHEUX, *Ballet in One Act*
BOOK: Boris Kochno, after Molière
MUSIC: Georges Auric
CHOREOGRAPHY: Leonide Massine
CURTAIN: Georges Braque
SETTING: Georges Braque
COSTUMES: Georges Braque
COMPANY: Ballet Russe (Diaghilev)
PREMIÈRE: Monte Carlo, 1924

277 FAIR AT SOROCHINSK
BOOK: After Gogol
MUSIC: Modeste Moussorgsky
CHOREOGRAPHY: George Balanchine

SETTING: Mstislav Dobujinsky
COSTUMES: Mstislav Dobujinsky
COMPANY: New Opera Co.
PREMIÈRE: New York, 1942

278 FAIR AT SOROCHINSK
BOOK: After Gogol
MUSIC: Modeste Moussorgsky; arr. Antal Dorati
CHOREOGRAPHY: David Lichine
SETTING: Nicolai Remisoff
COSTUMES: Nicolai Remisoff
COMPANY: Ballet Theatre
PREMIÈRE: New York, 1943

279 FAIR AT SOROCHINSK
BOOK: Mikhail Mordkin
MUSIC: Modeste Moussorgsky
CHOREOGRAPHY: Mikhail Mordkin
SETTING: Serge Soudeikine
COSTUMES: Serge Soudeikine
COMPANY: The Mordkin Ballet
PREMIÈRE: New York, 1930

280 FAIRY DOLL
MUSIC: Josef Bayer
CHOREOGRAPHY: Boris Novikoff
SETTING: Serge Soudeikine
COSTUMES: Serge Soudeikine
COMPANY: Pavlova Company
PREMIÈRE: Paris, 1923

281 THE FAIRY DOLL
MUSIC: Josef Bayer
CHOREOGRAPHY: Catherine Littlefield
SETTING: A. Jarin
COSTUMES: P. T. Champs
COMPANY: Philadelphia Opera Ballet
PREMIÈRE: Philadelphia, Pennsylvania, 1935

THE FAIRY DOLL
see also FÉE DES POUPÉES
PUPPENFEE

THE FAIRY'S KISS
see BAISER DE LA FÉE

FAIRY TALE
FAIRY TALES
see also LA BELLE AU BOIS DORMANT

282 FANCY FREE, *A Ballet in One Act concerning
   Three Sailors on Shore Leave*
BOOK: Jerome Robbins
MUSIC: Leonard Bernstein
CHOREOGRAPHY: Jerome Robbins
SETTINGS: Oliver Smith
COSTUMES: Kermit Love
COMPANY: Ballet Theatre
PREMIÈRE: New York, 1944

283 FANTASIA
Music: Johann Strauss
Choreography: Catherine Littlefield
Setting: Mary Fales
Costumes: Mary Fales
Company: Philadelphia Opera Ballet
Première: Chicago, Illinois, 1938

284 FANTASIA BRASILEIRA
Music: Francisco Mignone
Choreography: George Balanchine
Setting: Enrico Bianco
Costumes: Enrico Bianco
Company: The American Ballet Caravan
Première: Lima, Peru, 1941

285 LES FANTAISIES HONGROISES
Book: L. Markus
Music: Franz Liszt
Choreography: L. Markus
Setting: Gustáv Olâh and Zoltán Fülöp
Costumes: Gustáv Olâh and Zoltán Fülöp
Company: Hungarian State Ballet
Première: Budapest, 1934

286 FANTASY
Music: Frederic Chopin
Choreography: Keith Lester
Costumes: Beryl Dean
Company: The Ballet Guild
Première: London, 1941

287 FANTASY 1939
Book: Berta Ochsner and David Campbell
Music: David Campbell
Choreography: Berta Ochsner
Setting: Alexander Jones
Costumes: Alexander Jones
Company: W. P. A. Federal Theatre
Première: New York, 1939

288 LES FANTOCHES
Music: Robert Schumann
Choreography: Pauline Grant
Setting: Hein Heckroth
Costumes: Hein Heckroth
Company: New Russian Ballet
Première: Brighton, England, 1942

289 LA FARCE DU PONT NEUF
Book: Adolph Bolm
Music: Jeanne Clément Herscher
Choreography: Adolph Bolm
Setting: Jean Valmier
Costumes: Jean Valmier
Company: Chicago Allied Arts
Première: Chicago, [1926]

290 FASTES
Book: André Derain
Music: Henri Sauguet
Choreography: George Balanchine
Setting: André Derain
Costumes: André Derain
Company: Les Ballets 1933
Première: Paris, 1933

291 FAUN
Music: Claude Debussy
Choreography: Serge Lifar
Setting: Christian Bérard
Costumes: Christian Bérard
Company: Ballet Russe (Massine)
Première: New York, 1938

292 FÉE DES POUPÉES
Music: Josef Bayer
Choreography: Ivan Clustine
Setting: Mstislav Dobujinsky
Costumes: Mstislav Dobujinsky
Company: Pavlova Company
Première: United States of America, 1915

293 LES FEMMES DE BONNE HUMEUR, *Choreographic Comedy in One Act*
Book: After Carlo Goldoni
Music: Domenico Scarlatti; orch. Vincenzo Tommasini
Choreography: Leonide Massine
Setting: Léon Bakst
Costumes: Léon Bakst
Company: Ballet Russe (Diaghilev)
Première: Rome, 1917

294 LE FESTIN, *Suite of Dances*
Music: Rimsky-Korsakov, Tchaikowsky, Glinka, Glazounov, Moussorgsky
Choreography: Michel Fokine
Setting: Constantin Korovine
Costumes: Bakst, Benois, Bilibine, Korovine
Company: Ballet Russe (Diaghilev)
Première: Paris, 1909

295 LE FESTIN DE L'ARAIGNÉE, *Ballet-Pantomime*
Music: Albert Roussel
Choreography: Léo Staats
Setting: Maxime Dethomas
Costumes: Maxime Dethomas
Company: [Théâtre des Arts]
Première: Paris, 1913

296 LE FESTIN DE L'ARAIGNÉE, *Ballet-Pantomime*
Book: Gilbert de Voisins

MUSIC: Albert Roussel
CHOREOGRAPHY: A. Aveline
SETTING: Léon Leyritz
COSTUMES: Léon Leyritz
COMPANY: Théâtre National de L'Opéra
PREMIÈRE: Paris, 1939

297 LE FESTIN DE L'ARAIGNÉE, *Ballet in One Scene*
BOOK: Andrée Howard
MUSIC: Albert Roussel
CHOREOGRAPHY: Andrée Howard
SETTING: Michael Ayrton
COSTUMES: Michael Ayrton
COMPANY: Sadler's Wells Ballet
PREMIÈRE: London, 1944

298 FÊTE BOHÊME
MUSIC: Antonin Dvorak
CHOREOGRAPHY: Harold Turner
SETTING: Beryl Dean
COSTUMES: Beryl Dean
COMPANY: The International Ballet
PREMIÈRE: Glasgow, Scotland, 1941

299 FÊTE CHAMPÊTRE
MUSIC: Lully, Grétry, Rameau
CHOREOGRAPHY: Catherine Littlefield and Edward Caton
SETTING: A. Jarin
COSTUMES: J. Pascal
COMPANY: Philadelphia Opera Ballet
PREMIÈRE: Philadelphia, Pennsylvania, 1936

300 FÊTE ÉTRANGE, *Ballet in One Act and Two Scenes*
BOOK: Ronald Crichton
MUSIC: Gabriel Fauré; arr. Ronald Crichton
CHOREOGRAPHY: Andrée Howard
SETTING: Sophie Fedorovitch
COSTUMES: Sophie Fedorovitch
COMPANY: The London Ballet
PREMIÈRE: London, 1940

301 FÊTE POLONAISE
MUSIC: Michael Glinka
CHOREOGRAPHY: Ninette de Valois
SETTING: O. P. Smyth
COSTUMES: O. P. Smyth
COMPANY: Sadler's Wells Ballet
PREMIÈRE: London, 1931

302 FÊTES DE JADIS
MUSIC: François Couperin; arr. Richard Strauss
CHOREOGRAPHY: Constantin Tcherkas
SETTING: P. Lavalley
COSTUMES: P. Lavalley

COMPANY: Théâtre National de l'Opéra Comique
PREMIÈRE: Paris, 1943

303 FEU D'ARTIFICE
MUSIC: Igor Strawinsky
SETTINGS: Balla
COMPANY: Ballet Russe (Diaghilev)
PREMIÈRE: Rome, 1917

304 LA FILLE MAL GARDÉE, *Pantomime Ballet in Two Acts and Three Scenes*
BOOK: Jean Dauberval
MUSIC: Johann Wilhelm Hertel
CHOREOGRAPHY: Mikhail Mordkin
SETTING: Serge Soudeikine
COSTUMES: Serge Soudeikine
COMPANY: Mordkin Ballet
PREMIÈRE: New York [1938-39]

305 LA FILLE MAL GARDÉE, *Ballet in Two Acts and Four Scenes*
BOOK: Jean Dauberval
MUSIC: Johann Wilhelm Hertel
CHOREOGRAPHY: Bronislava Nijinska, after Dauberval
SETTING: Serge Soudeikine
COSTUMES: Serge Soudeikine
COMPANY: Ballet Theatre
PREMIÈRE: New York, 1940

306 FILLING STATION, *Ballet-Document in One Act*
BOOK: Lincoln Kirstein
MUSIC: Virgil Thomson; arr. Trude Rittmann
CHOREOGRAPHY: Lew Christensen
CURTAIN: Paul Cadmus
SETTING: Paul Cadmus
COSTUMES: Paul Cadmus
COMPANY: The American Ballet Caravan
PREMIÈRE: Hartford, Connecticut, 1938

307 LE FILS PRODIGUE
BOOK: Boris Kochno, after Biblical Story
MUSIC: Serge Prokofieff
CHOREOGRAPHY: George Balanchine
SETTING: Georges Rouault
COSTUMES: Georges Rouault
COMPANY: Ballet Russe (Diaghilev)
PREMIÈRE: Paris, 1929
LE FILS PRODIGUE
see also L'ENFANT PRODIGUE;
THE PRODIGAL SON

308 FIREBIRD
MUSIC: Igor Strawinsky
CHOREOGRAPHY: Adolph Bolm
SETTING: Nicolai Remisoff

COSTUMES: Nicolai Remisoff
COMPANY: Hollywood Bowl
PREMIÈRE: Hollywood, 1940

309 FIREBIRD, *Ballet in One Act and Three Scenes*
BOOK: After Michel Fokine
ARTISTIC COLLABORATION: Henry Clifford
MUSIC: Igor Strawinsky
CHOREOGRAPHY: Adolph Bolm
CURTAIN: Marc Chagall
SETTING: Marc Chagall
COSTUMES: Marc Chagall
COMPANY: Ballet Theatre
PREMIÈRE: New York, 1945

FIREBIRD
see also L'OISEAU DE FEU

310 THE FIRST SHOOT
BOOK: Oswald Sitwell
MUSIC: William Turner Walton
CHOREOGRAPHY: Frederick Ashton
SETTING: Cecil Beaton
COSTUMES: Cecil Beaton
COMPANY: C. B. Cochran Revue
PREMIÈRE: London, 1931

311 FLAMENCO
MUSIC: Robert Gerhard
CHOREOGRAPHY: Elsa Brunelleschi
SETTING: Hugh Stevenson
COSTUMES: Hugh Stevenson
COMPANY: Marie Rambert Company
PREMIÈRE: Reading, England, 1943

312 LA FLAMME
BOOK: Miriam Jaumeton-Epstein
MUSIC: Miriam Jaumeton-Epstein; orch. Pommerantzeff
CHOREOGRAPHY: Lubov Egorova
SETTING: Mireille Hunnebelle
COSTUMES: Mireille Hunnebelle
COMPANY: Les Archives Internationales de la Danse
PREMIÈRE: Paris, 1932

313 FLORENTINE PICTURE
BOOK: Frederick Ashton
MUSIC: Arcangelo Corelli
CHOREOGRAPHY: Frederick Ashton
SETTING: After Italian Masters
COSTUMES: After Italian Masters
COMPANY: Marie Rambert Company
PREMIÈRE: London, 1930

314 FOLK DANCE, *Character-Divertissement in One Act*
MUSIC: Emmanuel Chabrier

CHOREOGRAPHY: Douglas Coudy
COSTUMES: Charles Rain
COMPANY: The American Ballet Caravan
PREMIÈRE: Burlington, Vermont, 1936

315 LES FORAINS
BOOK: Boris Kochno
MUSIC: Henri Sauguet
CHOREOGRAPHY: Roland Petit
SETTING: Christian Bérard
COSTUMES: Christian Bérard
COMPANY: Les Ballets des Champs-Élysées
PREMIÈRE: Paris, 1945

316 THE FOUNTAIN OF BAKHCHISARAY,
Choreographic Poem in Four Acts
BOOK: N. D. Volkov, after Pushkin
MUSIC: B. V. Asafiev
CHOREOGRAPHY: Rostislav Zakharov
SETTING: V. M. Khodasevich
COMPANY: Soviet State Ballet
PREMIÈRE: Leningrad, 1934

317 LE FOYER DE LA DANSE, *Pantomimic Ballet
in One Act*
BOOK: Adolph Bolm, after Degas
MUSIC: Emmanuel Chabrier
CHOREOGRAPHY: Adolph Bolm
SETTING: Nicolai Remisoff
COSTUMES: Nicolai Remisoff
COMPANY: Chicago Allied Arts
PREMIÈRE: Chicago, Illinois, 1924

318 FOYER DE LA DANSE
BOOK: Frederick Ashton
MUSIC: Gerald Hugh Berners
CHOREOGRAPHY: Frederick Ashton
SETTING: After Degas
COSTUMES: After Degas
COMPANY: Marie Rambert Company
PREMIÈRE: London, 1931

319 FRANCESCA DA RIMINI, *Ballet in Two
Scenes*
BOOK: David Lichine and Henry Clifford, after
Dante
MUSIC: Peter Tchaikowsky
CHOREOGRAPHY: David Lichine
SETTING: Oliver Messel
COSTUMES: Oliver Messel
COMPANY: Ballet Russe (de Basil)
PREMIÈRE: London, 1937

320 FRANKIE AND JOHNNY, *An American Dance-
Melodrama in Seven Scenes*
BOOK: Michael Blandford and Jerome Moross
MUSIC: Jerome Moross

62

CHOREOGRAPHY: Ruth Page and Bentley Stone
SETTING: Clive Rickabaugh
COSTUMES: Paul DuPont
COMPANY: Chicago Federal Theatre
PREMIÈRE: Chicago, Illinois, 1938

321 THE FRESCOES OF ADJANTA, *Ballet in One Act and Three Scenes*
MUSIC: Alexandre Tcherepnine
CHOREOGRAPHY: Ivan Clustine
SETTING: O. Allegri, after Adjanta Frescoes
COMPANY: Pavlova Company
PREMIÈRE: New York, 1923

322 FROLICKING GODS
BOOK: Michel Fokine
MUSIC: Peter Tchaikowsky
CHOREOGRAPHY: Michel Fokine
SETTING: Joseph Urban
COSTUMES: John Reynolds
PREMIÈRE: New York, 1923

323 FUENSANTA
BOOK: Martin Luis Guzmán
MUSIC: Old Mexican
CHOREOGRAPHY: Nellie Campobello
SETTING: Roberto Montenegro
COSTUMES: Roberto Montenegro
COMPANY: Ballet of the City of Mexico
PREMIÈRE: México, D. F., 1943

324 THE FUGITIVE, *Ballet in Two Scenes*
BOOK: Hugh Stevenson
MUSIC: Leonard Salzedo
CHOREOGRAPHY: Andrée Howard
SETTING: Hugh Stevenson
COSTUMES: Hugh Stevenson
COMPANY: Marie Rambert Company
PREMIÈRE: Bedford, England, 1944

325 GAÎTÉ PARISIENNE, *Ballet in One Act*
BOOK: Etienne de Beaumont
MUSIC: Jacques Offenbach; orch. Manuel Rosenthal
CHOREOGRAPHY: Leonide Massine
SETTING: Etienne de Beaumont
COSTUMES: Etienne de Beaumont
COMPANY: Ballet Russe (de Basil)
PREMIÈRE: Monte Carlo, 1938

326 GALA PERFORMANCE, *Ballet in One Act and Two Scenes*
BOOK: Antony Tudor
MUSIC: Serge Prokofieff
CHOREOGRAPHY: Antony Tudor
SETTING: Hugh Stevenson
COSTUMES: Hugh Stevenson

COMPANY: The London Ballet
PREMIÈRE: London, 1938

327 GALA PERFORMANCE, *Ballet in One Act and Two Scenes*
MUSIC: Serge Prokofieff; orch. Paul Baron
CHOREOGRAPHY: Antony Tudor
SETTING: Nicolas de Molas
COSTUMES: Nicolas de Molas
COMPANY: Ballet Theatre
PREMIÈRE: New York, 1941

328 GALLANT ASSEMBLY
MUSIC: Giuseppe Tartini
CHOREOGRAPHY: Antony Tudor
SETTING: Hugh Stevenson
COSTUMES: Hugh Stevenson
COMPANY: Dance Theatre
PREMIÈRE: Oxford, England, 1937

329 GAUKELEI, *Dance Drama in Five Acts*
BOOK: Rudolf von Laban and Kurt Jooss
MUSIC: Frederic Cohen
CHOREOGRAPHY: Kurt Jooss
SETTING: Hein Heckroth
COSTUMES: Hein Heckroth
COMPANY: Folkwang Tanzbuehne
PREMIÈRE: Essen, Germany, 1930

330 GHOST TOWN, *An American Folk Ballet in One Scene, Prologue and Epilogue*
BOOK: Marc Platoff
MUSIC: Richard Rodgers
CHOREOGRAPHY: Marc Platoff
SETTING: Raoul Pène Du Bois
COSTUMES: Raoul Pène Du Bois
COMPANY: Ballet Russe (Massine)
PREMIÈRE: New York, 1939

331 GIFT OF THE MAGI, *Ballet in Six Scenes*
BOOK: Simon Semenoff, after O. Henry
MUSIC: Lukas Foss
CHOREOGRAPHY: Simon Semenoff
SETTING: Raoul Pène Du Bois
COSTUMES: Raoul Pène Du Bois
COMPANY: Ballet Theatre
PREMIÈRE: New York, 1945

332 GISELLE
BOOK: V. de Saint Georges and Théophile Gautier
MUSIC: Adolphe Adam
CHOREOGRAPHY: Marius Petipa
SETTING: Alexandre Benois
COSTUMES: Alexandre Benois
COMPANY: Ballet Russe (Diaghilev)
PREMIÈRE: Paris, 1910

333 GISELLE
   Book: V. de Saint Georges and Théophile
      Gautier
   Music: Adolphe Adam
   Choreography: Boris Romanoff, after Coralli
   Setting: Leon Zack
   Costumes: Leon Zack
   Company: Russian Romantic Theatre
   Première: Berlin, 1922

334 GISELLE
   Book: V. de Saint Georges and Théophile
      Gautier
   Music: Adolphe Adam
   Choreography: Nicholas Sergueff, after Coralli
   Setting: William Chappell
   Costumes: William Chappell
   Company: Sadler's Wells Ballet
   Première: London, 1934

335 GISELLE
   Book: V. de Saint Georges and Théophile
      Gautier
   Music: Adolphe Adam
   Choreography: Mikhail Mordkin
   Setting: Serge Soudeikine
   Costumes: Serge Soudeikine
   Company: Mordkin Ballet
   Première: New York, 1937

336 GISELLE, *Fantastic Ballet in Two Scenes*
   Book: V. de Saint Georges and Théophile
      Gautier
   Music: Adolphe Adam
   Choreography: Jean Coralli
   Setting: Eugene Berman
   Costumes: Eugene Berman
   Company: Ballet Russe (de Basil)
   Project: 1940

337 GISELLE, *Ballet in Two Acts*
   Book: V. de Saint Georges and Théophile
      Gautier
   Music: Adolphe Adam; orch. Eugene Fuerst
   Choreography: Anton Dolin, after Coralli
   Setting: Lucinda Ballard
   Costumes: Lucinda Ballard
   Company: Ballet Theatre
   Première: New York, 1940

338 GISELLE
   Book: V. de Saint Georges and Théophile
      Gautier
   Music: Adolphe Adam; orch. by Frederick
      Austin
   Choreography: Nicholas Sergueff, after Coralli

Setting: Doris Zinkeisen
Costumes: Doris Zinkeisen
Company: The International Ballet
Première: 1942

339 GISELLE, *Ballet in Two Acts*
   Book: V. de Saint Georges and Théophile
      Gautier
   Music: Adolphe Adam
   Choreography: [?]
   Setting: Hugh Stevenson
   Costumes: Hugh Stevenson
   Company: Marie Rambert Company
   Première: London, 1945

340 THE GLEN
   Music: Felix Mendelssohn
   Choreography: Keith Lester
   Setting: Eleanor Watts
   Costumes: Eleanor Watts
   Company: Arts Theatre Ballet
   Première: Manchester, England, 1940

341 THE GODS GO A-BEGGING
   Music: George Frederic Handel; arr. Thomas
      Beecham
   Choreography: Ninette de Valois
   Setting: Hugh Stevenson
   Costumes: Hugh Stevenson
   Company: Sadler's Wells Ballet
   Première: London, 1935

   The Gods go A-Begging
   see also Les Dieux Mendiants

342 THE GOLDEN AGE, *Ballet in Three Acts and
      Five Scenes*
   Book: A. V. Ivanovsky
   Music: Dimitri Shostakovitch
   Choreography: E. I. Kaplan and V. I. Vynonen
   Setting: V. M. Khodasevich
   Company: Soviet State Ballet
   Première: Leningrad, 1930

343 THE GOLDEN FLEECE
   Music: Alex North
   Choreography: Hanya Holm
   Costumes: Kurt Seligmann
   Company: Hanya Holm Group
   Première: New York, 1941

344 THE GOLDFISH, *Ballet in Seven Scenes*
   Book: Mikhail Mordkin, after Alexander
      Pushkin
   Music: Nicolas Tcherepnine
   Choreography: Mikhail Mordkin
   Setting: Serge Soudeikine

64

COSTUMES: Serge Soudeikine
COMPANY: The Mordkin Ballet
PREMIÈRE: New York, 1937

345 GOLD STANDARD
BOOK: Ruth Page and Nicolai Remisoff
MUSIC: Jacques Ibert
CHOREOGRAPHY: Ruth Page
SETTING: Nicolai Remisoff
COSTUMES: Nicolai Remisoff
COMPANY: Page-Stone Ballet
PREMIÈRE: Chicago, Illinois, 1934

THE GOOD-HUMORED LADIES
see LES FEMMES DE BONNE HUMEUR

346 GOYA PASTORAL
BOOK: Nicolas de Molas
MUSIC: Enrique Granados; orch. Harold Byrns
CHOREOGRAPHY: Antony Tudor
SETTING: Nicolas de Molas
COSTUMES: Nicolas de Molas
COMPANY: Lewisohn Stadium
PREMIÈRE: New York, 1940

347 GOYESCAS, A Ballet in One Scene
BOOK: Alden Jenkins
MUSIC: Enrique Granados; arr. Harold Byrns
CHOREOGRAPHY: José Fernandez
SETTING: Nicolas de Molas
COSTUMES: Nicolas de Molas
COMPANY: Ballet Theatre
PREMIÈRE: New York, 1940

348 GRADUATION BALL, Ballet in One Act
BOOK: David Lichine
MUSIC: Johann Strauss; orch. Antal Dorati
CHOREOGRAPHY: David Lichine
SETTING: Alexandre Benois
COSTUMES: Alexandre Benois
COMPANY: Ballet Russe (de Basil)
PREMIÈRE: Sydney, Australia, 1940

349 GRADUATION BALL, Ballet in One Act
BOOK: David Lichine
MUSIC: Johann Strauss; orch. Antal Dorati
CHOREOGRAPHY: David Lichine
SETTING: Mstislav Dobujinsky
COSTUMES: Mstislav Dobujinsky
COMPANY: Ballet Theatre
PREMIÈRE: Montreal, Canada, 1944

350 GRAZIANA, Ballet in Three Movements
MUSIC: Wolfgang Amadeus Mozart
CHOREOGRAPHY: John Taras
COSTUMES: Alvin Colt
COMPANY: Ballet Theatre
PREMIÈRE: New York, 1945

351 THE GREAT AMERICAN GOOF, A number
of Absurd and Poetic Events
BOOK: William Saroyan
MUSIC: Henry Brant
CHOREOGRAPHY: Eugene Loring
SETTING: Boris Aronson
COSTUMES: Boris Aronson
COMPANY: Ballet Theatre
PREMIÈRE: New York, 1940

352 THE GREEN TABLE, Dance of Death in Eight
Scenes
BOOK: Kurt Jooss
MUSIC: Frederic Cohen
CHOREOGRAPHY: Kurt Jooss
SETTING: Hein Heckroth
COSTUMES: Hein Heckroth
COMPANY: Jooss Ballet
PREMIÈRE: Paris, 1932

353 LA GRISI
MUSIC: Henri Thomas, after Métra
CHOREOGRAPHY: Georges Aveline
SETTING: André Dignimont
COSTUMES: André Dignimont
COMPANY: Théâtre National de l'Opéra
PREMIÈRE: Paris, 1935

354 LA GUIABLESSE
BOOK: Ruth Page, after Martinique Folk-legend
MUSIC: William Grant Still
CHOREOGRAPHY: Ruth Page
SETTING: Nicolai Remisoff
COSTUMES: Nicolai Remisoff
COMPANY: Page-Stone Ballet
PREMIÈRE: Chicago, Illinois, 1933

355 GUIGNOL ET PANDORA
BOOK: Serge Lifar
MUSIC: André Jolivet
CHOREOGRAPHY: Serge Lifar
CURTAIN: André Dignimont
SETTING: André Dignimont
COSTUMES: André Dignimont
COMPANY: Théâtre National de l'Opéra
PREMIÈRE: Paris, 1944

356 GUNS AND CASTANETS, Ballet in One Act
BOOK: Ruth Page, after Prosper Merimée
MUSIC: Georges Bizet; arr. Jerome Moross
CHOREOGRAPHY: Ruth Page and Bentley Stone
SETTING: Clive Rickabaugh
COSTUMES: John Pratt
COMPANY: Page-Stone Ballet
PREMIÈRE: Chicago, Illinois, 1939

357 HAMLET
Book: Robert Helpmann, after Shakespeare
Music: Peter Tchaikowsky
Choreography: Robert Helpmann
Setting: Leslie Hurry
Costumes: Leslie Hurry
Company: Sadler's Wells Ballet
Première: London, 1942

358 HARLEQUIN, *Ballet-Pantomime in the Spirit of the Italian Popular Comedy*
Music: Domenico Scarlatti; orch. Ariadna Mikeshina
Choreography: Eugene Loring
Costumes: Keith Martin
Company: The American Ballet Caravan
Première: New York, 1936

359 HARLEQUIN IN THE STREET
Book: Frederick Ashton
Music: François Couperin; orch. Gavin Gordon
Choreography: Frederick Ashton, after Jean-François Reynard
Setting: André Derain
Costumes: André Derain
Company: Sadler's Wells Ballet
Première: London, 1938

360 HARNASIE, *Ballet-Pantomime in Three Scenes*
Music: Karol Szymanowsky
Choreography: Serge Lifar
Setting: Irène Lorentowicz
Costumes: Irène Lorentowicz
Company: Théâtre National de l'Opéra
Première: Paris, 1936

361 HARNASIE, *Ballet in Three Scenes*
Music: Karol Szymanowski
Book: Jan Cieplinski
Choreography: Jan Cieplinski
Setting: Zofia Stryjenska
Company: The Polish Ballet
Première: [Paris,] 1937

362 HARRILD
Music: R. Garcia Morillo
Choreography: Louis de Bercher
Setting: Hector Basaldua
Costumes: Hector Basaldua
Company: Teatro Colon
Première: Buenos Aires, 1945

363 HARVEST TIME, *Pastoral Ballet*
Book: Bronislava Nijinska
Music: Henri Wieniawski; arr. Antal Dorati
Choreography: Bronislava Nijinska
Costumes: Enid Gilbert

Company: Ballet Theatre
Première: New York, 1945

364 THE HAUNTED BALLROOM, *Ballet in One Act and Two Scenes*
Book: Geoffrey Toye
Music: Geoffrey Toye
Choreography: Ninette de Valois
Setting: Motley
Costumes: Motley
Company: Sadler's Wells Ballet
Première: London, 1934

365 HEAR YE! HEAR YE!
Book: Ruth Page and Nicolai Remisoff
Music: Aaron Copland
Choreography: Ruth Page
Setting: Nicolai Remisoff
Costumes: Nicolai Remisoff
Company: Page-Stone Ballet
Première: Chicago, Illinois, 1934

366 HELEN OF TROY, *Ballet in Three Scenes with Prologue*
Book: David Lichine and Antal Dorati
Music: Jacques Offenbach
Choreography: Michel Fokine
Setting: Marcel Vertès
Costumes: Marcel Vertès
Company: Ballet Theatre
Première: México, D. F., 1942

THE HEROES
see THE SEVEN HEROES

367 HIGH YELLOW
Music: Spike Hughes
Choreography: Buddy Bradley and Frederick Ashton
Setting: Vanessa Bell
Costumes: William Chappell
Company: Camargo Society
Première: London, 1932

368 HISTOIRE D'UN PIERROT
Music: Mario Costa
Choreography: Cia Fornaroli
Setting: Guido Salvini
Costumes: Guido Salvini
Company: Italian Chamber Ballets
Première: [San Remo, Italy], 1933

HOBO OF THE HILLS
see THE DUKE OF SACRAMENTO

369 THE HOLY TORCH, *Ballet in Eleven Scenes*
Book: Erno von Dohnányi
Music: Erno von Dohnányi

66

CHOREOGRAPHY: Elsa von Galafres
SETTING: Zoltán Fülöp
COSTUMES: Zoltán Fülöp
COMPANY: Hungarian State Ballet
PREMIÈRE: Budapest, 1934

370 HOME LIFE OF THE GODS
MUSIC: Erik Satie
CHOREOGRAPHY: Catherine Littlefield
SETTING: Lazar Galpern
COSTUMES: Lazar Galpern
COMPANY: Philadelphia Opera Ballet
PREMIÈRE: Philadelphia, Pennsylvania, 1936

371 HOMMAGE À SCHUBERT
MUSIC: Franz Schubert
CHOREOGRAPHY: Boris Romanoff
SETTING: Hector Basaldua
COSTUMES: Hector Basaldua
COMPANY: Teatro Colon
PREMIÈRE: Buenos Aires, 1934

372 L'HOMME ET SON DÉSIR, *Plastic Poem*
BOOK: Paul Claudel
MUSIC: Darius Milhaud
CHOREOGRAPHER: Jean Borlin
SETTING: Andrée Parr
COSTUMES: Andrée Parr
COMPANY: Les Ballets Suédois
PREMIÈRE: Paris, 1921

THE HOUSE PARTY
see LES BICHES

373 HOROSCOPE, *Ballet in One Act*
BOOK: Constant Lambert
MUSIC: Constant Lambert
CHOREOGRAPHY: Frederick Ashton
SETTING: Sophie Fedorovitch
COSTUMES: Sophie Fedorovitch
COMPANY: Sadler's Wells Ballet
PREMIÈRE: London, 1938

374 H. P.
BOOK: Catherine Littlefield
MUSIC: Carlos Chavez
CHOREOGRAPHY: Catherine Littlefield
SETTING: Diego Rivera
COSTUMES: Diego Rivera
COMPANY: Philadelphia Opera Ballet
PREMIÈRE: Philadelphia, Pennsylvania, 1932

HUNDRED KISSES
see LES CENT BAISERS

375 IBERIA, *Spanish Scenes in Three Tableaux*
MUSIC: Isaac Albeniz; orch. D. E. Inghelbrecht
CHOREOGRAPHY: Jean Borlin

SETTING: Théophile-Alexandre Steinlen
COMPANY: Les Ballets Suédois
PREMIÈRE: Paris, 1920

376 IBERIAN MONOTONE
MUSIC: Maurice Ravel
CHOREOGRAPHY: Ruth Page
SETTING: Nicolai Remisoff
COSTUMES: Nicolai Remisoff
COMPANY: Page-Stone Ballet
PREMIÈRE: Ravinia, Illinois, 1930

IBERIAN MONOTONE
see also BOLERO

377 ICARE, *Neo-Classic Ballet in Two Scenes*
BOOK: Serge Lifar
RHYTHMS: Serge Lifar; orch. J. E. Szyfer
CHOREOGRAPHY: Serge Lifar
SETTING: Eugene Berman
COSTUMES: Eugene Berman
COMPANY: Ballet Russe (Massine)
PREMIÈRE: New York, 1937

378 ICARE, *Choreographic Legend in One Act*
BOOK: Serge Lifar
RHYTHMS: Serge Lifar; orch. J. E. Szyfer
CHOREOGRAPHY: Serge Lifar
SETTING: Paul-René Larthe
COSTUMES: Paul-René Larthe
COMPANY: Théâtre National de l'Opéra
PREMIÈRE: Paris, 1935

379 IGROUCHKI (RUSSIAN TOYS), *Ballet in One Scene*
BOOK: Michel Fokine
MUSIC: Nicholas Rimsky-Korsakov
CHOREOGRAPHY: Michel Fokine
SETTING: Nathalie Gontcharova
COSTUMES: Nathalie Gontcharova
COMPANY: [Gilda Gray Company]
PREMIÈRE: New York, 1921

380 ILGA, *Ballet in Four Acts*
BOOK: Oskar Grosbergs
MUSIC: Janis Vitolins
CHOREOGRAPHY: Osvalds Lemanis
SETTING: Niklaus Strunke
COSTUMES: Niklaus Strunke
COMPANY: National Opera
PREMIÈRE: Riga, Latvia, 1937

381 LES IMAGINAIRES
BOOK: David Lichine
MUSIC: Georges Auric
CHOREOGRAPHY: David Lichine
SETTING: Etienne de Beaumont
COSTUMES: Etienne de Beaumont

COMPANY: Ballet Russe (de Basil)
PREMIÈRE: Paris, 1934

382 IMPRESSIONS OF A BIG CITY, *Ballet in One Act and Three Scenes*
BOOK: Kurt Jooss
MUSIC: Alexander Tansman
CHOREOGRAPHY: Kurt Jooss
SETTING: Hein Heckroth
COSTUMES: Hein Heckroth
COMPANY: Jooss Ballet
PREMIÈRE: Cologne, Germany, 1932

383 IMPRESSIONS DE MUSIC-HALL, *Ballet in One Act*
MUSIC: Gabriel Pierné
CHOREOGRAPHY: Bronislava Nijinska
SETTING: Maxime Dethomas
COSTUMES: Maxime Dethomas
COMPANY: Théâtre National de l'Opéra
PREMIÈRE: Paris, 1927

384 LA INFANTA
BOOK: Margarete Wallmann
MUSIC: Armando Schiuma
CHOREOGRAPHY: Margarete Wallmann
SETTING: Hector Basaldua
COSTUMES: Hector Basaldua
COMPANY: Teatro Colon
PREMIÈRE: Buenos Aires, 1939

385 INTERPLAY, *Ballet in One Act and Four Movements*
MUSIC: Morton Gould
CHOREOGRAPHY: Jerome Robbins
SETTING: Oliver Smith
COSTUMES: Irene Sharaff
COMPANY: Ballet Theatre
PREMIÈRE: New York, 1945

386 THE INVISIBLE WIFE
BOOK: Legend of New England
MUSIC: Benjamin Britten
CHOREOGRAPHY: Eugene Loring
SETTING: Waldo Pierce
COSTUMES: Waldo Pierce
COMPANY: The Dance Players
PREMIÈRE: New York, 1942

387 INVITATION TO THE DANCE
MUSIC: Carl-Maria von Weber
CHOREOGRAPHY: Piotr Zaylich
SETTING: Nadia Benois
COSTUMES: Nadia Benois
COMPANY: Pavlova Company
PREMIÈRE: London, 1913

THE IRON FOUNDRY
see MECHANICAL BALLET

388 ISLAMEY
MUSIC: Mily Balakirev; orch. S. M. Liapunov
CHOREOGRAPHY: Michel Fokine
SETTING: Boris Anisfeld
COMPANY: Maryinsky Theatre
PREMIÈRE: St. Petersburg, 1912

389 ISTAR, *Ballet in One Act*
MUSIC: Vincent d'Indy
CHOREOGRAPHY: Léo Staats
SETTING: Léon Bakst
COSTUMES: Léon Bakst
COMPANY: Ida Rubinstein Ballet
PREMIÈRE: Paris, 1925

390 ITALIAN SUITE
MUSIC: Édouard Lalo
CHOREOGRAPHY: Ninette de Valois
SETTING: Phyllis Dolton
COSTUMES: Phyllis Dolton
COMPANY: Sadler's Wells Ballet
PREMIÈRE: London, 1931

391 ITALIAN SUITE
BOOK: Anton Dolin
MUSIC: Domenico Cimarosa
CHOREOGRAPHY: Anton Dolin
SETTING: Nicolas de Molas
COSTUMES: Nicolas de Molas
COMPANY: Ballet Theatre
PREMIÈRE: New York, 1940

392 ITALIAN SYMPHONY, *Ballet in Four Scenes*
BOOK: David Lichine
MUSIC: Felix Mendelssohn
CHOREOGRAPHY: David Lichine
SETTING: Eugene Berman
COSTUMES: Eugene Berman
COMPANY: Ballet Russe (de Basil)
PROJECT: 1940

393 THE JACKDAW AND THE PIGEONS
MUSIC: Hugh Bradford
CHOREOGRAPHY: Ninette de Valois
SETTING: William Chappell
COSTUMES: William Chappell
COMPANY: Sadler's Wells Ballet
PREMIÈRE: London, 1931

394 JACK-IN-THE-BOX
MUSIC: Erik Satie; orch. Darius Milhaud
CHOREOGRAPHY: George Balanchine
SETTING: André Derain
COSTUMES: André Derain

COMPANY: Les Soireés de Paris
PREMIÈRE: Paris, 1924

THE JAR
see LA JARRE

395 JARDIN AUX LILAS, *Ballet in One Act*
BOOK: Antony Tudor
MUSIC: Ernest Chausson
CHOREOGRAPHY: Antony Tudor
SETTING: Hugh Stevenson
COSTUMES: Hugh Stevenson
COMPANY: Marie Rambert Company
PREMIÈRE: London, 1936

396 JARDIN PUBLIC, *Ballet in One Act*
BOOK: André Gide
MUSIC: Vladimir Dukelsky
CHOREOGRAPHY: Leonide Massine
COSTUMES: Jean Lurçat
COMPANY: Ballet Russe (de Basil)
PREMIÈRE: Paris, 1935

397 JARDIN PUBLIC, *Ballet in One Act*
BOOK: Vladimir Dukelsky and Leonide Massine
MUSIC: Vladimir Dukelsky
CHOREOGRAPHY: Leonide Massine
SETTING: Alice Halicka
COSTUMES: Alice Halicka
COMPANY: Ballet Russe (de Basil)
PREMIÈRE: Paris, 1936

398 LES JARDINS D'ARANJUEZ
MUSIC: Fauré, Ravel, Chabrier
CHOREOGRAPHY: Leonide Massine
SETTING: Socrate
COSTUMES: José-Maria Sert
COMPANY: Ballet Russe (Diaghilev)
PREMIÈRE: Madrid, 1918

LES JARDINS D'ARANJUEZ
see also LAS MENIÑAS

399 LA JARRE, *Ballet in One Act*
BOOK: Luigi Pirandello
MUSIC: Alfredo Casella
CHOREOGRAPHY: Jean Borlin
SETTING: Georges de Chirico
COSTUMES: Georges de Chirico
COMPANY: Les Ballets Suédois
PREMIÈRE: Paris, 1924

400 LA JARRE, *Ballet in One Act*
BOOK: Luigi Pirandello
MUSIC: Alfredo Casella
CHOREOGRAPHY: Ninette de Valois
SETTING: William Chappell
COSTUMES: William Chappell

COMPANY: Sadler's Wells Ballet
PREMIÈRE: London, 1934

401 JEU DE CARTES
BOOK: Igor Schwezoff
MUSIC: Robert de Roos
CHOREOGRAPHY: Igor Schwezoff
SETTING: David Grey
COSTUMES: David Grey
COMPANY: Ballet Schwezoff
PREMIÈRE: Amsterdam, 1935

402 JEU DE CARTES
MUSIC: Igor Strawinsky
CHOREOGRAPHY: Janine Charrat
SETTING: Pierre Roy
COSTUMES: Pierre Roy
COMPANY: Les Ballets des Champs-Elysées
PREMIÈRE: Paris, 1945

JEU DE CARTES
see also THE CARD PARTY

403 JEUNESSE
BOOK: André Cœuroy
MUSIC: Pierre Octave Ferroud
CHOREOGRAPHY: Serge Lifar
SETTING: Jean Godebsky
COSTUMES: Jean Godebsky
COMPANY: Théâtre National de l'Opéra
PREMIÈRE: Paris, 1933

404 JEUX, *Ballet in One Act*
BOOK: Vaslav Nijinsky
MUSIC: Claude Debussy
CHOREOGRAPHY: Vaslav Nijinsky
SETTING: Léon Bakst
COSTUMES: Léon Bakst
COMPANY: Ballet Russe (Diaghilev)
PREMIÈRE: Paris, 1913

405 JEUX, *Ballet in One Act*
MUSIC: Claude Debussy
CHOREOGRAPHY: Jean Borlin
SETTING: Pierre Bonnard
COMPANY: Les Ballets Suédois
PREMIÈRE: Paris, 1920

406 JEUX D'ENFANTS, *Ballet in One Act*
BOOK: Boris Kochno
MUSIC: Georges Bizet
CHOREOGRAPHY: Leonide Massine
CURTAIN: Joan Miro
SETTING: Joan Miro
COSTUMES: Joan Miro
COMPANY: Ballet Russe (de Basil)
PREMIÈRE: Monte Carlo, 1932

69

407 THE JEW IN THE BUSH
Music: Gavin Gordon
Choreography: Ninette de Valois
Setting: Bertram Guest
Costumes: Bertram Guest
Company: Sadler's Wells Ballet
Première: London, 1931

408 JINX
Book: Lew Christensen
Music: Benjamin Britten; arr. Colin McFee
Choreography: Lew Christensen
Settings: George Bockman
Costumes: George Bockman
Company: The Dance Players
Première: New York, 1942

409 JOAN DE ZARISSA
Book: Werner Egk
Music: Werner Egk
Choreography: Serge Lifar
Settings: Yves Brayer
Costumes: Yves Brayer
Company: Théâtre National de l'Opéra
Première: Paris, 1942

410 JOAN OF ARC
Music: James O. Turner
Choreography: John Regan
Settings: Elizabeth Agombar
Costumes: Elizabeth Agombar
Company: Three Arts Ballet
Première: Calcutta, India, 1945

411 JOB, *Masque for Dancing in Eight Scenes*
Book: Geoffrey Keyes
Music: Ralph Vaughan Williams
Choreography: Ninette de Valois
Settings: Gwendolyn Raverat
Costumes: Gwendolyn Raverat
Masks: Hedley Briggs
Company: The Camargo Society
Première: London, 1931

412 JOHANN STRAUSS, TO-NIGHT
Book: Kurt Jooss
Music: Frederic Cohen, after Johann Strauss
Choreography: Kurt Jooss
Costumes: George Kirsta
Company: Jooss Ballet
Première: London, 1935

413 JOSEPH AND POTIPHAR
Book: [George Balanchine]
Music: Richard Strauss
Choreography: George Balanchine
Settings: Kjeld Abell

Costumes: Kjeld Abell
Company: Royal Theatre
Première: Copenhagen, Denmark, 1930

Josephslegende
see also La Légende de Joseph

414 JOSEPHSLEGENDE
Book: Hugo von Hofmannsthal and Harry Kessler
Music: Richard Strauss
Choreography: Heinrich Kroeller
Setting: Emil Pirchan
Costumes: Emil Pirchan
Company: State Opera, Berlin
Première: Berlin, 1922

415 JOSZI THE WISE
Book: E. Mohacsi and L. Márkus
Music: G. Kósa
Choreography: Jan Cieplinsky
Setting: Zoltán Fülöp
Costumes: Zoltán Fülöp
Company: Hungarian State Ballet
Première: Budapest, 1933

416 JOTA ARAGONESA
Music: Michael Glinka
Choreography: Michel Fokine
Setting: Mariano Andreù
Costumes: Mariano Andreù
Company: Ballet Russe (Blum)
Première: London, 1937

417 LE JOUR
Book: Jules Supervielle
Music: Maurice Jaubert
Choreography: Serge Lifar
Setting: Jean Ernotte
Costumes: Jean Ernotte
Company: Théâtre National de l'Opéra
Première: Paris, 1943

418 JUDGMENT OF PARIS
Book: Frederick Ashton
Music: Lennox Berkeley
Choreography: Frederick Ashton
Setting: William Chappell
Costumes: William Chappell
Company: Sadler's Wells Ballet
Première: London, 1938

419 JUDGMENT OF PARIS
Book: Hugh Laing
Music: Kurt Weill
Choreography: Antony Tudor
Costumes: Hugh Laing

COMPANY: Marie Rambert Company
PREMIÈRE: [London,] 1938

420 JUDGMENT OF PARIS, *Satiric Ballet in One Act*
BOOK: Hugh Laing
MUSIC: Kurt Weill
CHOREOGRAPHY: Antony Tudor
SETTING: Lucinda Ballard
COSTUMES: Lucinda Ballard
COMPANY: Ballet Theatre
PREMIÈRE: New York, 1940

421 JUKE-BOX, *Jazz Ballet in One Act*
BOOK: Lincoln Kirstein
MUSIC: Alec Wilder
CHOREOGRAPHY: William Dollar
SETTING: Tom Lee
COSTUMES: Tom Lee
COMPANY: The American Ballet
PREMIÈRE: New York, 1941

422 KARAGUEZ
MUSIC: Marcel Mihailovic
CHOREOGRAPHY: Adolph Bolm
SETTING: Michel Larionow
COSTUMES: Michel Larionow
COMPANY: Chicago Allied Arts
PREMIÈRE: Chicago, Illinois, 1924-1927

423 KATERINA, THE SERF BALLERINA, *Ballet in Three Acts and Seven Scenes*
BOOK: L. M. Lavrovsky
MUSIC: Klementia Korchmarev, after Rubinstein and Adam
CHOREOGRAPHY: L. M. Lavrovsky
SETTING: B. M. Erbstein
COSTUMES: B. M. Erbstein
COMPANY: Soviet State Theatre
PREMIÈRE: Leningrad, Moscow, 1927

424 KERMESSE
MUSIC: Lavande
CHOREOGRAPHY: Constantin Tcherkas
SETTING: Roger Wild
COSTUMES: Roger Wild
COMPANY: Théâtre National de l'Opéra Comique
PREMIÈRE: Paris, 1943

425 KIKIMORA
MUSIC: Anatol Liadov
CHOREOGRAPHY: Leonide Massine
SETTINGS: Michel Larionow
COSTUMES: Michel Larionow
COMPANY: Ballet Russe (Diaghilev)
PREMIÈRE: San Sebastian, Spain, 1916

426 EINE KLEINE NACHTMUSIK
MUSIC: Wolfgang Amadeus Mozart
CHOREOGRAPHY: Leon Wojcikovsky
SETTING: Michel Kedziora
COSTUMES: Michel Kedziora
COMPANY: The Polish Ballet
PREMIÈRE: [Paris], 1938-1939

427 KRAZY KAT, *A Jazz Pantomime*
MUSIC: John Alden Carpenter
CHOREOGRAPHY: Adolph Bolm
SETTING: George Herriman
COSTUMES: George Herriman
PREMIÈRE: New York, 1922

428 KURUC FAIRY TALE, *Ballet in Three Acts*
BOOK: Harsanyi Zsolt
MUSIC: Zoltán Kordály
CHOREOGRAPHY: Aurél Milloss and Ressö Brada
SETTING: Gustáv Oláh
COMPANY: Hungarian State Ballet
PREMIÈRE: Budapest, 1935

429 LABYRINTH, *Ballet in Four Scenes*
BOOK: Salvador Dali
MUSIC: Franz Schubert
CHOREOGRAPHY: Leonide Massine
SETTING: Salvador Dali
COSTUMES: Salvador Dali
COMPANY: Ballet Russe (Massine)
PREMIÈRE: New York, 1941

430 LE LAC DES CYGNES, *Ballet in Two Scenes*
BOOK: V. P. Begitchev and Geltser
MUSIC: Peter Tchaikowsky
CHOREOGRAPHY: Michel Fokine, after Petipa and Ivanov
SETTING: FIRST SCENE: Constantin Korovine
SETTING: SECOND SCENE: Alexander Golovine
COSTUMES: Alexander Golovine
COMPANY: Ballet Russe (Diaghilev)
PREMIÈRE: London, 1911

431 LE LAC DES CYGNES, *Ballet in Two Acts*
BOOK: V. P. Begitchev and Geltser
MUSIC: Peter Tchaikowsky
CHOREOGRAPHY: Nicholas Sergueff, after Petipa and Ivanov
SETTINGS: Hugh Stevenson
COSTUMES: Hugh Stevenson
COMPANY: Sadler's Wells Ballet
PREMIÈRE: London, 1934

432 LE LAC DES CYGNES, *Ballet in Two Acts*
BOOK: V. P. Begitchev and Geltser
MUSIC: Peter Tchaikowsky
CHOREOGRAPHY: Nicholas Sergueff, after Petipa and Ivanov

SETTINGS: William Chappell
COSTUMES: William Chappell
COMPANY: The International Ballet
PREMIÈRE: [London], 1941

433 LE LAC DES CYGNES, *Ballet in Two Acts*
BOOK: V. P. Begitchev and Geltser
MUSIC: Peter Tchaikowsky
CHOREOGRAPHY: Nicholas Sergueff, after Petipa and Ivanov
SETTINGS: Leslie Hurry
COSTUMES: Leslie Hurry
COMPANY: Sadler's Wells Ballet
PREMIÈRE: London, 1943

434 LE LAC DES CYGNES, *Ballet in One Scene*
MUSIC: Peter Tchaikowsky
CHOREOGRAPHY: Igor Schwezoff, after Petipa and Ivanov
SETTING: Collomb
COSTUMES: Igor Schwezoff
COMPANY: Teatro Municipal
PREMIÈRE: Rio de Janeiro, 1945

LE LAC DES CYGNES
see also SWAN LAKE

435 LADIES' BETTER DRESSES
MUSIC: Herbert Kingsley
CHOREOGRAPHY: Catherine Littlefield
SETTINGS: R. Starke
COSTUMES: Joy Michael
COMPANY: Philadelphia Opera Ballet
PREMIÈRE: Chicago, Illinois, 1938

436 LADY INTO FOX, *Ballet in One Act and Three Scenes*
BOOK: Andrée Howard, after David Garnett
MUSIC: Arthur Honegger; arr. Charles Lynch
CHOREOGRAPHY: Andrée Howard
SETTINGS: Nadia Benois
COSTUMES: Nadia Benois
COMPANY: Marie Rambert Company
PREMIÈRE: London, 1939

437 LADY OF SHALOTT, *Ballet in One Scene*
BOOK: After Alfred Tennyson
MUSIC: Jan Sibelius
CHOREOGRAPHY: Frederick Ashton
SETTINGS: William Chappell
COSTUMES: William Chappell
COMPANY: Marie Rambert Company
PREMIÈRE: London, 1931

438 LARVEN
BOOK: Kurt Jooss
MUSIC: Percussion; arr. Kurt Jooss
CHOREOGRAPHY: Kurt Jooss

SETTING: Hein Heckroth
COSTUMES: Hein Heckroth
COMPANY: Neue Tanzbuehne
PREMIÈRE: Muenster, Germany, 1925

439 LAST FLOWER
BOOK: After James Thurber
MUSIC: Nicolas Nabokov
CHOREOGRAPHY: William Dollar
SETTING: Stewart Chaney
COSTUMES: Stewart Chaney
COMPANY: Ballet International
PREMIÈRE: New York, 1944

440 LAURENCIA
BOOK: After Lope de Vega
MUSIC: Alexander Krein
CHOREOGRAPHY: Vakhtang Chabukiani
SETTINGS: S. Virsaladze
COSTUMES: S. Virsaladze
COMPANY: [Kirov State Opera]
PREMIÈRE: Leningrad, 1939

441 LA LEÇON APPRISE
BOOK: Wendy Toye
MUSIC: Darius Milhaud
CHOREOGRAPHY: Wendy Toye
SETTING: Joseph Carl
COSTUMES: Joseph Carl
COMPANY: The London Ballet
PREMIÈRE: London, 1940

442 LÉDA
BOOK: Frederick Ashton
MUSIC: Christoph Willibald Gluck
CHOREOGRAPHY: Frederick Ashton
SETTINGS: William Chappell
COSTUMES: William Chappell
COMPANY: Marie Rambert Company
PREMIÈRE: London, 1930

443 LA LÉGENDE DE CRACOVIE, *Ballet in Two Scenes*
BOOK: Ludwik-Horonin Morstin
MUSIC: Michal Kondracki
CHOREOGRAPHY: Bronislava Nijinska
SETTINGS: Teresa Ruszkowska
COSTUMES: Teresa Ruszkowska
COMPANY: The Polish Ballet
PREMIÈRE: Paris, 1937-1938

444 LEGEND OF THE SILVER BIRCH
MUSIC: Adrian Beecham
CHOREOGRAPHY: Lydia Sokolova
SETTINGS: Nadia Benois
COSTUMES: Nadia Benois
COMPANY: Allied Ballets
PREMIÈRE: London, 1942

445 LA LÉGENDE DU BOULEAU (Berioska)
Book: Boris Kniasoff
Music: [Fedor] Konstantinoff
Choreography: Boris Kniasoff
Settings: Mireille Hunnebelle
Costumes: Mireille Hunnebelle
Company: Archives Internationales de la Danse
Première: Paris, 1932

446 LA LÉGENDE DE JOSEPH, *Spectacle Ballet in One Act*
Book: Hugo von Hofmannsthal and Harry Kessler
Music: Richard Strauss
Choreography: Michel Fokine
Setting: José-Maria Sert
Costumes: Léon Bakst
Company: Ballet Russe (Diaghilev)
Première: Paris, 1914

La Légende de Joseph
see also Josephslegende

447 LET THE RIGHTEOUS BE GLAD
Book: Catherine Littlefield
Music: Negro Spirituals; arr. J. Donath
Choreography: Catherine Littlefield
Setting: Angelo Pinto
Costumes: Salvatore Pinto
Company: Philadelphia Opera Ballet
Première: Philadelphia, Pennsylvania, 1937

448 LA LIBELLULE, *Ballet in One Act*
Book: Guy de Téramond
Music: Gabriel Pierné
Choreography: Constantin Tcherkas
Settings: Paul-René Larthe
Costumes: Paul-René Larthe
Company: Théâtre National de l'Opéra Comique
Première: Paris, 1940

Lieutenant Kije
see Russian Soldier

Lilac Garden
see Jardin aux Lilas

449 LE LION AMOUREUX
Book: David Lichine and Henry Clifford
Music: Karol Rathaus
Choreography: David Lichine
Settings: Pierre Roy
Costumes: Pierre Roy
Company: Ballet Russe (de Basil)
Première: 1937

450 LITTLE CIRCUS
Music: Jacques Offenbach

Choreography: Adolph Bolm
Setting: Nicolai Remisoff
Costumes: Nicolai Remisoff
Company: Chicago Allied Arts
Première: Chicago, Illinois, 1925

451 LA LITURGIE, *Originally 7 Acts*
Book: Biblical Story
Music: For Entr'actes to be commissioned from Igor Strawinsky
Choreography: Leonide Massine
Settings: Nathalie Gontcharova
Costumes: Nathalie Gontcharova
Company: Ballet Russe (Diaghilev)
Project: 1915

452 LITTLE JOHNNY IN TOP-BOOTS, *Ballet in One Act and Three Scenes*
Book: Ervin Clementis
Music: Jenö Kenessey
Choreography: Gyula Harangozó
Settings: Zoltán Fülöp
Costumes: Gustáv Oláh
Company: Hungarian State Ballet
Première: Budapest, 1937

Lord of Burleigh
see My Lord of Burleigh

453 LOST ILLUSIONS, *Choreographic Novel*
Book: After Honoré de Balzac
Music: B. A. Asafiev
Choreography: R. V. Zakarov
Settings: V. V. Dmitriev
Costumes: V. V. Dmitriev
Company: Soviet State Ballet
Première: Leningrad, 1936

Love the Sorcerer
see El Amor Brujo

454 LOVE SONG
Book: Ruth Page
Music: Franz Schubert; orch. Wesley LaViolette, Rudolph Ganz
Choreography: Ruth Page
Setting: Nicolai Remisoff
Costumes: Nicolai Remisoff
Company: Chicago Opera Company
Première: Chicago, Illinois, 1935

455 LUMAWIG E LA SAETTA
Book: Maner Lualdi
Music: Adriano Lualdi
Choreography: Boris Romanoff
Settings: Mario Cito Filomarino
Costumes: Mario Cito Filomarino

COMPANY: Royal Opera House
PREMIÈRE: Rome, 1937

456 LUNA PARK
BOOK: Boris Kochno
MUSIC: Gerald Hugh Berners
CHOREOGRAPHY: George Balanchine
SETTINGS: Christopher Wood
COSTUMES: Christopher Wood
COMPANY: C. B. Cochran's Review
PREMIÈRE: London, 1930

LUTTE ETERNELLE
see THE ETERNAL STRUGGLE

457 LYSISTRATA OR THE STRIKE OF WIVES
BOOK: After Aristophanes
MUSIC: Serge Prokofieff
CHOREOGRAPHY: Antony Tudor
SETTINGS: William Chappell
COSTUMES: William Chappell
COMPANY: Marie Rambert Company
PREMIÈRE: London, 1932

458 MADEMOISELLE ANGOT, *Ballet in Three Scenes*
BOOK: Charles Lecocq
MUSIC: Charles Lecocq; arr. Efrem Kurtz; orch. Richard Mohaupt
CHOREOGRAPHY: Leonide Massine
SETTING: Mstislav Dobujinsky
COSTUMES: Mstislav Dobujinsky
COMPANY: Ballet Theatre
PREMIÈRE: New York, 1943

459 MAD TRISTAN, *The First Paranoic Ballet Based on the Eternal Myth of Love in Death, Two Scenes*
BOOK: Salvador Dali
MUSIC: Richard Wagner; orch. Ivan Boutnikoff
CURTAIN: Salvador Dali
SETTINGS: Salvador Dali
COSTUMES: Salvador Dali
CHOREOGRAPHY: Leonide Massine
COMPANY: Ballet International
PREMIÈRE: New York, 1944

460 MAGIC, *Ballet-Serenata in One Scene*
MUSIC: Wolfgang Amadeus Mozart
CHOREOGRAPHY: George Balanchine
SETTING: Pavel Tchelitchew
COSTUMES: Pavel Tchelitchew
COMPANY: Felia Doubrowska and American Ballet Company
PREMIÈRE: Hartford, Connecticut, 1936

THE MAGIC SWAN
see LE LAC DES CYGNES

461 MAGYAR ABRANDOK, *Ballet in Three Acts*
BOOK: L. Markús
MUSIC: Franz Liszt
CHOREOGRAPHY: Jan Cieplinsky
SETTING: Zoltán Fülöp
COSTUMES: Gustáv Oláh
COMPANY: Hungarian State Ballet
PREMIÈRE: Budapest, 1933

462 MAISON DE FOUS
BOOK: Jean Borlin
MUSIC: Viking Dahl
CHOREOGRAPHY: Jean Borlin
SETTINGS: Nils de Dardel
COSTUMES: Nils de Dardel
COMPANY: Les Ballets Suédois
PREMIÈRE: Paris, 1920

463 MANDRAGORA
MUSIC: Karol Szymanowsky
CHOREOGRAPHY: Adolph Bolm
SETTING: Nicolai Remisoff
COSTUMES: Nicolai Remisoff
COMPANY: Chicago Allied Arts
PREMIÈRE: Chicago, Illinois, 1925

464 THE MAN FROM MIDIAN
SETTING: Winthrop Palmer
MUSIC: Stefan Wolpe
CHOREOGRAPHY: Eugene Loring
DECOR: Doris Rosenthal
COSTUMES: Doris Rosenthal
COMPANY: The Dance Players
PREMIÈRE: Washington, D. C., 1942

465 MARCHAND D'OISEAUX
BOOK: Hélène Perdriat
MUSIC: Germaine Tailleferre
CHOREOGRAPHY: Jean Borlin
SETTING: Hélène Perdriat
COSTUMES: Hélène Perdriat
COMPANY: Les Ballets Suédois
PREMIÈRE: Paris, 1923

466 LE MARIAGE D'AURORE, *Ballet in One Act*
BOOK: Marius Petipa
MUSIC: Peter Tchaikowsky
CHOREOGRAPHY: Bronislava Nijinska, after Petipa
SETTING: Léon Bakst
COSTUMES: Léon Bakst and Alexandre Benois
COMPANY: Ballet Russe (Diaghilev)
PREMIÈRE: Paris, 1922

LE MARIAGE D'AURORE
see also AURORA'S WEDDING

467 LES MARIÉS DE LA TOUR EIFFEL
BOOK: Jean Cocteau
MUSIC: Auric, Honegger, Milhaud, Poulenc, Tailleferre
CHOREOGRAPHY: Jean Borlin
SETTING: Irène Lagut
COSTUMES: Jean Hugo
MASKS: Jean Hugo
COMPANY: Les Ballets Suédois
PREMIÈRE: Paris, 1921

468 MARS AND VENUS
MUSIC: Domenico Scarlatti; arr. Constant Lambert
CHOREOGRAPHY: Frederick Ashton
SETTING: William Chappell
COSTUMES: William Chappell
COMPANY: Marie Rambert Company
PREMIÈRE: London, 1931

469 MASQUE OF THE RED DEATH
BOOK: Soudeikine, after Edgar Allen Poe
MUSIC: Nicolas Tcherepnine
CURTAIN: Serge Soudeikine
SETTINGS: Serge Soudeikine
COSTUMES: Serge Soudeikine
COMPANY: Ballet Russe (Diaghilev)
PROJECT: 1914

470 LES MASQUES
BOOK: Frederick Ashton
MUSIC: Francis Poulenc
CHOREOGRAPHY: Frederick Ashton
SETTING: Sophie Fedorovitch
COSTUMES: Sophie Fedorovitch
COMPANY: Marie Rambert Company
PREMIÈRE: London, 1933

471 LES MATELOTS, *Ballet in Five Scenes*
BOOK: Boris Kochno
MUSIC: Georges Auric
CHOREOGRAPHY: Leonide Massine
SETTING: Pedro Pruna
COSTUMES: Pedro Pruna
COMPANY: Ballet Russe (Diaghilev)
PREMIÈRE: Paris, 1925

472 MAY COLIN
MUSIC: Arnold Bax
CHOREOGRAPHY: Harold Turner
SETTING: Guy Sheppard
COSTUMES: Guy Sheppard
COMPANY: Arts Theatre Ballet
PREMIÈRE: London, 1940

473 MAZURKA
BOOK: Igor Schwezoff
MUSIC: Frederic Chopin
CHOREOGRAPHY: Igor Schwezoff
SETTING: David Grey
COSTUMES: David Grey
COMPANY: Ballet Schwezoff
PREMIÈRE: The Hague, Holland, [1934]

474 MECHANICAL BALLET, *A Ballet in One Act*
BOOK: Adolph Bolm
MUSIC: Alexander Mossolov
CHOREOGRAPHY: Adolph Bolm
COSTUMES: John Hambleton
COMPANY: Ballet Theatre
PREMIÈRE: New York, 1940

MECHANICAL BALLET
see also BALLET MÉCANIQUE

475 MÉKHÂNO
MUSIC: Juan José Castro
CHOREOGRAPHY: Paul Petroff
SETTING: Hector Basaldua
COSTUMES: Hector Basaldua
COMPANY: Teatro Colon
PREMIÈRE: Buenos Aires, 1936

476 MEMORIES, *Ballet in One Act and Prologue*
BOOK: Winthrop Palmer
MUSIC: Johannes Brahms; orch. Maurice Baron
CHOREOGRAPHY: Simon Semenoff
SETTING: Raoul Pène Du Bois
COSTUMES: Raoul Pène Du Bois
COMPANY: Ballet International
PREMIÈRE: New York, 1944

477 LAS MENIÑAS
MUSIC: Gabriel Fauré
CHOREOGRAPHY: Leonide Massine
SETTING: Socrate
COSTUMES: José-Maria Sert
COMPANY: Ballet Russe (Diaghilev)
PREMIÈRE: San Sebastian, Spain, 1916

478 MEPHISTO VALSE
MUSIC: Franz Liszt
CHOREOGRAPHY: Vaslav Nijinsky
SETTING: Robert Edmond Jones
COSTUMES: Robert Edmond Jones
COMPANY: Ballet Russe (Diaghilev)
PROJECT: 1916

479 MEPHISTO VALSE
MUSIC: Franz Liszt
CHOREOGRAPHY: Frederick Ashton
SETTING: Sophie Fedorovitch
COSTUMES: Sophie Fedorovitch
COMPANY: Marie Rambert Company
PREMIÈRE: London, 1931

480 MEPHISTO VALSE
MUSIC: Franz Liszt
CHOREOGRAPHY: Michel Fokine
SETTING: Nathalie Gontcharova
COSTUMES: Nathalie Gontcharova
COMPANY: Théâtre National de l'Opéra
Comique
PREMIÈRE: Paris, 1935

481 MERCURE
BOOK: Etienne de Beaumont
MUSIC: Erik Satie
CHOREOGRAPHY: Leonide Massine
SETTING: Pablo Picasso
COSTUMES: Pablo Picasso
COMPANY: Les Soirées de Paris
PREMIÈRE: Paris, 1924

482 MERCURE
BOOK: Frederick Ashton
MUSIC: Erik Satie
CHOREOGRAPHY: Frederick Ashton
SETTING: William Chappell
COSTUMES: William Chappell
COMPANY: Marie Rambert Company
PREMIÈRE: London, 1931

483 LA MÈRE L'OYE
MUSIC: Maurice Ravel
CHOREOGRAPHY: Constantin Tcherkas
SETTING: Léon Leyritz
COSTUMES: Léon Leyritz
COMPANY: Théâtre National de l'Opéra
Comique
PREMIÈRE: Paris, 1942

484 MERMAID, *Ballet in Four Scenes*
BOOK: After Hans Christian Andersen
MUSIC: Maurice Ravel
CHOREOGRAPHY: Andrée Howard and Susan
Salaman
SETTING: Andrée Howard
COSTUMES: Andrée Howard
COMPANY: The Ballet Club
PREMIÈRE: London, 1934

485 MIDAS, *Ballet in One Act*
BOOK: Léon Bakst, after Ovid
MUSIC: Maximilien Steinberg
CHOREOGRAPHY: Michel Fokine
SETTING: Mstislav Dobujinsky
COSTUMES: Mstislav Dobujinsky
COMPANY: Ballet Russe (Diaghilev)
PREMIÈRE: Paris, 1914

486 MIDAS, *Ballet in One Act*
BOOK: Léon Bakst, after Ovid

MUSIC: Maximilien Steinberg
CHOREOGRAPHY: Michel Fokine
SETTING: Léon Bakst
COSTUMES: Léon Bakst
COMPANY: Ballet Russe (Diaghilev)
PREMIÈRE: Paris, 1914

487 MIDAS
MUSIC: Elizabeth Lutyens
CHOREOGRAPHY: Celia Franca
SETTING: del Renzio
COSTUMES: del Renzio
COMPANY: Ballet Trois Arts
PREMIÈRE: Hammersmith, England, 1939

THE MIDNIGHT SUN
see SOLEIL DE MINUIT

488 MILLE E UNA NOTTE, *Ballet in Seven Acts*
BOOK: Guiseppe Adami
MUSIC: Victor de Sabeta
CHOREOGRAPHY: Max Terpis
SETTING: Caramba
COSTUMES: Caramba
COMPANY: Scala Opera Ballet
PREMIÈRE: Milan, 1930

489 LES MILLIONS D'ARLEQUIN
MUSIC: Riccardo Drigo
CHOREOGRAPHY: Boris Romanoff
SETTING: Hosiasson and Bobermann
COSTUMES: Hosiasson and Bobermann
COMPANY: Russian Romantic Theatre
PREMIÈRE: Berlin, 1922

490 THE MINOTAUR
MUSIC: Charles Naginski
CHOREOGRAPHY: Erick Hawkins
COSTUMES: Leslie Powell
COMPANY: The American Ballet Caravan
PREMIÈRE: New York, 1939

491 THE MINSTREL
BOOK: Catherine Littlefield
MUSIC: Claude Debussy
CHOREOGRAPHY: Catherine Littlefield
SETTING: Angelo Pinto
COSTUMES: Salvatore Pinto
COMPANY: Philadelphia Opera Ballet
PREMIÈRE: Haverford, Pennsylvania, 1936

492 MIRACLE IN THE GORBALS, *Ballet in One
Scene*
BOOK: Michael Benthall
MUSIC: Arthur Bliss
CHOREOGRAPHY: Robert Helpmann
CURTAIN: Edward Burra
SETTING: Edward Burra

COSTUMES: Edward Burra
COMPANY: Sadler's Wells Ballet
PREMIÈRE: London, 1944

493 MIRAGES
MUSIC: Claude Debussy
CHOREOGRAPHY: David Lichine
SETTING: Eugene Berman
COSTUMES: Eugene Berman
COMPANY: Ballet Russe (de Basil)
PROJECT: 1942

494 LES MIRAGES
BOOK: A.-M. Cassandre
MUSIC: Henri Sauguet
CHOREOGRAPHY: [Serge Lifar]
SETTING: A.-M. Cassandre
COSTUMES: A.-M. Cassandre
COMPANY: Théâtre National de l'Opéra
PROJECT: 1944

495 THE MIRROR, *Dance Drama in Eight Scenes*
BOOK: Kurt Jooss
MUSIC: Frederic Cohen
CHOREOGRAPHY: Kurt Jooss
COSTUMES: Hein Heckroth
COMPANY: Jooss Ballet
PREMIÈRE: Manchester, England, 1935

496 MOMENT PERPÉTUEL
BOOK: Igor Schwezoff
MUSIC: Francis Poulenc
CHOREOGRAPHY: Igor Schwezoff
SETTING: David Grey
COSTUMES: David Grey
COMPANY: Ballet Schwezoff
PREMIÈRE: Amsterdam, 1935

497 MOONLIGHT SONATA
BOOK: Leonide Massine
MUSIC: Ludwig van Beethoven
CHOREOGRAPHY: Leonide Massine
SETTING: Serge Soudeikine
COSTUMES: Serge Soudeikine
COMPANY: Ballet Theatre
PREMIÈRE: Chicago, Illinois, 1944

498 MOUVEMENT TRAGIQUE, *Ballet in One Scene*
BOOK: Igor Schwezoff
MUSIC: Alexander Scriabine
CHOREOGRAPHY: Igor Schwezoff
SETTING: David Grey
COSTUMES: David Grey
COMPANY: Ballet Schwezoff
PREMIÈRE: The Hague, Holland, 1934

499 MOZARTIANA, *Ballet in Five Movements*
MUSIC: Wolfgang Amadeus Mozart; orch. Peter Tchaikowsky
CHOREOGRAPHY: George Balanchine
SETTING: Christian Bérard
COSTUMES: Christian Bérard
COMPANY: Les Ballets 1933
PREMIÈRE: Paris, 1933

500 MUCKLE MOU'D MEG
MUSIC: John Gough
CHOREOGRAPHY: Margery Middleton
SETTING: Cecile Walton
COSTUMES: Cecile Walton
COMPANY: Edinburgh Ballet Club
PREMIÈRE: Edinburgh, Scotland, 1945

501 LA MUSE S'AMUSE
MUSIC: Déodat de Séverac
CHOREOGRAPHY: Andrée Howard
SETTING: Andrée Howard
COSTUMES: Andrée Howard
COMPANY: Marie Rambert Company
PREMIÈRE: London, 1936

MUSICAL CHAIRS
see COMMEDIA BALLETICA

502 MUTE WIFE
BOOK: After Anatole France
MUSIC: Niccolo Paganini; orch. Vittorio Rieti
CHOREOGRAPHY: Antonia Cobos
SETTING: Rico Lebrun
COSTUMES: Rico Lebrun
COMPANY: Ballet International
PREMIÈRE: New York, 1944

503 MY LORD OF BURLEIGH
BOOK: Edwin Evans
MUSIC: Felix Mendelssohn
CHOREOGRAPHY: Frederick Ashton
SETTING: George Sheringham
COSTUMES: George Sheringham
COMPANY: The Camargo Society
PREMIÈRE: London, 1931

504 MY LORD OF BURLEIGH
MUSIC: Felix Mendelssohn; arr. Edwin Evans
CHOREOGRAPHER: Frederick Ashton
SETTING: Derek Hill
COSTUMES: Derek Hill
COMPANY: Sadler's Wells Ballet
PREMIÈRE: [London,] 1937

505 MYSTERY OF PYRAMID
MUSIC: Alexandre Tcherepnine
CHOREOGRAPHY: Kirsanova

SETTING: Mstislav Dobujinsky
COSTUMES: Mstislav Dobujinsky
COMPANY: Lithuanian State Ballet
PREMIÈRE: Kaunas, Lithuania, 1938

506 NARCISSE, *Ballet in One Act*
BOOK: Léon Bakst
MUSIC: Nicolas Tcherepnine
CHOREOGRAPHY: Michel Fokine
SETTING: Léon Bakst
COSTUMES: Léon Bakst
COMPANY: Ballet Russe (Diaghilev)
PREMIÈRE: Paris, 1911

507 NARCISSUS AND ECHO
MUSIC: Arthur Bliss
CHOREOGRAPHY: Ninette de Valois
SETTING: William Chappell
COSTUMES: William Chappell
COMPANY: Sadler's Wells Ballet
PREMIÈRE: [London], 1932

508 THE NEW YORKER, *Ballet in Three Scenes*
BOOK: Rea Irwin and Leonide Massine
MUSIC: George Gershwin; orch. David Raksin
CHOREOGRAPHY: Leonide Massine
SETTING: Rea Irwin
COMPANY: Ballet Russe (de Basil)
PREMIÈRE: New York, 1940

509 THE NIGHTINGALE, *Ballet in Three Acts*
BOOK: J. O. Slonimsky and A. N. Yermolayev, after Zmitrok Biadulia
MUSIC: M. E. Kroshner
CHOREOGRAPHY: Alexei N. Yermolayev
SETTING: B. A. Matrunin
COMPANY: Festival of Byelo-Russian Art
PREMIÈRE: Moscow, 1940

510 NIKOTINA
MUSIC: Vitezslav Novák
CHOREOGRAPHY: Jelizaveta Nikolská
SETTING: Antonin Heythum
COSTUMES: Antonin Heythum
COMPANY: National Theatre
PREMIÈRE: Prague, 1937

NOBILISSIMA VISIONE
see SAINT FRANCIS

511 NOCE A OJCÓW, *Ballet in One Scene*
MUSIC: K. Kurpinski; Stefani
CHOREOGRAPHY: Piotr Zaylich
SETTING: Michel Kedziora
COSTUMES: Michel Kedziora
COMPANY: The Polish Ballet
PREMIÈRE: [Paris, 1937]

512 LES NOCES, *Russian Choreographic Scenes in Four Tableaux*
BOOK: Igor Strawinsky
MUSIC: Igor Strawinsky
CHOREOGRAPHY: Bronislava Nijinska
SETTING: Nathalie Gontcharova
CURTAIN: Nathalie Gontcharova
COSTUMES: Nathalie Gontcharova
COMPANY: Ballet Russe (Diaghilev)
PREMIÈRE: Paris, 1923

513 LES NOCES, *Ballet in Four Scenes*
MUSIC: Igor Strawinsky
CHOREOGRAPHY: Elizabeth Anderson
CONSTRUCTIVIST SETTINGS: Serge Soudeikine
COSTUMES: Serge Soudeikine
COMPANY: League of Composers
PREMIÈRE: New York, 1929

514 LES NOCES DE PSYCHÉ ET L'AMOUR
MUSIC: Johann Sebastian Bach; orch. Arthur Honegger
CHOREOGRAPHER: Bronislava Nijinska
SETTING: Alexandre Benois
COSTUMES: Alexandre Benois
COMPANY: Ida Rubinstein Ballet
PREMIÈRE: Paris, 1928

515 LES NOCES RUSSES
MUSIC: Michail Glinka and Nicholas Rimsky-Korsakov
CHOREOGRAPHY: Boris Romanoff
SETTING: Pavel Tchelitchew
COSTUMES: Pavel Tchelitchew
COMPANY: Russian Romantic Theatre
PREMIÈRE: Berlin, 1922

516 NOCTURNE, *Ballet in One Act*
BOOK: Etienne de Beaumont
MUSIC: J. P. Rameau; arr. Roger Desormière
CHOREOGRAPHY: David Lichine
SETTING: Etienne de Beaumont
COSTUMES: Etienne de Beaumont
COMPANY: Ballet Russe (de Basil)
PREMIÈRE: Paris, 1933

517 NOCTURNE
BOOK: Edward Sackville-West
MUSIC: Frederick Delius
CHOREOGRAPHY: Frederick Ashton
SETTING: Sophie Fedorovitch
CURTAIN: Sophie Fedorovitch
COSTUMES: Sophie Fedorovitch
COMPANY: The Sadler's Wells Ballet
PREMIÈRE: London, 1936

518 LES NUAGES, *Allegoric Ballet in One Act*
MUSIC: Claude Debussy

CHOREOGRAPHY: Nini Theilade
COSTUMES: Willem de Kooning
COMPANY: Ballet Russe (Massine)
PREMIÈRE: New York, 1940

519 LES NUAGES
MUSIC: Claude Debussy
CHOREOGRAPHY: Nini Theilade
SETTING: Eugene Berman
COSTUMES: Eugene Berman
COMPANY: Ballet Russe (de Basil)
PROJECT: 1942

520 LES NUAGES
MUSIC: Henri Sauguet
CHOREOGRAPHY: Serge Lifar
SETTING: A.-M. Cassandre
COSTUMES: A.-M. Cassandre
COMPANY: Théâtre National de l'Opéra
PREMIÈRE: Paris, [1944]

521 LA NUIT DE LA SAINT-JEAN, *Ballet in One Act*
BOOK: Jean Borlin
MUSIC: Hugo Alfvén
CHOREOGRAPHY: Jean Borlin
CURTAIN: Nils de Dardel
SETTINGS: Nils de Dardel
COSTUMES: Nils de Dardel
COMPANY: Les Ballets Suédois
PREMIÈRE: Paris, 1920

522 LA NUIT DE LA SAINT-JEAN, *Ballet in Two Acts*
BOOK: Ventura Gasol
MUSIC: Robert Gerhard
SETTING: Joan Junyer
COSTUMES: Joan Junyer
COMPANY: Ballet Russe (de Basil)
PROJECT: 1939

523 NURSERY SUITE
MUSIC: Edward Elgar
CHOREOGRAPHY: Ninette de Valois
SETTING: Nancy Allen
COSTUMES: Nancy Allen
COMPANY: Sadler's Wells Ballet
PREMIÈRE: [London], 1932

524 THE NUTCRACKER, *A Fairy Tale Ballet in Two Acts and Three Scenes*
BOOK: Alexandra Fedorova
MUSIC: Peter Tchaikowsky
CHOREOGRAPHY: A. Fedorova, after Lev Ivanov
SETTING: Alexandre Benois
COSTUMES: Alexandre Benois

COMPANY: Ballet Russe (Denham)
PREMIÈRE: New York, 1940

THE NUTCRACKER
see also CASSE-NOISETTE

525 NUTCRACKER SUITE
BOOK: Leon Leonidoff
MUSIC: Peter Tchaikowsky
CHOREOGRAPHY: Florence Rogge
SETTING: Serge Soudeikine
COSTUMES: Serge Soudeikine
COMPANY: Radio City Music Hall
PREMIÈRE: New York, 1937

526 OAK STREET BEACH
MUSIC: Clarence Loomis
CHOREOGRAPHER: Ruth Page
SETTING: Nicolai Remisoff
COSTUMES: Nicolai Remisoff
COMPANY: Ravinia Opera Company
PREMIÈRE: Ravinia, Illinois, 1928

OBEAH
see BLACK RITUAL

527 OBERTURA REPUBLICANA
BOOK: Martin Luis Guzmán
MUSIC: Carlos Chavez
CHOREOGRAPHY: [Nellie Campobello]
SETTING: José Clemente Orozco
COSTUMES: José Clemente Orozco
COMPANY: Ballet of the City of México
PREMIÈRE: México, D. F., [1945]

528 ODE, *Ballet in One Act and Three Scenes*
BOOK: Boris Kochno
MUSIC: Nicolas Nabokov
CHOREOGRAPHY: Leonide Massine
SETTING: Pavel Tchelitchew
COSTUMES: Pavel Tchelitchew
COMPANY: Ballet Russe (Diaghilev)
PREMIÈRE: Paris, 1928

529 ODE TO GLORY, *Choreographic Ode*
BOOK: Yurek Shabelevski
MUSIC: Frederic Chopin
CHOREOGRAPHY: Yurek Shabelevski
SETTING: Michel Baronov
COSTUMES: Michel Baronov
COMPANY: Ballet Theatre
PREMIÈRE: New York, 1940

530 OFFENBACHIANA
MUSIC: Juan José Castro, after Jacques Offenbach
CHOREOGRAPHY: Margarete Wallmann
SETTING: Hector Basaldua

COSTUMES: Hector Basaldua
COMPANY: Teatro Colon
PREMIÈRE: Buenos Aires, 1941

531 OFFERLUNDEN, *Ballet-Pantomime*
BOOK: Jean Borlin
MUSIC: Algot Haquinius
CHOREOGRAPHY: Jean Borlin
SETTING: Gunnar Hallstroem
COSTUMES: Gunnar Hallstroem
COMPANY: Les Ballets Suédois
PREMIÈRE: Paris, 1923

532 L'OISEAU DE FEU, *Fantastic Ballet in One Act*
BOOK: Michel Fokine
MUSIC: Igor Strawinsky
CHOREOGRAPHY: Michel Fokine
SETTING: Alexander Golovine
COSTUMES: A. Golovine and Léon Bakst
COMPANY: Ballet Russe (Diaghilev)
PREMIÈRE: Paris, 1910

533 L'OISEAU DE FEU, *A Russian Fairy Tale*
BOOK: Michel Fokine
MUSIC: Igor Strawinsky
CHOREOGRAPHY: After Michel Fokine
SETTING: Nathalie Gontcharova
COSTUMES: Nathalie Gontcharova
COMPANY: Ballet Russe (de Basil)
PREMIÈRE: [Monte Carlo], 1934

L'OISEAU DE FEU
see also FIREBIRD

534 L'OISEAU ET LE PRINCE
MUSIC: Peter Tchaikowsky
CHOREOGRAPHY: After Marius Petipa
DECORS: Léon Bakst
COSTUMES: Léon Bakst
COMPANY: Ballet Russe (Diaghilev)
PREMIÈRE: London, 1919

535 OLD MILAN
BOOK: G. Adami
MUSIC: F. Vittadini
CHOREOGRAPHY: Leonide Massine
SETTING: Antonio Rovescalli and G. B. Santoni
COSTUMES: Antonio Rovescalli and G. B. Santoni
COMPANY: Scala Opera Ballet
PREMIÈRE: Milan, 1935

536 OLD RUSSIAN FOLK-LORE, *Ballet in One Act*
MUSIC: Nicolas Tcherepnine
CHOREOGRAPHY: Laurent Novikoff

SETTING: Ivan Bilibine
COSTUMES: Ivan Bilibine
COMPANY: Pavlova Company
PREMIÈRE: New York, 1923

537 OLD VIENNA
BOOK: Adolph Bolm
MUSIC: Ludwig van Beethoven
CHOREOGRAPHY: Adolph Bolm
SETTING: Nicolai Remisoff
COSTUMES: Nicolai Remisoff
COMPANY: Chamber Music Society
PREMIÈRE: Washington, D. C., 1928

538 ON STAGE, *Ballet in One Act*
BOOK: Mary and Michael Kidd
MUSIC: Norman Dello Joio
CHOREOGRAPHY: Michael Kidd
SETTING: Oliver Smith
COSTUMES: Alvin Colt
COMPANY: Ballet Theatre
PREMIÈRE: New York, 1945

539 L'ORCHESTRE EN LIBERTÉ
MUSIC: Henry Sauveplane
CHOREOGRAPHY: Serge Lifar
SETTING: Paul Colin
COSTUMES: Paul Colin
COMPANY: Théâtre National de l'Opéra
PREMIÈRE: Paris, 1931

540 ORIANE ET LE ROI D'AMOUR, *Ballet in Two Acts*
BOOK: Claude Seran
MUSIC: Florent Schmitt
CHOREOGRAPHER: Serge Lifar
DECOR: Pedro Pruna
COSTUMES: Pedro Pruna
COMPANY: Théâtre National de l'Opéra
PREMIÈRE: Paris, 1938

541 LES ORIENTALES
BOOK: Michel Fokine
MUSIC: Glazounov, Arensky, Grieg, Borodine
CHOREOGRAPHY: Michel Fokine, after Petipa
SETTING: Constantin Korovine
COSTUMES: Constantin Korovine
COMPANY: Ballet Russe (Diaghilev)
PREMIÈRE: Paris, 1910

542 ORIGIN OF DESIGN
MUSIC: George Frederic Handel; arr. Thomas Beecham
CHOREOGRAPHY: Ninette de Valois
SETTING: William Chappell
COSTUMES: William Chappell
COMPANY: Sadler's Wells Ballet
PREMIÈRE: [London], 1932

543 ORPHEUS, *Opera-Ballet in Two Acts and Four Scenes*
BOOK: Ranieri de Calzabigi
MUSIC: Christoph Willibald Gluck
CHOREOGRAPHY: George Balanchine
SETTING: Pavel Tchelitchew
COSTUMES: Pavel Tchelitchew
COMPANY: The American Ballet Company
PREMIÈRE: New York, 1936

544 ORPHEUS AND EURYDICE
BOOK: Michel Fokine
MUSIC: Christoph Willibald Gluck
CHOREOGRAPHY: Michel Fokine
SETTING: Alexander Golovine
COSTUMES: Alexander Golovine
COMPANY: Russian Imperial Ballet
PREMIÈRE: St. Petersburg, 1911

545 ORPHEUS AND EURYDICE, *Ballet in Two Acts*
BOOK: Ninette de Valois, after Gluck's Opera
MUSIC: Christoph Willibald Gluck
CHOREOGRAPHY: Ninette de Valois
SETTING: Sophie Fedorovitch
COSTUMES: Sophie Fedorovitch
COMPANY: Sadler's Wells Ballet
PREMIÈRE: London, 1941

546 OUR LADY'S JUGGLER
BOOK: Andrée Howard
MUSIC: Ottorino Respighi
CHOREOGRAPHY: Andrée Howard and Susan Salaman
SETTING: Susan Salaman
COSTUMES: Susan Salaman
COMPANY: The Ballet Club
PREMIÈRE: London, 1933

547 PAGANINI, *Fantastic Ballet in One Act and Three Scenes*
BOOK: Serge Rachmaninoff and Michel Fokine
MUSIC: Serge Rachmaninoff
CHOREOGRAPHY: Michel Fokine
SETTING: Serge Soudeikine
COSTUMES: Serge Soudeikine
COMPANY: Ballet Russe (de Basil)
PREMIÈRE: London, 1939

548 PANDORA
BOOK: Kurt Jooss
MUSIC: Robert Gerhard
CHOREOGRAPHY: Kurt Jooss
COSTUMES: Hein Heckroth
COMPANY: Jooss Ballet
PREMIÈRE: London, 1944

549 PAPILLONS, *Ballet in One Act*
BOOK: Michel Fokine
MUSIC: Robert Schumann; orch. Nicolas Tcherepnine
CHOREOGRAPHY: Michel Fokine
SETTING: Mstislav Dobujinsky
COSTUMES: Léon Bakst
COMPANY: Ballet Russe (Diaghilev)
PREMIÈRE: Paris, 1914

550 PARABLE IN BLUE, *A Pent-House Ballet*
MUSIC: Martin Gabowitz
CHOREOGRAPHY: Catherine Littlefield
SETTING: George C. Jenkins
COSTUMES: Lee Gainsborough
COMPANY: Philadelphia Opera Ballet
PREMIÈRE: Philadelphia, Pennsylvania, 1937

551 PARADE, *Realistic Ballet in One Scene*
BOOK: Jean Cocteau
MUSIC: Erik Satie
CHOREOGRAPHY: Leonide Massine
SETTING: Pablo Picasso
CURTAIN: Pablo Picasso
COSTUMES: Pablo Picasso
COMPANY: Ballet Russe (Diaghilev)
PREMIÈRE: Paris, 1917

552 PARADE
MUSIC: Erik Satie
CHOREOGRAPHY: Mariette de Meyenburg
SETTING: Mariette de Meyenburg
COSTUMES: Mariette de Meyenburg
COMPANY: Municipal Theatre
PREMIÈRE: Basle, Switzerland, 1935

553 PARAPHRASES SUR LES VALSES DE SCHUBERT
MUSIC: Serge Prokofieff, after Franz Schubert
CHOREOGRAPHY: Boris Romanoff
SETTING: Bobermann and Hosiasson
COSTUMES: Bobermann and Hosiasson
COMPANY: Russian Romantic Theatre
PREMIÈRE: Berlin, 1922

554 PARIS-SOIR
MUSIC: Francis Poulenc
CHOREOGRAPHY: Walter Gore
SETTING: Eve Swinstead-Smith
COSTUMES: Eve Swinstead-Smith
COMPANY: Marie Rambert Company
PREMIÈRE: London, 1939

555 PARNASSUS ON MONTMARTRE
MUSIC: Erik Satie
CHOREOGRAPHY: Adolph Bolm
SETTING: Nicolai Remisoff

COSTUMES: Nicolai Remisoff
COMPANY: Chicago Allied Arts
PREMIÈRE: Chicago, Illinois, 1926

PARTY AT THE MANOR
see COMPANY AT THE MANOR

556 LE PAS D'ACIER, *Ballet in Two Scenes*
BOOK: Serge Prokofieff and Georges Jakuloff
MUSIC: Serge Prokofieff
CHOREOGRAPHY: Leonide Massine
CONSTRUCTIONS: Georges Jakuloff
COMPANY: Ballet Russe (Diaghilev)
PREMIÈRE: Paris, 1927

557 LE PAS D'ACIER, *Ballet in One Scene*
BOOK: Lee Simonson
MUSIC: Serge Prokofieff
CHOREOGRAPHY: Edwin Strawbridge
CONSTRUCTION: Lee Simonson
COSTUMES: Lee Simonson
COMPANY: The Strawbridge Ballet
PREMIÈRE: Philadelphia, Pennsylvania, 1931

558 PAS DE DÉESSES
MUSIC: Cesar Pugni; arr. Leighton Lucas
CHOREOGRAPHY: Keith Lester
SETTING: John Guthrie and Hugh Stevenson
COSTUMES: John Guthrie and Hugh Stevenson
COMPANY: Marie Rambert Company
PREMIÈRE: London, 1939

559 PASSIONATE PAVANE
BOOK: Frederick Ashton
MUSIC: John Dowland
CHOREOGRAPHY: Frederick Ashton
SETTING: William Chappell
COSTUMES: William Chappell
COMPANY: The Arts Theatre
PREMIÈRE: London, 1930

560 LA PASTORALE
BOOK: Boris Kochno
MUSIC: Georges Auric
CHOREOGRAPHY: George Balanchine
SETTING: Pedro Pruna
CURTAIN: Pedro Pruna
COSTUMES: Pedro Pruna
COMPANY: Ballet Russe (Diaghilev)
PREMIÈRE: Paris, 1926

561 PASTORELA
BOOK: José Ambrosio Martinez; words Rafael Alvarez
MUSIC: Paul Bowles
CHOREOGRAPHY: Lew Christensen
COSTUMES: Alvin Colt

COMPANY: The American Ballet Caravan
PREMIÈRE: Rio de Janeiro, 1941

562 LES PATINEURS
MUSIC: Giacomo Meyerbeer
CHOREOGRAPHY: Frederick Ashton
SETTING: William Chappell
COSTUMES: William Chappell
COMPANY: Sadler's Wells Ballet
PREMIÈRE: London, 1937

563 PAUSA
BOOK: Gloria Campobello
MUSIC: Ludwig van Beethoven
CHOREOGRAPHY: Gloria Campobello
SETTING: José Clemente Orozco
COSTUMES: José Clemente Orozco
COMPANY: Ballet of the City of México
PREMIÈRE: México, D. F., 1945

564 PAVANE
MUSIC: Maurice Ravel
CHOREOGRAPHY: Ruth Page
SETTING: Nicolai Remisoff
COSTUMES: Nicolai Remisoff
COMPANY: Ravinia Opera Company
PREMIÈRE: Ravinia, Illinois, 1929

565 PAVANE (ON THE DEATH OF AN INFANTA)
BOOK: Kurt Jooss
MUSIC: Maurice Ravel
CHOREOGRAPHY: Kurt Jooss
COSTUMES: Sigurd Leeder
COMPANY: Jooss Ballet
PREMIÈRE: Essen, Germany, 1929

566 PAVANE
MUSIC: Gabriel Fauré
CHOREOGRAPHY: Serge Lifar
SETTING: José-Maria Sert
COSTUMES: José-Maria Sert
COMPANY: Ballet Russe (de Basil)
PREMIÈRE: [Paris], 1940

567 PAVANE POUR UNE INFANTE DÉFUNTE
MUSIC: Maurice Ravel
CHOREOGRAPHY: Bentley Stone
SETTING: Hugh Stevenson
COSTUMES: Hugh Stevenson
COMPANY: Marie Rambert Company
PREMIÈRE: Biarritz, France, 1937

568 PAVILLON, *Ballet in One Act*
BOOK: Boris Kochno
MUSIC: Alexander Borodine; orch. Antal Dorati
CHOREOGRAPHY: David Lichine
SETTING: Cecil Beaton

COSTUMES: Cecil Beaton
COMPANY: Ballet Russe (de Basil)
PREMIÈRE: London, 1936

569 LE PAVILLON D'ARMIDE, *Ballet in One Act and Three Scenes*
BOOK: Alexandre Benois
MUSIC: Nicolas Tcherepnine
CHOREOGRAPHY: Michel Fokine
SETTINGS: Alexandre Benois
COSTUMES: Alexandre Benois
COMPANY: Ballet Russe (Diaghilev)
PREMIÈRE: Paris, 1909

570 PERHAPS TOMORROW, *Ballet in One Act and Three Scenes*
BOOK: István Juhász
MUSIC: Jenö Kenessey
CHOREOGRAPHY: Gyula Harangozó
SETTING: Aladár Olgyay
COMPANY: Metropolitan Art Theatre
PREMIÈRE: Budapest, 1937

571 LA PÉRI
BOOK: Michel Fokine
MUSIC: Paul Dukas
CHOREOGRAPHY: Michel Fokine
SETTING: Léon Bakst
COSTUMES: Léon Bakst
COMPANY: Ballet Russe (Diaghilev)
PREMIÈRE: Paris, 1911

572 LA PÉRI, *A Dance Poem*
MUSIC: Paul Dukas
CHOREOGRAPHY: Ivan Clustine
SETTING: Hubert Stowitts
COSTUMES: Hubert Stowitts
COMPANY: Pavlova Company
PREMIÈRE: Paris, 1912

573 LA PÉRI
BOOK: Paul Dukas
MUSIC: Paul Dukas
CHOREOGRAPHY: Frederick Ashton
SETTING: William Chappell
COSTUMES: William Chappell
COMPANY: Marie Rambert Company
PREMIÈRE: London, 1931

574 LA PÉRI
MUSIC: Paul Dukas
CHOREOGRAPHY: Frank Staff
SETTING: Nadia Benois
COSTUMES: Nadia Benois
COMPANY: Marie Rambert Company
PREMIÈRE: London, 1938

575 PERSÉPHONE, *Melodrama in Three Parts*
BOOK: André Gide
MUSIC: Igor Strawinsky
CHOREOGRAPHY: Kurt Jooss
SETTING: Alexandre Benois
COSTUMES: Alexandre Benois
COMPANY: Ida Rubinstein Ballet
PREMIÈRE: Paris, 1934

576 PERSEUS
MUSIC: Stanley Bate
CHOREOGRAPHY: John Regan
SETTING: del Renzio
COSTUMES: del Renzio
COMPANY: Ballet Trois Arts
PREMIÈRE: London, 1939

577 PERSEUS, *Classical Story in Seven Scenes*
MUSIC: Stanley Bate
CHOREOGRAPHY: Keith Lester
SETTING: Pamela Boden
COSTUMES: Pamela Boden
COMPANY: Arts Theatre Ballet
PREMIÈRE: [London], 1940

578 PERSEUS
MUSIC: James O. Turner
CHOREOGRAPHY: John Regan
SETTING: Elizabeth Agombar
COSTUMES: Elizabeth Agombar
COMPANY: Ballet Trois Arts
PREMIÈRE: Westcliffe, England, 1940

579 PERSIAN BALLET
BOOK: Kurt Jooss
MUSIC: Egon Wellesz
CHOREOGRAPHY: Kurt Jooss
SETTING: Hein Heckroth
COSTUMES: Hein Heckroth
COMPANY: Jooss Ballet
PREMIÈRE: Donaueschingen, Germany, 1924

580 PETER AND THE WOLF, *Ballet in One Act*
BOOK: Serge Prokofieff
MUSIC: Serge Prokofieff
CHOREOGRAPHY: Adolph Bolm
SETTING: Lucinda Ballard
COSTUMES: Lucinda Ballard
COMPANY: Ballet Theatre
PREMIÈRE: New York, 1940

581 PETER AND THE WOLF, *Ballet in One Act*
MUSIC: Serge Prokofieff
CHOREOGRAPHY: Frank Staff
SETTING: Guy Sheppard
COSTUMES: Guy Sheppard

COMPANY: Marie Rambert Company
PREMIÈRE: Cambridge, England, 1940

582 LA PETITE FADETTE
BOOK: Deryck Lynham
MUSIC: Gabriel Fauré
CHOREOGRAPHY: Molly Lake
SETTING: Beryl Dean
COSTUMES: Sylvia Green
COMPANY: Ballet Guild
PREMIÈRE: London, 1942

583 LE PETIT ELFE FERME L'ŒIL
MUSIC: Florent Schmitt
CHOREOGRAPHY: Chasles
SETTING: André Hellé
COSTUMES: André Hellé
COMPANY: Théâtre National de l'Opéra
   Comique
PREMIÈRE: Paris, 1924

584 LES PETITS RIENS
BOOK: Frederick Ashton
MUSIC: Wolfgang Amadeus Mozart
CHOREOGRAPHY: Frederick Ashton
SETTING: William Chappell
COSTUMES: William Chappell
COMPANY: Marie Rambert Company
PREMIÈRE: London, 1935

585 LE PETIT TRIANON
MUSIC: George Frederic Handel
CHOREOGRAPHY: John Regan
SETTING: Elizabeth Agombar
COSTUMES: Elizabeth Agombar
COMPANY: Ballet Trois Arts
PREMIÈRE: Notting Hill Gate, England, 1941

586 PETROUCHKA, *Burlesque in One Act and
   Four Scenes*
BOOK: Igor Strawinsky and Alexandre Benois
MUSIC: Igor Strawinsky
CHOREOGRAPHY: Michel Fokine
SETTING: Alexandre Benois
COSTUMES: Alexandre Benois
COMPANY: Ballet Russe (Diaghilev)
PREMIÈRE: Paris, 1911

587 PETROUCHKA
MUSIC: Igor Strawinsky
CHOREOGRAPHY: Adolph Bolm
SETTING: Serge Soudeikine
COSTUMES: Serge Soudeikine
COMPANY: Metropolitan Opera Company
PREMIÈRE: New York, 1925

588 PETROUCHKA
MUSIC: Igor Strawinsky

CHOREOGRAPHY: Adolph Bolm
SETTING: Nicolai Remisoff
COSTUMES: Nicolai Remisoff
COMPANY: Adolph Bolm Ballet
PREMIÈRE: [Chicago, Illinois, 1926]

589 PETROUCHKA
MUSIC: Igor Strawinsky
CHOREOGRAPHY: Kurt Jooss
SETTING: Hein Heckroth
COSTUMES: Hein Heckroth
COMPANY: Jooss Ballet
PREMIÈRE: Essen, Germany, 1930

590 PETRUSCHKA
BOOK: [Yvonne Georgi]
MUSIC: Igor Strawinsky
CHOREOGRAPHY: Yvonne Georgi
SETTING: George Kirsta
COSTUMES: George Kirsta
COMPANY: [The Netherlands Ballet]
PREMIÈRE: Hannover, Germany

591 PICTURES AT AN EXHIBITION, *Choreo-
   graphic Pictures*
MUSIC: Modeste Moussorgsky; orch. Ivan Bout-
   nikoff
CHOREOGRAPHY: Bronislava Nijinska
SETTING: Boris Aronson
COSTUMES: Boris Aronson
COMPANY: Ballet International
PREMIÈRE: New York, 1944

592 PICTURES OF GOYA
MUSIC: Enrique Granados; arr. Antal Dorati
CHOREOGRAPHY: Argentinita and Pilar Lopez
SETTING: Federico Rey
COSTUMES: Federico Rey
COMPANY: Ballet Theatre
PREMIÈRE: New York, 1943

593 PILLAR OF FIRE
BOOK: Antony Tudor
MUSIC: Arnold Schoenberg
CHOREOGRAPHY: Antony Tudor
SETTING: Jo Mielziner
COSTUMES: Jo Mielziner
COMPANY: Ballet Theatre
PREMIÈRE: New York, 1942

594 PINOCCHIO, *Ballet Pantomime in Two Acts
   and Six Scenes*
BOOK: Dorothy Coit, after Collodi
MUSIC: M. Wood Hill
CHOREOGRAPHY: Felicia Sorel
SETTING: Willy Pogany
COSTUMES: Willy Pogany

84

COMPANY: American Ballet Guild
PREMIÈRE: New York, 1931

595 PLAGES, *Ballet in One Act — A Ballet of the Open Air*
BOOK: After René Kerdyk
MUSIC: Jean Françaix
CHOREOGRAPHY: Leonide Massine
SETTING: Raoul Dufy
COSTUMES: Raoul Dufy
COMPANY: Ballet Russe (de Basil)
PREMIÈRE: Monte Carlo, 1933

596 PLANETOMANIA
BOOK: Mona Inglesby
MUSIC: Norman Demuth
CHOREOGRAPHY: Mona Inglesby
SETTING: Doris Zinkeisen
COSTUMES: Doris Zinkeisen
COMPANY: The International Ballet
PREMIÈRE: Birmingham, England, 1941

597 THE PLANETS
MUSIC: Gustav Holst
CHOREOGRAPHY: Antony Tudor
SETTING: Hugh Stevenson
COSTUMES: Hugh Stevenson
COMPANY: Marie Rambert Company
PREMIÈRE: London, 1934

598 POCAHONTAS, *Ballet-Pantomime in One Act*
BOOK: Lincoln Kirstein
MUSIC: Elliot Carter, Jr.
CHOREOGRAPHY: Lew Christensen
COSTUMES: Karl Free
COMPANY: The American Ballet Caravan
PREMIÈRE: Middlebury, Vermont, 1936

599 LE POÈTE, *Romantic Reverie*
BOOK: Boris Kochno
MUSIC: Benjamin Godard; arr. Charles Koechlin
CHOREOGRAPHY: Roland Petit
SETTING: Lucien Couteau
COSTUMES: Lucien Couteau
COMPANY: Ballet des Champs-Élysées
PREMIÈRE: Paris, 1945

POKER GAME
see CARD PARTY

POLOVTSIAN DANCES
see PRINCE IGOR
DANSES POLOVTSIENNES

600 POMONA
BOOK: Constant Lambert
MUSIC: Constant Lambert
CHOREOGRAPHY: Frederick Ashton

SETTING: John Banting
COMPANY: The Camargo Society
PREMIÈRE: London, 1930

601 POMONA
BOOK: Constant Lambert
MUSIC: Constant Lambert
CHOREOGRAPHY: Frederick Ashton
SETTING: Vanessa Bell
COSTUMES: Vanessa Bell
COMPANY: Sadler's Wells Ballet
PREMIÈRE: [London], 1933

602 PORT SAID, *Ballet in One Act*
MUSIC: Constantin Konstantinov
CHOREOGRAPHY: Leon Wojzikovsky
SETTING: Michel Larionow
COSTUMES: Michel Larionow
COMPANY: Ballet Russe (de Basil)
PREMIÈRE: London, 1935

603 PRAIRIE
BOOK: After Carl Sandburg
MUSIC: Norman Dello Joio
CHOREOGRAPHY: Eugene Loring
SETTING: George Bockman
COSTUMES: George Bockman
COMPANY: The Dance Players
PREMIÈRE: Washington, D. C., 1942

PRÉLUDE À L'APRÈS-MIDI D'UN FAUNE
see L'APRÈS-MIDI D'UN FAUNE

604 LES PRÉLUDES
MUSIC: Franz Liszt
CHOREOGRAPHY: Michel Fokine
SETTING: Boris Anisfeld
COSTUMES: Boris Anisfeld
COMPANY: Pavlova Company
PREMIÈRE: London, 1913

605 LES PRÉSAGES
BOOK: Leonide Massine
MUSIC: Peter Tchaikowsky
CHOREOGRAPHY: Leonide Massine
SETTINGS: André Masson
COSTUMES: André Masson
COMPANY: Ballet Russe (de Basil)
PREMIÈRE: Monte Carlo, 1933

606 PRIMEIRO BAILE, *Ballet in One Scene*
BOOK: Igor Schwezoff
MUSIC: Joseph Lanner; orch. Francisco Mignone
CHOREOGRAPHY: Igor Schwezoff
SETTING: Collomb
COSTUMES: David Grey
COMPANY: Teatro Municipal
PREMIÈRE: Rio de Janeiro, 1945

607 THE PRINCE CARVED FROM WOOD
Music: Béla Bartók
Choreography: Jan Cieplinsky
Setting: Gustáv Oláh and Zoltán Fülöp
Costumes: Gustáv Oláh and Zoltán Fülöp
Company: Hungarian State Ballet
Première: Budapest, 1935

The Prince Carved from Wood
see also El Principe de Madera

608 LE PRINCE EN BOIS
Music: Béla Bartók
Choreography: Milca Mayerova
Setting: Feuerstein
Costumes: Feuerstein
Company: Théâtre Libéré
Première: [Prague], 1933

609 PRINCE GOUDAL'S FESTIVAL, Ballet in One Act
Music: Anton Rubinstein; orch. Maurice Baron
Choreography: Boris Romanoff
Setting: Mstislav Dobujinsky
Costumes: Mstislav Dobujinsky
Company: Ballet International
Première: New York, 1944

610 PRINCE IGOR, Polovtsian Dances
Music: Alexander Borodine
Choreography: Nicholas Zverev
Setting: Mstislav Dobujinsky
Costumes: Mstislav Dobujinsky
Company: Lithuanian Ballet
Première: Kaunas, Lithuania, 1932

611 PRINCE IGOR
Music: Alexander Borodine
Choreography: Baratov
Setting: F. F. Fedorovsky
Costumes: F. F. Fedorovsky
Company: Soviet Theatre
Première: Moscow, 1934

612 PRINCE IGOR, Polovtsian Dances
Music: Alexander Borodine
Choreography: Catherine Littlefield
Setting: A. Jarin
Company: Philadelphia Opera Ballet
Première: Philadelphia, Pennsylvania, 1936

Prince Igor
see also Danses Polovtsiennes

613 LA PRINCESSE AU JARDIN
Book: Henri Vuillermoz and Gabriel Grovlez
Music: Gabriel Grovlez
Choreography: Serge Lifar

Setting: Paul Bony
Costumes: Paul Bony
Company: Théâtre National de l'Opéra
Première: Paris, 1941

614 LA PRINCESSE CYGNE
Music: Nicholas Rimsky-Korsakov
Choreography: Bronislava Nijinska
Setting: Alexandre Benois
Costumes: Alexandre Benois
Company: Ida Rubinstein Ballet
Première: Paris, 1928

615 LA PRINCESSE CYGNE
Music: Nicholas Rimsky-Korsakov
Choreography: Bronislava Nijinska
Setting: B. Bilinsky
Costumes: B. Bilinsky
Company: Théâtre de la Danse (Nijinska)
Première: Paris, 1932

616 EL PRINCIPE DE MADERA
Music: Belá Bartók
Choreography: Jan Cieplinsky
Setting: Hector Basaldua
Costumes: Hector Basaldua
Company: Teatro Colon
Première: Buenos Aires, 1936

El Principe de Madera
see also The Prince Carved from Wood

617 THE PRISONER IN THE CAUCASUS, Ballet in Three Acts and Seven Scenes with a Prologue
Book: After Alexander Pushkin
Music: B. V. Asafiev
Choreography: L. M. Lavrovsky
Setting: V. M. Khodasevich
Costumes: V. M. Khodasevich
Company: Soviet State Theatre
Première: Leningrad, 1938

618 THE PRODIGAL SON, A Legend in Dance in Two Acts and Four Scenes
Book: Kurt Jooss
Music: Frederic Cohen
Choreography: Kurt Jooss
Setting: Hein Heckroth
Costumes: Hein Heckroth
Company: Jooss Ballet
Première: Rotterdam, Holland, 1933

619 THE PRODIGAL SON, Dramatic Ballet in Five Scenes
Music: César Franck
Choreography: Catherine Littlefield

86

COSTUMES: Lazar Galpern
COMPANY: Philadelphia Opera Ballet
PREMIÈRE: Philadelphia, Pennsylvania, 1936

620 THE PRODIGAL SON, *Ballet in One Act and Three Scenes*
MUSIC: Serge Prokofieff
CHOREOGRAPHY: David Lichine
SETTING: Georges Rouault
COSTUMES: Georges Rouault
COMPANY: Ballet Russe (de Basil)
PREMIÈRE: Sydney, Australia, 1938

621 THE PRODIGAL SON, *A Legend in Dance in Two Acts and Four Scenes*
BOOK: Kurt Jooss
MUSIC: Frederic Cohen
CHOREOGRAPHY: Kurt Jooss
COSTUMES: Dimitri Bouchêne
COMPANY: Jooss Ballet
PREMIÈRE: England, 1938

THE PRODIGAL SON
see also LE FILS PRODIGUE
L'ENFANT PRODIGUE

622 PROCRIS AND CEPHALUS
MUSIC: André Grétry
CHOREOGRAPHY: Ninette de Valois
SETTING: William Chappell
COSTUMES: William Chappell
COMPANY: The Camargo Society
PREMIÈRE: [London, 1931]

623 PROMENADE
MUSIC: Joseph Haydn; arr. Edwin Evans
CHOREOGRAPHY: Ninette de Valois
SETTING: Hugh Stevenson
COSTUMES: Hugh Stevenson
COMPANY: Sadler's Wells Ballet
PREMIÈRE: Edinburgh, Scotland, 1943

624 PROMENADES DANS ROME
MUSIC: Marcel-Samuel Rousseau
CHOREOGRAPHY: Serge Lifar
SETTING: After Leopold Robert
COSTUMES: After Leopold Robert
COMPANY: Théâtre National de l'Opéra
PREMIÈRE: Paris, 1937

625 PROMETEO
BOOK: Serge Lifar
MUSIC: Ludwig van Beethoven
CHOREOGRAPHY: Serge Lifar
SETTING: Hector Basaldua
COSTUMES: Hector Basaldua
COMPANY: Teatro Colon
PREMIÈRE: Buenos Aires, 1934

626 PROMÉTHÉE
BOOK: Serge Lifar
MUSIC: Ludwig van Beethoven
CHOREOGRAPHY: Serge Lifar
SETTING: A. Schervachidze
COSTUMES: A. Schervachidze
COMPANY: Théâtre National de l'Opéra
PREMIÈRE: Paris, 1929

627 PROMÉTHÉE
BOOK: Marcel Silver
MUSIC: Alexander Scriabine
CHOREOGRAPHY: Aida Barona
SETTING: Benno Prival
COSTUMES: Helen Rose
COMPANY: Hollywood Ballet
PREMIÈRE: Hollywood, 194?

628 PROMETHEUS
MUSIC: Ludwig van Beethoven
CHOREOGRAPHY: Ninette de Valois
SETTING: John Banting
COSTUMES: John Banting
COMPANY: Sadler's Wells Ballet
PREMIÈRE: [London], 1936

629 THE PROSPECT BEFORE US, *Ballet in Seven Scenes*
BOOK: Ninette de Valois
MUSIC: William Boyce; arr. Constant Lambert
CHOREOGRAPHY: Ninette de Valois
SETTINGS: Roger Furse
COSTUMES: Roger Furse
COMPANY: Sadler's Wells Ballet
PREMIÈRE: London, 1940

630 PROTÉE, *Neo-Classic Ballet in One Act*
BOOK: David Lichine and Henry Clifford
MUSIC: Claude Debussy
CHOREOGRAPHY: David Lichine
SETTING: Georges de Chirico
COSTUMES: Georges de Chirico
COMPANY: Ballet Russe (de Basil)
PREMIÈRE: London, 1938

631 PULCINELLA, *Ballet in One Act*
MUSIC: Igor Strawinsky, after Pergolesi
CHOREOGRAPHY: Leonide Massine
SETTING: Pablo Picasso
CURTAIN: Pablo Picasso
COSTUMES: Pablo Picasso
COMPANY: Ballet Russe (Diaghilev)
PREMIÈRE: Paris, 1920

632 PULCINELLA
MUSIC: Igor Strawinsky
CHOREOGRAPHY: Kurt Jooss

SETTING:Hein Heckroth
COSTUMES: Hein Heckroth
COMPANY: Jooss Ballet
PREMIÈRE: Essen, Germany, 1932

633 PUPPENFEE
BOOK: Kurt Jooss
MUSIC: Josef Bayer
CHOREOGRAPHY: Kurt Jooss
SETTING: Hein Heckroth
COSTUMES: Hein Heckroth
COMPANY: Jooss Ballet
PREMIÈRE: Essen, Germany, 1931

PUPPENFEE
see also THE FAIRY DOLL

634 PYRAMUS AND THISBE
MUSIC: Fritz Behrens
CHOREOGRAPHY: William Christensen
SETTING: Russell Hartley
COSTUMES: Russell Hartley
COMPANY: San Francisco Ballet
PREMIÈRE: San Francisco, 1945

635 QUADRILLE
BOOK: Boris Kochno
MUSIC: Georges Auric
CHOREOGRAPHY: Roger Fenonjois
SETTING: Valentine Hugo
COSTUMES: Valentine Hugo
COMPANY: Ballets des Champs-Elysées
PREMIÈRE: Paris, 1945

636 QUEST, Ballet in Three Scenes
MUSIC: Johann Sebastian Bach; orch. Antal
    Dorati
CHOREOGRAPHY: Nina Verchinina
SETTING: Carl Kent, after Francesco Cristofa-
    netti
COSTUMES: Carl Kent, after Francesco Cristo-
    fanetti
COMPANY: Ballet Russe (de Basil)
PREMIÈRE: [New York, 1940]

637 THE QUEST, Ballet in Five Scenes
BOOK: Doris Langley Moore, after Spencer
MUSIC: William Turner Walton
CHOREOGRAPHY: Frederick Ashton
SETTING: John Piper
COSTUMES: John Piper
COMPANY: Sadler's Wells Ballet
PREMIÈRE: London, 1943

638 QUINTET, A Ballet Operetta in Six Scenes
MUSIC: Raymond Scott
CHOREOGRAPHY: Anton Dolin
SETTING: Lucinda Ballard

COSTUMES: Lucinda Ballard
COMPANY: Ballet Theatre
PREMIÈRE: New York, 1940

639 RAILROADS ON PARADE
BOOK: Edward Hungerford
MUSIC: Kurt Weill
CHOREOGRAPHY: Bill Matons
SETTING: Harry Horner, Howard Ketcham,
    A. Sheldon Pennoyer
COSTUMES: Harry Horner, Howard Ketcham,
    A. Sheldon Pennoyer
COMPANY: The World's Fair
PREMIÈRE: New York, 1939

640 THE RAKE
BOOK: Inspired by Hogarth
MUSIC: Roger Quitter
CHOREOGRAPHY: Leonide Massine
SETTING: William Nicholson
COSTUMES: William Nicholson
COMPANY: C. B. Cochran's Revue
PREMIÈRE: London, 1925

641 THE RAKE'S PROGRESS, Ballet in Six Scenes
BOOK: Gavin Gordon
MUSIC: Gavin Gordon
CHOREOGRAPHY: Ninette de Valois
SETTING: Rex Whistler, after Hogarth
ACT-DROP: Rex Whistler, after Hogarth
COSTUMES: Rex Whistler, after Hogarth
COMPANY: Sadler's Wells Ballet
PREMIÈRE: London, 1935

642 THE RAPE OF THE LOCK
BOOK: After Alexander Pope
MUSIC: Joseph Haydn
CHOREOGRAPHY: Andrée Howard
SETTING: Andrée Howard
COSTUMES: Andrée Howard
COMPANY: The Ballet Club
PREMIÈRE: London, 1935

643 LE RAPPEL, Ballet in Three Scenes
MUSIC: Boleslaw Woytowicz
CHOREOGRAPHY: Bronislava Nijinska
SETTING: Irène Lorentowicz
COSTUMES: Irène Lorentowicz
COMPANY: The Polish Ballet
PREMIÈRE: Paris, 1937

644 RAYMONDA
BOOK: L. Pashov and M. Petipa
MUSIC: Alexander Glazounov
CHOREOGRAPHY: Nicolas Zverev, after Petipa
SETTING: Mstislav Dobujinsky
COSTUMES: Mstislav Dobujinsky

COMPANY: Lithuanian State Ballet
PREMIÈRE: Kaunas, Lithuania, 1934

645 RÉCAMIER
BOOK: Frederick Ashton
MUSIC: Franz Schubert
CHOREOGRAPHY: Frederick Ashton
SETTING: William Chappell
COSTUMES: William Chappell
COMPANY: C. B. Cochran Revue
PREMIÈRE: London, 1932

646 THE RED POPPY, *Ballet in Three Acts and Six Scenes*
BOOK: M. T. Kurilko
MUSIC: Reinhold Gliere
CHOREOGRAPHY: L. A. Larchiune and V. O. Khomirov
SETTING: M. T. Kurilko
COSTUMES: M. T. Kurilko
COMPANY: Bolshoi Theatre
PREMIÈRE: Moscow, 1927

647 RED POPPY, *Ballet in Three Scenes with a Prologue*
BOOK: Igor Schwezoff
MUSIC: Reinhold Gliere; arr. Arthur Cohn
CHOREOGRAPHY: Igor Schwezoff
SETTING: Boris Aronson
COSTUMES: Boris Aronson
COMPANY: Ballet Russe (Denham)
PREMIÈRE: Cleveland, Ohio, 1943

648 REGATTA
BOOK: Frederick Ashton
MUSIC: Gavin Gordon
CHOREOGRAPHY: Frederick Ashton
SETTING: William Chappell
COSTUMES: William Chappell
COMPANY: Sadler's Wells Ballet
PREMIÈRE: [London], 1931

649 RELÂCHE, *Instantaneous Ballet in Two Acts and A Cinematographic Entr'acte*
BOOK: Francis Picabia
MUSIC: Erik Satie
CHOREOGRAPHY: Jean Borlin
ENTR'ACTE: René Clair
SETTING: Francis Picabia
COSTUMES: Francis Picabia
COMPANY: Les Ballets Suédois
PREMIÈRE: Paris, 1924

650 REMINISCENCE, *Classic Ballet in One Act*
MUSIC: Paul Godard; orch. Henry Brant
CHOREOGRAPHY: George Balanchine
SETTING: Serge Soudeikine

COSTUMES: Serge Soudeikine
COMPANY: The American Ballet
PREMIÈRE: New York, 1935

651 EL RENACUAJO PAESADOR
MUSIC: Silvestre Revueltas
CHOREOGRAPHY: Anna Sokolow
SETTING: Carlos Mérida
COSTUMES: Carlos Mérida
COMPANY: Anna Sokolow Ballet
PREMIÈRE: México, D. F., 1940

652 LE RENARD, *Ballet in One Act*
BOOK: Igor Strawinsky
MUSIC: Igor Strawinsky
CHOREOGRAPHY: Bronislava Nijinska
SETTING: Michel Larionow
COSTUMES: Michel Larionow
COMPANY: Ballet Russe (Diaghilev)
PREMIÈRE: Paris, 1922

653 LE RENARD, *Ballet in One Act*
MUSIC: Igor Strawinsky
CHOREOGRAPHY: Serge Lifar
CONSTRUCTIVIST SETTING: Michel Larionow
COSTUMES: Michel Larionow
COMPANY: Ballet Russe (Diaghilev)
PREMIÈRE: Paris, 1929

654 LE RENDEZ-VOUS
BOOK: Jacques Prévert
MUSIC: Pierre Kosma
CHOREOGRAPHY: Roland Petit
CURTAIN: Pablo Picasso
SETTING: Brassai
COSTUMES: Mayo
COMPANY: Ballets des Champs-Elysées
PREMIÈRE: Paris, 1945

655 LES RENDEZ-VOUS
BOOK: Frederick Ashton
MUSIC: Daniel Auber; arr. Constant Lambert
CHOREOGRAPHY: Frederick Ashton
SETTING: William Chappell
COSTUMES: William Chappell
COMPANY: The Camargo Society
PREMIÈRE: London, 1933

656 REVOLUTION
BOOK: Gladys Spencer-Curling
MUSIC: Frederic Chopin
CHOREOGRAPHY: Anton Dolin
SETTING: Gladys Spencer-Curling
COSTUMES: Gladys Spencer-Curling
COMPANY: Nemchinova-Dolin Company
PREMIÈRE: London, 1928

657 RHAPSODIE ESPAGNOL
MUSIC: Maurice Ravel
SETTING: Nathalie Gontcharova
COSTUMES: Nathalie Gontcharova
COMPANY: Ballet Russe (Diaghilev)
PROJECT: 1916

658 RHAPSODY IN BLUE, *Ballet in One Act*
BOOK: Anton Dolin
MUSIC: George Gershwin
CHOREOGRAPHY: Anton Dolin
SETTING: Gladys Spencer-Curling
COSTUMES: Gladys Spencer-Curling
COMPANY: Nemchinova-Dolin Ballet
PREMIÈRE: Paris, 1928

659 RHAPSODY IN BLUE
BOOK: Astrid Malmborg
MUSIC: George Gershwin
CHOREOGRAPHY: Astrid Malmborg
SETTING: Sandro Malmquist
COSTUMES: Sandro Malmquist
COMPANY: Archives Internationales de la Danse
PREMIÈRE: Paris, 1932

660 RIO GRANDE
BOOK: Constant Lambert
MUSIC: Constant Lambert
CHOREOGRAPHY: Frederick Ashton
SETTING: Edward Burra
COSTUMES: Edward Burra
COMPANY: The Camargo Society
PREMIÈRE: London, 1931

THE RITES OF SPRING
see LE SACRE DE PRINTEMPS

661 THE RIVALS
BOOK: Chinese Legend
MUSIC: Henry Eichheim
CHOREOGRAPHY: Adolph Bolm
SETTING: Nicolai Remisoff
COSTUMES: Nicolai Remisoff
COMPANY: Chicago Allied Arts
PREMIÈRE: Chicago, Illinois, 1925

662 ROBES PIERRE AND CO., *Criminal Dance Sketch*
BOOK: Georgi-Kreutzberg
MUSIC: Frederick Wilckens
CHOREOGRAPHY: Yvonne Georgi
SETTING: Emil Pirchan
COSTUMES: Emil Pirchan
COMPANY: The Netherlands Ballet
PREMIÈRE: [Hannover, Germany], 1928

663 RODEO or THE COURTING AT BURNT RANCH, *Ballet in Two Scenes and an Interlude*
BOOK: Agnes De Mille
MUSIC: Aaron Copland
CHOREOGRAPHY: Agnes De Mille
SETTING: Oliver Smith
COSTUMES: Kermit Love
COMPANY: Ballet Russe (Massine)
PREMIÈRE: New York, 1942

664 LE ROI NU, *Ballet in One Act and Four Scenes*
BOOK: Serge Lifar, after Hans Christian Andersen
MUSIC: Jean Françaix
CHOREOGRAPHY: Serge Lifar
SETTING: Pedro Pruna
COSTUMES: Pedro Pruna
COMPANY: Théâtre National de l'Opéra
PREMIÈRE: Paris, 1936

665 LE ROI NU
BOOK: After Hans Christian Andersen
MUSIC: Jean Françaix
CHOREOGRAPHY: Ninette de Valois
SETTING: Hedley Briggs
COSTUMES: Hedley Briggs
COMPANY: Sadler's Wells Ballet
PREMIÈRE: London, 1938

666 THE ROMANCE OF A MUMMY
BOOK: Anna Pavlova, after Théophile Gautier
MUSIC: Nicolas Tcherepnine
CHOREOGRAPHY: Ivan Clustine
SETTING: Ivan Bilibine
COSTUMES: Ivan Bilibine
COMPANY: Pavlova Company
PREMIÈRE: London, 1925

667 THE ROMANTIC AGE
MUSIC: Vincenzo Bellini; orch. Antal Dorati
CHOREOGRAPHY: Anton Dolin
SETTING: Lucinda Ballard
COSTUMES: Carlos Mérida
COMPANY: Ballet Theatre
PREMIÈRE: New York, 1942

668 ROMANTIC VARIATIONS
MUSIC: Camille Saint-Saëns
CHOREOGRAPHY: Catherine Littlefield
COSTUMES: J. Pascal
COMPANY: Philadelphia Opera Ballet
PREMIÈRE: Philadelphia, Pennsylvania, 1936

669 ROMEO AND JULIET
MUSIC: Constant Lambert

CHOREOGRAPHY: Bronislava Nijinska
ENTR'ACTE: George Balanchine
CURTAIN: Joan Miro
SETTINGS: Max Ernst
COSTUMES: Max Ernst and Joan Miro
COMPANY: Ballet Russe (Diaghilev)
PREMIÈRE: Monte Carlo, 1926

670 ROMEO AND JULIET, *Dance Poem in One Act and Six Scenes*
BOOK: G. Harangozó, after Shakespeare
MUSIC: Peter Tchaikowsky
CHOREOGRAPHY: Gyula Harangozó
SETTING: Gustáv Oláh
COSTUMES: Gustáv Oláh
COMPANY: Hungarian State Ballet
PREMIÈRE: Budapest, 1939

671 ROMEO AND JULIET, *Ballet in Three Acts*
BOOK: After Shakespeare
MUSIC: Serge Prokofieff; arr. S. Radlov
CHOREOGRAPHY: Leonid Lavrovsky
SETTING: Peter Williams
COSTUMES: Peter Williams
COMPANY: Kirov State Theatre
PREMIÈRE: Leningrad, 1940

672 ROMEO AND JULIET, *Narrative Ballet in One Act*
BOOK: Antony Tudor, after Shakespeare
MUSIC: Frederick Delius; arr. Antal Dorati
CHOREOGRAPHY: Antony Tudor
SETTINGS: Eugene Berman
COSTUMES: Eugene Berman
COMPANY: Ballet Theatre
PREMIÈRE: New York, 1942

LA ROMERIA DE LOS CORNUDOS
see THE CUCKOLD'S FAIR

673 ROOM No. 13, *Comic Ballet*
BOOK: Kurt Jooss
MUSIC: Frederic Cohen
CHOREOGRAPHY: Kurt Jooss
SETTING: Hein Heckroth
COSTUMES: Hein Heckroth
COMPANY: Folkwang Tanzbuehne
PREMIÈRE: Essen, Germany, 1929

674 LE ROSEAU
BOOK: After Persian Tale
MUSIC: Daniel Lazarus
CHOREOGRAPHY: Jean Borlin
SETTING: After Persian Miniatures
COSTUMES: After Persian Miniatures
COMPANY: Les Ballets Suédois
PREMIÈRE: Paris, 1924

675 LE ROSSIGNOL
BOOK: Igor Strawinsky, after Hans C. Andersen
MUSIC: Igor Strawinsky
CHOREOGRAPHY: George Balanchine
SETTING: Henri Matisse
COSTUMES: Henri Matisse
COMPANY: Ballet Russe (Diaghilev)
PREMIÈRE: Paris, 1920

676 LE ROSSIGNOL ET LA ROSE, *Ballet in One Act*
BOOK: After Oscar Wilde
MUSIC: Janis Kalnins
CHOREOGRAPHY: Osvalds Lemanis
SETTING: Peters Rozlapa
COSTUMES: Peters Rozlapa
COMPANY: National Opera
PREMIÈRE: Riga, Latvia, 1938

677 ROUGE ET NOIR, *Ballet in Four Movements and One Scene*
BOOK: Leonide Massine
MUSIC: Dimitry Shostakovich
CHOREOGRAPHY: Leonide Massine
SETTING: Henri Matisse
COSTUMES: Henri Matisse
COMPANY: Ballet Russe (Massine)
PREMIÈRE: Monte Carlo, 1939

678 RUMANIAN WEDDING
MUSIC: Georges Enesco
CHOREOGRAPHY: William Christensen
SETTING: J. C. Taylor
COSTUMES: J. C. Taylor
COMPANY: Portland Symphony Orchestra
PREMIÈRE: Portland, Oregon, 1936

679 RUSSIAN SOLDIER, *Ballet in One Act and Five Scenes*
BOOK: Michel Fokine
MUSIC: Serge Prokofieff
CHOREOGRAPHY: Michel Fokine
SETTINGS: Mstislav Dobujinsky
COSTUMES: Mstislav Dobujinsky
COMPANY: Ballet Theatre
PREMIÈRE: Boston, Massachusetts, 1942

RUSSIAN TOYS,
see IGROUCHKI

680 LE SACRE DU PRINTEMPS, *A Picture of Ancient Russia in Two Acts*
BOOK: Igor Strawinsky and Nicholas Roerich
MUSIC: Igor Strawinsky
CHOREOGRAPHY: Vaslav Nijinsky
COSTUMES: Nicholas Roerich
SETTING: Nicholas Roerich

COMPANY: Ballet Russe (Diaghilev)
PREMIÈRE: Paris, 1913

681 SADKO, *Tableau Sous-Marin*
MUSIC: Nicholas Rimsky-Korsakov
CHOREOGRAPHY: Michel Fokine
SCENERY: Boris Anisfeld
COSTUMES: Boris Anisfeld
COMPANY: Ballet Russe (Diaghilev)
PREMIÈRE: Paris, 1911

682 SADKO
MUSIC: Nicholas Rimsky-Korsakov
CHOREOGRAPHY: Adolph Bolm
SETTING: Boris Anisfeld
COSTUMES: Nathalie Gontcharova
COMPANY: Ballet Russe (Diaghilev)
PREMIÈRE: Paris, 1916

683 SAILOR'S LOVE
BOOK: Sigurd Leeder
MUSIC: Folk melodies; arr. Martin Penny
CHOREOGRAPHY: Sigurd Leeder
SETTING: Hein Heckroth
COSTUMES: Hein Heckroth
COMPANY: Jooss Ballet
PREMIÈRE: [London], 1936

684 SAINT FRANCIS (NOBILISSIMA VIS-
IONE), *Choreographic Legend in One Act
and Five Scenes*
BOOK: Paul Hindemith and Leonide Massine
MUSIC: Paul Hindemith
CHOREOGRAPHY: Leonide Massine
SETTINGS: Pavel Tchelitchew
COSTUMES: Pavel Tchelitchew
COMPANY: Ballet Russe (Massine)
PREMIÈRE: London, 1938

685 SALADE, *Ballet in Two Acts with Songs*
BOOK: Albert Flament
MUSIC: Darius Milhaud
CHOREOGRAPHY: Leonide Massine
SETTING: Georges Braque
COSTUMES: Georges Braque
COMPANY: Les Soirées de Paris
PREMIÈRE: Paris, 1924

686 SALADE, *Ballet in Two Acts with Songs*
BOOK: Albert Flament
MUSIC: Darius Milhaud
CHOREOGRAPHY: Remislavsky-Nikolska
SETTING: Antonin Heythum
COSTUMES: Antonin Heythum
COMPANY: National Theatre
PREMIÈRE: Prague, 1926

687 SALADE
BOOK: Albert Flament
MUSIC: Darius Milhaud
CHOREOGRAPHY: Serge Lifar
SETTING: André Derain
COSTUMES: André Derain
COMPANY: Théâtre National de l'Opéra
PREMIÈRE: Paris, 1935

SALOME
see LA TRAGÉDIE DE SALOMÉ

688 SAPPHO
MUSIC: Claude Debussy
CHOREOGRAPHY: Leila Hyde
SETTING: Nicholas E. Koutoulakis
COSTUMES: Nicholas E. Koutoulakis
COMPANY: Arts Theatre Ballet
PREMIÈRE: London, 1940

689 SARATOGA
BOOK: Jaromir Weinberger
MUSIC: Jaromir Weinberger
CHOREOGRAPHY: Leonide Massine
SETTING: Oliver Smith
COSTUMES: Alvin Colt
COMPANY: Ballet Russe (Massine)
PREMIÈRE: New York, 1941

690 SCARAMOUCHE, *Ballet in Two Scenes*
BOOK: Paul Knudsen
MUSIC: Jan Sibelius
CHOREOGRAPHY: Osvalds Lemanis
SETTING: Niklaus Strunke
COSTUMES: Niklaus Strunke
COMPANY: National Opera
PREMIÈRE: Riga, Latvia, 1936

691 SCHEHERAZADE, *Choreographic Drama in
One Act*
BOOK: Léon Bakst and Michel Fokine
MUSIC: Nicholas Rimsky-Korsakov
CHOREOGRAPHY: Michel Fokine
SETTING: Léon Bakst
COSTUMES: Léon Bakst
COMPANY: Ballet Russe (Diaghilev)
PREMIÈRE: Paris, 1910

692 SCHEHERAZADE
BOOK: Léon Bakst and Michel Fokine
MUSIC: Nicholas Rimsky-Korsakov
CHOREOGRAPHY: Michel Fokine
CURTAIN: Valentin Serov
SETTING: Léon Bakst
COSTUMES: Léon Bakst
COMPANY: Ballet Russe (Diaghilev)
PREMIÈRE: Paris, 1913

693 SCHLAGOBERS, *Ballet in Two Acts*
BOOK: Richard Strauss
MUSIC: Richard Strauss
CHOREOGRAPHY: Heinrich Kroeller
SETTING: Ada Nigrin
COSTUMES: Ada Nigrin
COMPANY: Vienna State Opera
PREMIÈRE: Vienna, 1924

694 THE SCORPIONS OF YSIT
MUSIC: Gavin Gordon
CHOREOGRAPHY: Ninette de Valois
SETTING: Sophie Fedorovitch
COSTUMES: Sophie Fedorovitch
COMPANY: Sadler's Wells Ballet
PREMIÈRE: London, 1932

695 SCULPTURE NÈGRE
CHOREOGRAPHY: Jean Borlin
SETTING: Paul Colin
COSTUMES: Paul Colin
COMPANY: Les Ballets Suédois
PREMIÈRE: Paris, 1929

696 SCUOLA DI BALLO, *A Comedy*
BOOK: After Carlo Goldoni
MUSIC: Luigi Boccherini; orch. Jean Français
CHOREOGRAPHY: Leonide Massine
SETTING: Etienne de Beaumont
COSTUMES: Etienne de Beaumont
COMPANY: Soirées de Paris
PREMIÈRE: Paris, 1924

697 THE SEASONS
MUSIC: Alexander Glazounov
CHOREOGRAPHY: Frank Staff
SETTING: William Chappell
COSTUMES: William Chappell
COMPANY: Arts Theatre Ballet
PREMIÈRE: London, 1940

698 SEBASTIAN, *Ballet in One Act and Three Scenes*
BOOK: Edward Caton
MUSIC: Gian-Carlo Menotti
CHOREOGRAPHY: Edward Caton
SETTING: Oliver Smith
COSTUMES: Milena
COMPANY: The Ballet International
PREMIÈRE: New York, 1944

699 THE SELFISH GIANT (AZ ONZÖ ORIÁS)
BOOK: After Oscar Wilde
MUSIC: Jenö von Hubay
CHOREOGRAPHY: Ressö Brada
SETTING: Zoltán Fülöp
COSTUMES: Zoltán Fülöp

COMPANY: Hungarian State Ballet
PREMIÈRE: Budapest

700 SEMIRAMIS
BOOK: After Paul Valéry
MUSIC: Arthur Honegger
CHOREOGRAPHY: Michel Fokine
SETTING: Jakovleff
COSTUMES: Jakovleff
COMPANY: Ida Rubinstein Ballet
PREMIÈRE: Paris, 1934

701 SENTIMENTAL COLLOQUY
MUSIC: Paul Bowles
CHOREOGRAPHY: André Eglevsky
SETTING: Salvador Dali
COSTUMES: Salvador Dali
COMPANY: Ballet International
PREMIÈRE: New York, 1944

702 LES SEPT PÉCHÉS CAPITAUX
BOOK: Bert Brecht
MUSIC: Kurt Weill
CHOREOGRAPHY: George Balanchine
SETTING: Caspar Neher
COSTUMES: Caspar Neher
COMPANY: Les Ballets 1933
PREMIÈRE: Paris, 1933

703 SERENADE, *Ballet in Three Movements*
MUSIC: Peter Tchaikowsky
CHOREOGRAPHY: George Balanchine
COSTUMES: Jean Lurçat
COMPANY: The American Ballet
PREMIÈRE: Hartford, Connecticut, 1934

704 SERENADE
MUSIC: Peter Tchaikowsky
CHOREOGRAPHY: George Balanchine
SETTING: Gaston Longchamp
COSTUMES: Jean Lurçat
COMPANY: Ballet Russe (Blum)
PREMIÈRE: New York, 1935

705 SERENADE
MUSIC: Hugo Wolf
CHOREOGRAPHY: Harold Turner
SETTING: Diana Gould
COSTUMES: Diana Gould
COMPANY: Arts Theatre Ballet
PREMIÈRE: London, 1940

THE SEVEN CAPITAL SINS
see LES SEPT PÉCHÉS CAPITAUX

706 THE SEVEN DAUGHTERS OF THE MOUNTAIN KING
BOOK: Lermontov; arr. Michel Fokine and Boris Anisfeld

MUSIC: Alexander Spendiarov
CHOREOGRAPHY: Michel Fokine
SETTING: Boris Anisfeld
COSTUMES: Boris Anisfeld
COMPANY: Pavlova Company
PREMIÈRE: Berlin, 1913

707 THE SEVEN HEROES, *Comic Ballet in Three Parts*
BOOK: Kurt Jooss, after Grimm
MUSIC: Frederic Cohen, after Henry Purcell
CHOREOGRAPHY: Kurt Jooss
SETTING: Hein Heckroth
COSTUMES: Hein Heckroth
COMPANY: Jooss Ballet
PREMIÈRE: Maastricht, Holland, 1933

708 THE SEVENTH SYMPHONY, *Choreographic Symphony in Four Scenes*
BOOK: Leonide Massine
MUSIC: Ludwig van Beethoven
CHOREOGRAPHY: Leonide Massine
SETTING: Christian Bérard
COSTUMES: Christian Bérard
COMPANY: Ballet Russe (Massine)
PREMIÈRE: Monte Carlo, 1938

709 SHOW PIECE, *Ballet Work-Out in One Act*
MUSIC: Robert McBride
CHOREOGRAPHY: Erick Hawkins
COSTUMES: Keith Martin
COMPANY: The American Ballet Caravan
PREMIÈRE: Bar Harbor, Maine, 1937

710 SIANG-SIN
MUSIC: Georges Hue
CHOREOGRAPHY: Léo Staats
SETTING: René Piot
COSTUMES: René Piot
COMPANY: Théâtre National de l'Opéra
PREMIÈRE: Paris, 1942

711 SIEBA
BOOK: Luigi Manzotti
MUSIC: R. Marenco
CHOREOGRAPHY: Luigi Manzotti
SETTING: Antonio Rovescalli and G. B. Santoni
COSTUMES: Caramba
COMPANY: Scala Opera Ballet
PREMIÈRE: Milan, 1933

712 SIESTA
BOOK: Frederick Ashton
MUSIC: William Turner Walton
CHOREOGRAPHY: Frederick Ashton
SETTING: Sophie Fedorovitch
COSTUMES: Sophie Fedorovitch

COMPANY: Sadler's Wells Ballet
PREMIÈRE: London, 1936

713 SILVER BIRCH
MUSIC: Adrian Beecham
CHOREOGRAPHY: Lydia Sokolova
SETTING: Nadia Benois
COSTUMES: Nadia Benois
COMPANY: Allied Ballets
PREMIÈRE: Golders Green, England, 1942

714 SIMPLE SYMPHONY, *Ballet in One Scene and Four Movements*
MUSIC: Benjamin Britten
CHOREOGRAPHY: Walter Gore
SETTING: Ronald Wilson
COSTUMES: Ronald Wilson
COMPANY: Marie Rambert Company
PREMIÈRE: Bristol, England, 1944

715 SINGING EARTH
MUSIC: Joseph Hawes
CHOREOGRAPHY: Kurt Graff
COSTUMES: John Pratt
COMPANY: Kurt Graff Ballet
PREMIÈRE: Chicago, Illinois, 1939

716 SKATING RINK
BOOK: Riciotto Canudo
MUSIC: Arthur Honegger
CHOREOGRAPHY: Jean Borlin
CURTAIN: Fernand Léger
SETTING: Fernand Léger
COSTUMES: Fernand Léger
COMPANY: Les Ballets Suédois
PREMIÈRE: Paris, 1922

717 SKYSCRAPERS, *A Ballet of Modern American Life in Six Scenes*
MUSIC: John Alden Carpenter
CHOREOGRAPHY: Samuel Lee; Frank Wilson for 1926
SETTING: Robert Edmond Jones
COSTUMES: Robert Edmond Jones
COMPANY: Chicago Opera Company
PREMIÈRE: Chicago, Illinois, 1920

718 SLAVONIKA, *Ballet in One Act*
BOOK: Vania Psota
MUSIC: Antonin Dvorak
CHOREOGRAPHY: Vania Psota
COSTUMES: Alvin Colt
COMPANY: Ballet Theatre
PREMIÈRE: New York, 1941

719 THE SLEEPING BEAUTY
MUSIC: Peter Tchaikowsky

CHOREOGRAPHY: Laurent Novikoff, after Petipa
SETTING: Serge Soudeikine
COSTUMES: Serge Soudeikine
COMPANY: Pavlova Company
PREMIÈRE: Paris, 1923

720 THE SLEEPING BEAUTY
MUSIC: Peter Tchaikowsky
CHOREOGRAPHY: Nicholas Zverev, after Petipa
SETTING: Mstislav Dobujinsky
COSTUMES: Mstislav Dobujinsky
COMPANY: Lithuanian Ballet
PREMIÈRE: Kaunas, Lithuania, 1934

721 THE SLEEPING BEAUTY, *Ballet in Three Acts and Five Scenes*
BOOK: Catherine Littlefield
MUSIC: Peter Tchaikowsky
CHOREOGRAPHY: Catherine Littlefield
SETTING: R. Deshays
COSTUMES: Lee Gainsborough
COMPANY: Philadelphia Opera Ballet
PREMIÈRE: Philadelphia, Pennsylvania, 1937

722 THE SLEEPING PRINCESS
BOOK: Rudolf von Laban
MUSIC: Johann Strauss
CHOREOGRAPHY: Rudolf von Laban
SETTING: Benno von Arendt
COSTUMES: Benno von Arendt
COMPANY: State Chamber of Culture
PREMIÈRE: Berlin, 1934

723 THE SLEEPING PRINCESS, *Classic Ballet in Three Acts*
MUSIC: Peter Tchaikowsky
CHOREOGRAPHY: Nicolas Sergueff, after Petipa
SETTING: Nadia Benois
COSTUMES: Nadia Benois
COMPANY: Sadler's Wells Ballet
PREMIÈRE: London, 1939

THE SLEEPING PRINCESS
THE SLEEPING BEAUTY
see also LA BELLE AU BOIS DORMANT
AURORA'S WEDDING
THE FAIRY TALE

724 THE SNOW MAIDEN, *Ballet in One Act and Four Scenes*
BOOK: S. J. Denham
MUSIC: Alexander Glazounov
CHOREOGRAPHY: Bronislava Nijinska
SETTING: Boris Aronson
COSTUMES: Boris Aronson
COMPANY: Ballet Russe (Massine)
PREMIÈRE: New York, 1941

725 THE SNOW QUEEN
BOOK: After Hans Christian Andersen
MUSIC: Murray Cutter
CHOREOGRAPHY: Catherine Littlefield
SETTING: A. Jarin
COSTUMES: P. T. Champs
COMPANY: Philadelphia Opera Ballet
PREMIÈRE: Philadelphia, Pennsylvania, 1935

726 THE SOLDIER AND THE GYPSY, *Character Ballet in Seven Scenes*
MUSIC: Manuel de Falla
CHOREOGRAPHY: Douglas Coudy
COSTUMES: Charles Rain
COMPANY: The American Ballet Caravan
PREMIÈRE: Hartford, Connecticut, 1936

727 SOLEIL DE NUIT, *Russian Scenes and Dances in One Act*
BOOK: Leonide Massine
MUSIC: Nicholas Rimsky-Korsakov
CHOREOGRAPHY: Leonide Massine
SETTING: Michel Larionow
COSTUMES: Michel Larionow
COMPANY: Ballet Russe (Diaghilev)
PREMIÈRE: Paris, 1915

728 UN SONGE
MUSIC: Guillaume Lekeu
CHOREOGRAPHY: Frank Staff
SETTING: Ronald Wilson
COSTUMES: Ronald Wilson
COMPANY: Marie Rambert Company
PREMIÈRE: London, 1945

729 SONG OF OUR LAND, *Ballet in Three Scenes*
BOOK: Bronislava Nijinska
MUSIC: Roman Palester
CHOREOGRAPHY: Bronislava Nijinska
SETTING: Waclaw Borowski
COSTUMES: Waclaw Borowski
COMPANY: The Polish Ballet

730 LES SONGES
BOOK: André Derain
MUSIC: Darius Milhaud
CHOREOGRAPHY: George Balanchine
SETTING: André Derain
COSTUMES: André Derain
COMPANY: Les Ballets 1933
PREMIÈRE: Paris, 1933

731 SPANISH CAPRICCIO
BOOK: Leonide Massine
MUSIC: Nicholas Rimsky-Korsakov
CHOREOGRAPHY: Leonide Massine
SETTING: Mariano Andreù

COSTUMES: Mariano Andreù
COMPANY: Ballet Russe (de Basil)
PREMIÈRE: Monte Carlo, 1938
SPANISH CAPRICCIO
see also CAPRICCIO ESPAGNOL

732 SPECTRE DE L'AMOUR
MUSIC: Ch. Malecka
CHOREOGRAPHY: Angiola Sartorio
SETTING: Antonin Heythum
COSTUMES: Antonin Heythum
COMPANY: Triennale Milano
PREMIÈRE: Milan, 1935

733 LE SPECTRE DE LA ROSE, *Choreographic Tableau in One Act*
BOOK: J.-L. Vaudoyer, after Théophile Gautier
MUSIC: Carl-Maria von Weber; orch. Hector Berlioz
CHOREOGRAPHY: Michel Fokine
SETTING: Léon Bakst
COSTUMES: Léon Bakst
COMPANY: Ballet Russe (Diaghilev)
PREMIÈRE: Paris, 1911

734 LE SPECTRE DE LA ROSE, *Ballet in One Act*
MUSIC: Carl-Maria von Weber
CHOREOGRAPHY: Tamar Karsavina
SETTING: Rex Whistler
COSTUMES: Rex Whistler
COMPANY: Sadler's Wells Company
PREMIÈRE: London, 1944

735 A SPRING TALE, *Romantic Ballet in Four Parts*
BOOK: Kurt Jooss
MUSIC: Frederic Cohen
CHOREOGRAPHY: Kurt Jooss
COSTUMES: Hein Heckroth
COMPANY: Jooss Ballet
PREMIÈRE: Stratford-on-Avon, England, 1939

736 THE STORY OF THE SOLDIER
BOOK: Ruth Page
MUSIC: Igor Strawinsky
CHOREOGRAPHY: Ruth Page
SETTING: Nicolai Remisoff
COSTUMES: Nicolai Remisoff
COMPANY: Page-Stone Ballet
PREMIÈRE: Chicago, Illinois, 1931

737 SUITE EN BLANC
MUSIC: Édouard Lalo
CHOREOGRAPHY: Serge Lifar
SETTING: André Dignimont
COSTUMES: André Dignimont

COMPANY: Théâtre National de l'Opéra
PREMIÈRE: Paris, 1943

738 SUITE 1929
BOOK: Kurt Jooss
MUSIC: Frederic Cohen
CHOREOGRAPHY: Kurt Jooss
COSTUMES: Hein Heckroth
COMPANY: Folkwang Tanzbuehne Essen
PREMIÈRE: Essen, Germany, 1929

739 SUITE OF AIRS
MUSIC: Henry Purcell
CHOREOGRAPHY: Antony Tudor
COSTUMES: Nadia Benois
COMPANY: Marie Rambert Company
PREMIÈRE: London, 1939

740 SUR LE BORYSTHÈNE, *Choreographic Poem*
BOOK: Serge Lifar
MUSIC: Serge Prokofieff
CHOREOGRAPHY: Serge Lifar
CONSTRUCTIVIST SETTING: Michel Larionow
COSTUMES: Nathalie Gontcharova
COMPANY: Théâtre National de l'Opéra
PREMIÈRE: Paris, 1932

741 SWAN LAKE, *Second Act*
MUSIC: Peter Tchaikowsky
CHOREOGRAPHY: After Petipa and Ivanov
SETTING: Duncan Grant, after Inigo Jones
COSTUMES: Duncan Grant, after Inigo Jones
COMPANY: The Camargo Society
PREMIÈRE: London, 1932

742 SWAN LAKE, *Choreographic Poem in One Act*
MUSIC: Peter Tchaikowsky
CHOREOGRAPHY: Anton Dolin, after Petipa
SETTING: Augustus Vincent Tack
COSTUMES: Lucinda Ballard
COMPANY: Ballet Theatre
PREMIÈRE: New York, 1940

743 SWAN LAKE, *Choreographic Poem in One Act*
BOOK: V. P. Begitchev and Geltser
MUSIC: Peter Tchaikowsky; orch. Vittorio Rieti
CHOREOGRAPHY: Anton Dolin, after Petipa
SETTINGS: Lee Simonson
COSTUMES: Lucinda Ballard
COMPANY: Ballet Theatre
PREMIÈRE: New York, 1941

744 SWAN LAKE
MUSIC: Peter Tchaikowsky; orch. G. Creatore
CHOREOGRAPHY: Anatol Vilzak, after Petipa
SETTING: Eugene Dunkel
COSTUMES: Grace Houston

COMPANY: Ballet International
PREMIÈRE: New York, 1944

745 SWAN LAKE
BOOK: Fedor Lopukov
MUSIC: Peter Tchaikowsky
CHOREOGRAPHY: Fedor Lopukov, after Petipa
SETTING: Boris Volkov
COSTUMES: Boris Volkov
COMPANY: Soviet State Ballet
PREMIÈRE: Leningrad, [1944-45]

SWAN LAKE
see also LAC DES CYGNES

746 LES SYLPHIDES, *Romantic Rêverie in One Act*
BOOK: Michel Fokine
MUSIC: Frederic Chopin
CHOREOGRAPHY: Michel Fokine
SETTING: Alexandre Benois
COSTUMES: Alexandre Benois
COMPANY: Ballet Russe (Diaghilev)
PREMIÈRE: Paris, 1909

747 LES SYLPHIDES
BOOK: Michel Fokine
MUSIC: Frederic Chopin; orch. Maurice Ravel
CHOREOGRAPHY: Vaslav Nijinsky; after Michel Fokine
SETTING: Boris Anisfeld
COSTUMES: Boris Anisfeld
COMPANY: Vaslav Nijinsky Company
PREMIÈRE: London, 1914

748 LES SYLPHIDES
BOOK: Michel Fokine
MUSIC: Frederic Chopin
CHOREOGRAPHY: Michel Fokine
SETTING: Georges Braque
COSTUMES: Alexandre Benois
COMPANY: Ballet Russe (Diaghilev)
PREMIÈRE: Paris, 1925

749 LES SYLPHIDES
BOOK: Michel Fokine
MUSIC: Frederic Chopin
CHOREOGRAPHY: Nicholas Zverev, after Fokine
SETTING: Mstislav Dobujinsky
COSTUMES: Mstislav Dobujinsky
COMPANY: The Lithuanian Ballet
PREMIÈRE: London, 1935

750 LES SYLPHIDES
BOOK: Michel Fokine
MUSIC: Frederic Chopin; orch. Frederick Austin
CHOREOGRAPHY: Michel Fokine

SETTING: Rex Whistler
COSTUMES: Rex Whistler
COMPANY: The International Ballet
PREMIÈRE: London, [1941]

751 LES SYLPHIDES
BOOK: Michel Fokine
MUSIC: Frederic Chopin; orch. Benjamin Britten
CHOREOGRAPHY: Michel Fokine
SETTING: Augustus Vincent Tack
COSTUMES: Lucinda Ballard
COMPANY: Ballet Theatre
PREMIÈRE: New York, 1941

752 LES SYLPHIDES, *Ballet in One Act*
BOOK: Michel Fokine
MUSIC: Frederic Chopin; orch. Maurice Baron
CHOREOGRAPHY: Michel Fokine; supervised Vera Fokine
SETTING: Eugene Dunkel
COSTUMES: Grace Houston
COMPANY: The Ballet International
PREMIÈRE: New York, 1944

753 LES SYLPHIDES, *A Romantic Reverie in One Act*
BOOK: Michel Fokine
MUSIC: Frederic Chopin; orch. Vittorio Rieti
CHOREOGRAPHY: Michel Fokine
SETTING: A. Schervachidze, after Corot
COSTUMES: O. Larose
COMPANY: Ballet Russe (de Basil)
PREMIÈRE: [New York, 1940]

754 SYLVIA
MUSIC: Léo Delibes
CHOREOGRAPHY: Serge Lifar
SETTING: Maurice Brianchon
COSTUMES: Maurice Brianchon
COMPANY: Théâtre National de l'Opéra
PREMIÈRE: Paris, 1941

755 SYMPHONIE FANTASTIQUE, *Ballet in Five Scenes*
BOOK: Hector Berlioz
MUSIC: Hector Berlioz
CHOREOGRAPHY: Leonide Massine
SETTING: Christian Bérard
COSTUMES: Christian Bérard
COMPANY: Ballet Russe (de Basil)
PREMIÈRE: London, 1936

756 SZENT FÁKLYA (*The Holy Torch*)
BOOK: Elsa von Galafres
MUSIC: Erno von Dohnányi
CHOREOGRAPHY: Elsa von Galafres
SETTING: Zoltán Fülöp

COSTUMES: Zoltán Fülöp
COMPANY: Hungarian State Ballet
PREMIÈRE: Budapest, 1934

757 TALLY-HO OR THE FRAIL QUARRY, *Ballet in One Act*
BOOK: Agnes de Mille
MUSIC: Christoph Willibald Gluck; arr. Paul Nordoff
CHOREOGRAPHY: Agnes de Mille
SETTING: Motley
COSTUMES: Motley
COMPANY: Ballet Theatre
PREMIÈRE: New York, 1944

758 TANZ SUITE
BOOK: Kurt Jooss
MUSIC: Ernst Toch
CHOREOGRAPHY: Kurt Jooss
SETTING: Hein Heckroth
COSTUMES: Hein Heckroth
COMPANY: Neue Tanzbuehne
PREMIÈRE: Muenster, Germany, 1924

759 TARANTELLA
MUSIC: Gioachino Rossini; orch. Ottorino Respighi
CHOREOGRAPHY: William Christensen
SETTING: San Francisco Opera Company
COSTUMES: San Francisco Opera Company
COMPANY: Santa Rosa Symphony
PREMIÈRE: [Santa Rosa, California], 1937

760 THE TARTANS
BOOK: Frederick Ashton
MUSIC: William Boyce
CHOREOGRAPHY: Frederick Ashton
SETTING: William Chappell
COSTUMES: William Chappell
COMPANY: The Arts Theatre
PREMIÈRE: London, 1930

761 TEMPELOPFER DER ATORAGA, *Choreographic Tragedy in One Act*
MUSIC: Alexander Glazounov
CHOREOGRAPHY: Boris Romanoff
SETTING: Pavel Tchelitchew
COSTUMES: Pavel Tchelitchew
COMPANY: Russian Romantic Theatre
PREMIÈRE: Berlin, 1922

762 LA TENTATION DE LA BERGÈRE OU L'AMOUR VAINQUEUR, *Ballet in One Act*
MUSIC: Michel de Montclair; orch. Casadesus
CHOREOGRAPHY: Bronislava Nijinska
SETTING: Juan Gris

CURTAIN: Juan Gris
COSTUMES: Juan Gris
COMPANY: Ballet Russe (Diaghilev)
PREMIÈRE: Monte Carlo, 1924

763 TERMINAL, *Ballet in One Act*
BOOK: Catherine Littlefield
MUSIC: Herbert Kingsley; orch. Albert Boss
CHOREOGRAPHY: Catherine Littlefield
SETTING: Angelo Pinto
COSTUMES: Salvatore Pinto
COMPANY: Philadelphia Opera Ballet
PREMIÈRE: Paris, 1937

764 THAMAR, *Choreographic Drama in One Act*
BOOK: Léon Bakst
MUSIC: Mily Balakirev
CHOREOGRAPHY: Michel Fokine
SETTING: Léon Bakst
COSTUMES: Léon Bakst
COMPANY: Ballet Russe (Diaghilev)
PREMIÈRE: Paris, 1912

765 A THOUSAND TIMES NEIGH
BOOK: Edward Mabley
MUSIC: Tom Bennett
CHOREOGRAPHY: William Dollar
SETTING: Walter Dorwin Teague
COSTUMES: Alvin Colt
COMPANY: The American Ballet Caravan
PREMIÈRE: New York, 1940

THREE-CORNERED HAT
see LE TRICORNE

766 THE THREE FAT MEN, *Ballet in Four Acts and Eight Scenes*
BOOK: I. Olecha
MUSIC: Victor A. Oransky
CHOREOGRAPHY: Igor A. Moiseyev
SETTING: B. A. Matrunin
COSTUMES: B. A. Matrunin
COMPANY: Soviet State Ballet
PREMIÈRE: Moscow, 1935

767 THREE VIRGINS AND A DEVIL, *Ballet in One Act*
BOOK: Ramon Reed, after Boccaccio
MUSIC: Arr. Ottorino Respighi
CHOREOGRAPHY: Agnes de Mille
SETTING: Arne Lundborg, after Margaret Harris
COSTUMES: Motley
COMPANY: Ballet Theatre
PREMIÈRE: New York, 1941

768 TIL EULENSPIEGEL
BOOK: Vaslav Nijinsky

MUSIC: Richard Strauss
CHOREOGRAPHY: Vaslav Nijinsky
SETTING: Robert Edmond Jones
COSTUMES: Robert Edmond Jones
COMPANY: Ballet Russe (Diaghilev)
PREMIÈRE: New York, 1916

769 TIME TABLE, *Realistic Ballet in One Act*
BOOK: Lincoln Kirstein
MUSIC: Aaron Copland
CHOREOGRAPHY: Antony Tudor
SETTING: James Morcom
COSTUMES: James Morcom
COMPANY: The American Ballet
PREMIÈRE: Rio de Janeiro, 1941

770 LE TOMBEAU DE COUPERIN
BOOK: Jean Borlin
MUSIC: Maurice Ravel
CHOREOGRAPHY: Jean Borlin
SETTING: Pierre Laprade
COSTUMES: Pierre Laprade
COMPANY: Les Ballets Suédois
PREMIÈRE: Paris, 1920

771 LE TOURNOIS SINGULIER
BOOK: After Louise Labé
MUSIC: Roland Manuel
CHOREOGRAPHY: Jean Borlin
SETTING: Foujita
COSTUMES: Foujita
COMPANY: Les Ballets Suédois
PREMIÈRE: Paris, 1924

772 LA TRAGÉDIE DE SALOMÉ
BOOK: Serge Soudeikine and Lumier
MUSIC: Florent Schmitt
CHOREOGRAPHY: Boris Romanoff
SETTINGS: Serge Soudeikine
COSTUMES: Serge Soudeikine
COMPANY: Ballet Russe (Diaghilev)
PREMIÈRE: Paris, 1913

773 THE TRAGEDY OF FASHION
BOOK: Ashley Dukes
MUSIC: Eugene Goossens
CHOREOGRAPHY: Frederick Ashton
SETTING: Sophie Fedorovitch
COSTUMES: Sophie Fedorovitch
COMPANY: Sadler's Wells Ballet
PREMIÈRE: London, 1926

774 TRAGEDY OF THE 'CELLO
MUSIC: Alexandre Tansman
CHOREOGRAPHY: Adolph Bolm
SETTING: Nicolai Remisoff
COSTUMES: Nicolai Remisoff

COMPANY: Chicago Allied Arts
PREMIÈRE: Chicago, Illinois, 1927

775 TRAGOEDIE, *Dance Drama in Five Acts*
BOOK: Kurt Jooss
MUSIC: Frederic Cohen
CHOREOGRAPHY: Kurt Jooss
SETTING: Hein Heckroth
COSTUMES: Hein Heckroth
COMPANY: Neue Tanzbuehne
PREMIÈRE: Muenster, Germany, 1926

776 TRAIN BLEU, *Operette Dansée in One Act*
BOOK: Jean Cocteau
MUSIC: Darius Milhaud
CHOREOGRAPHY: Bronislava Nijinska
SETTING: H. Laurens
CURTAIN: Pablo Picasso
COSTUMES: Gabrielle Chanel
COMPANY: Ballet Russe (Diaghilev)
PREMIÈRE: Paris, 1924

777 TRANSCENDENCE
BOOK: Lincoln Kirstein
MUSIC: Franz Liszt; arr. and orch. George
    Antheil
CHOREOGRAPHY: George Balanchine
SETTING: Franklin C. Watkins
COSTUMES: Franklin C. Watkins
COMPANY: The American Ballet
PREMIÈRE: Hartford, Connecticut, 1934

778 LE TRAPÈZE
MUSIC: Serge Prokofieff
CHOREOGRAPHY: Boris Romanoff
SETTING: Leon Zack
COSTUMES: Leon Zack
COMPANY: Russian Romantic Theatre
PREMIÈRE: Berlin, [1922]

779 TREPAK
MUSIC: Léo Delibes
CHOREOGRAPHY: Bronislava Nijinska
SETTING: Pablo Picasso
COSTUMES: Pablo Picasso
COMPANY: Ballet Russe (Diaghilev)
PREMIÈRE: Monte Carlo, 1924

780 TREPAK
BOOK: Mordkin, Soudeikine, Tcherepnine
MUSIC: Alexandre Tcherepnine
CHOREOGRAPHY: Mikhail Mordkin
SETTING: Serge Soudeikine
COSTUMES: Serge Soudeikine
COMPANY: The Mordkin Ballet
PREMIÈRE: New York, 1938

781 THE TRIADIC BALLET, *Ballet in Three Parts*
BOOK: Oskar Schlemmer
MUSIC: Paul Hindemith, Music for Mechanical Organ
CHOREOGRAPHY: Oskar Schlemmer; collab. Albert Burger and Elsa Hoetzel
SETTING: Oskar Schlemmer
COSTUMES: Oskar Schlemmer
COMPANY: Bauhaus Weimar
PREMIÈRE: Stuttgart, Germany, 1922

782 LE TRICORNE
BOOK: Martinez Sierra, after Alarcon
MUSIC: Manuel de Falla
CHOREOGRAPHY: Leonide Massine
CURTAIN: Pablo Picasso
SETTING: Pablo Picasso
COSTUMES: Pablo Picasso
COMPANY: Ballet Russe (Diaghilev)
PREMIÈRE: London, 1919

783 LE TRICORNE
BOOK: Martinez Sierra
MUSIC: Manuel de Falla
CHOREOGRAPHY: Lizzie Maudrick
SETTING: Mario Cito Filomarino
COSTUMES: Mario Cito Filomarino
COMPANY: Scala Opera Ballet
PREMIÈRE: Milan, 1933

784 LE TRICORNE
BOOK: Margarete Wallmann, after Alarcon
MUSIC: Manuel de Falla
CHOREOGRAPHY: Margarete Wallmann
CURTAIN: Hector Basaldua
SETTINGS: Hector Basaldua
COSTUMES: Hector Basaldua
COMPANY: Teatro Colon
PREMIÈRE: Buenos Aires, 1941

785 LE TRIOMPHE DE L'AMOUR, *Ballet in Three Acts*
BOOK: Voldemars Komisars
MUSIC: Janis Medius
CHOREOGRAPHY: Osvalds Lemanis
SETTING: Ludolfs Liberts
COSTUMES: Ludolfs Liberts
COMPANY: National Opera
PREMIÈRE: Riga, Latvia, 1935

786 THE TRIUMPH OF HOPE, *Ballet in Four Acts*
BOOK: Jean de Botton
MUSIC: César Frank
CHOREOGRAPHY: William Christensen

SETTING: Jean de Botton
COSTUMES: Jean de Botton
COMPANY: San Francisco Opera
PREMIÈRE: San Francisco, 1944

787 THE TRIUMPH OF NEPTUNE, *Pantomimic Ballet in Two Acts and Six Scenes*
BOOK: Sacheverell Sitwell
MUSIC: Gerald Hugh Berners
CHOREOGRAPHY: George Balanchine
SETTING: A. Schervachidze
COSTUMES: A. Schervachidze
COMPANY: Ballet Russe (Diaghilev)
PREMIÈRE: London, 1926

788 LES TROIS MIRACLES DU PAUVRE PÊCHEUR
BOOK: Ladislas Markus and Eugene Mochacsi
MUSIC: George Kósa
CHOREOGRAPHY: Jan Cieplinski
SETTING: Gustáv Olâh
COSTUMES: Gustáv Olâh
COMPANY: Hungarian State Ballet
PREMIÈRE: Budapest, 1933

789 THE TRUTH ABOUT THE RUSSIAN DANCERS
BOOK: James M. Barrie
MUSIC: Arnold Bax
CHOREOGRAPHY: Tamar Karsavina
SETTING: Paul Nash
COSTUMES: Paul Nash
COMPANY: Karsavina Company
PREMIÈRE: London, 1920

790 TWELFTH NIGHT
BOOK: After Shakespeare
MUSIC: Edvard Grieg; orch. Julian Clifford and Ernest Irving
CHOREOGRAPHY: Andrée Howard
SETTING: Doris Zinkeisen
COSTUMES: Doris Zinkeisen
COMPANY: The International Ballet
PREMIÈRE: Liverpool, England, 1942

791 TWO ROSES, *Ballet in Three Acts*
BOOK: Mukhamed Rabiyev
MUSIC: A. Lensky
CHOREOGRAPHY: Kasyan Goleizovsky
SETTING: V. Ryndine
COSTUMES: V. Ryndine
COMPANY: Tadjikstan Festival of Art
PREMIÈRE: Moscow, 1941

792 UIRAPURA
MUSIC: Hector Villa-Lobos
CHOREOGRAPHY: Ricardo Nemanoff

SETTING: Hector Basaldua
COSTUMES: Hector Basaldua
COMPANY: Teatro Colon
PREMIÈRE: Buenos Aires, 1935

793 UMBRAL
BOOK: José Clemente Orozco and Gloria Campobello
MUSIC: Franz Schubert
CHOREOGRAPHY: Gloria Campobello
SETTING: José Clemente Orozco
COSTUMES: José Clemente Orozco
COMPANY: Ballet of the City of México
PREMIÈRE: México, D. F., 1943

794 UNDERTOW, *Ballet in Three Acts*
BOOK: Antony Tudor, after John Van Druten
MUSIC: William Schuman
CHOREOGRAPHY: Antony Tudor
SETTINGS: Raymond Breinin
COSTUMES: Raymond Breinin
COMPANY: Ballet Theatre
PREMIÈRE: New York, 1945

795 UNION PACIFIC, *An American Ballet in One Act and Four Scenes*
BOOK: Archibald MacLeish
MUSIC: Nicholas Nabokov; orch. Edward Powell
CHOREOGRAPHY: Leonide Massine
SETTING: Albert Johnson
COSTUMES: Irene Sharaff
COMPANY: Ballet Russe (de Basil)
PREMIÈRE: Philadelphia, Pennsylvania, 1934

796 VALENTINE'S EVE
BOOK: Frederick Ashton
MUSIC: Maurice Ravel
CHOREOGRAPHY: Frederick Ashton
SETTING: Sophie Fedorovitch
COSTUMES: Sophie Fedorovitch
COMPANY: Marie Rambert Company
PREMIÈRE: London, 1935

797 LA VALSE, *Choreographic Poem in One Act*
BOOK: Bronislava Nijinska
MUSIC: Maurice Ravel
CHOREOGRAPHY: Bronislava Nijinska
SETTING: Alexandre Benois
COSTUMES: Alexandre Benois
COMPANY: Ballet Russe (Diaghilev)
PREMIÈRE: Paris, 1929

798 VALSE FINALE
MUSIC: Maurice Ravel
CHOREOGRAPHY: Walter Gore
SETTING: Sophie Fedorovitch
COSTUMES: Sophie Fedorovitch

COMPANY: Marie Rambert Company
PREMIÈRE: London, 1938

799 LES VALSES DE BEETHOVEN
MUSIC: Ludwig van Beethoven; orch. Nicholas Nabokov
CHOREOGRAPHY: George Balanchine
SETTING: Emilio Terry
COSTUMES: Emilio Terry
COMPANY: Les Ballets 1933
PREMIÈRE: Paris, 1933

800 VARIATIONS, *Ballet in Three Parts*
MUSIC: Ludwig van Beethoven
CHOREOGRAPHY: Bronislava Nijinska
SETTING: George Annenkov
COSTUMES: George Annenkov
COMPANY: Théâtre de Danse (Nijinska)
PREMIÈRE: Paris, 1932

801 VARIATIONS
MUSIC: Johann Sebastian Bach
CHOREOGRAPHY: William Dollar
COSTUMES: Walter Gifford
COMPANY: The American Ballet Caravan
PREMIÈRE: Athens, Georgia, 1938

802 VENUSBERG
BOOK: (Tannhäuser)
MUSIC: Richard Wagner
CHOREOGRAPHY: Nechybová
SETTING: Antonin Heythum
COSTUMES: Antonin Heythum
COMPANY: Municipal Theatre
PREMIÈRE: Olomuc, Czechoslovakia, 1927

803 LA VEUVE DANS LE MIROIR
BOOK: Kjeld Abell
MUSIC: Bernhard Christensen
CHOREOGRAPHY: Börje Ralov
SETTING: Kjeld Abell
COSTUMES: Kjeld Abell
COMPANY: Royal Theatre
PREMIÈRE: Copenhagen, 1934

804 LA VIE DE POLICHINELLE
BOOK: Claude Seran
MUSIC: Nicholas Nabokov
CHOREOGRAPHY: Serge Lifar
SETTING: Pedro Pruna
COSTUMES: Pedro Pruna
COMPANY: Théâtre National de l'Opéra
PREMIÈRE: Paris, 1934

805 VIENNA — 1814
BOOK: Leonide Massine
MUSIC: Carl-Maria von Weber; orch. Russell Bennett

CHOREOGRAPHY: Leonide Massine
SETTING: Stewart Chaney
COSTUMES: Stewart Chaney
COMPANY: Ballet Russe (de Basil)
PREMIÈRE: New York, 1940

806 VIENNESE WALTZ, *Ballet in Three Scenes*
MUSIC: Johann Strauss
CHOREOGRAPHY: Catherine Littlefield
SETTING: A. Jarin
COSTUMES: P. T. Champs
COMPANY: Philadelphia Opera Ballet
PREMIÈRE: Philadelphia, Pennsylvania, 1936

807 LES VIERGES FOLLES, *Ballet-Pantomime in One Act*
BOOK: Kurt Atterberg and Einar Nerman
MUSIC: Kurt Atterberg
CHOREOGRAPHY: Jean Borlin
SETTINGS: Einar Nerman
COSTUMES: Einar Nerman
COMPANY: Les Ballets Suédois
PREMIÈRE: Paris, 1920

808 VOICES OF SPRING
BOOK: Mikhail Mordkin
MUSIC: Johann Strauss; arr. Mois Zlatin
CHOREOGRAPHY: Mikhail Mordkin
SETTING: Lee Simonson
COSTUMES: Lee Simonson
COMPANY: The Mordkin Ballet
PREMIÈRE: [New York], 1938

809 VOLTI LA LANTERN, *Ballet in Three Scenes and Two Interludes*
BOOK: Emidio Mucci
MUSIC: Ezio Carabella
CHOREOGRAPHY: Boris Romanoff
SETTING: Ettore Palidori
COSTUMES: Ettore Palidori
COMPANY: Royal Opera House
PREMIÈRE: Rome, 1934

810 WALTZ ACADEMY, *Ballet in One Act*
MUSIC: Vittorino Rieti
CHOREOGRAPHY: George Balanchine
SETTING: Oliver Smith
COSTUMES: Alvin Colt
COMPANY: Ballet Theatre
PREMIÈRE: Boston, Massachusetts, 1944

811 THE WANDERER
MUSIC: Franz Schubert
CHOREOGRAPHY: Frederick Ashton
SETTING: Graham Sutherland
COSTUMES: Graham Sutherland

COMPANY: Sadler's Wells Ballet
PREMIÈRE: London, 1941

THE WANDERER
see also ERRANTE

THE WAYWARD DAUGHTER
see LA FILLE MAL GARDÉE

812 A WEDDING BOUQUET
BOOK: Choral words: Gertrude Stein
MUSIC: Gerald Hugh Berners
CHOREOGRAPHY: Frederick Ashton
SETTING: Gerald Hugh Berners
COSTUMES: Gerald Hugh Berners
COMPANY: Sadler's Wells Ballet
PREMIÈRE: London, 1937

813 WESELE W. OJCOWIE, *Ballet in One Act*
MUSIC: Karol Kurpinski
CHOREOGRAPHY: Piotr Zaylich
SETTING: Marian Walontynowicz
COSTUMES: Michel Kedziora
COMPANY: The Polish Ballet

THE WIDOW IN THE MIRROR
see LA VEUVE DANS LE MIROIR

814 THE WISE AND THE FOOLISH VIRGINS
BOOK: Biblical Story
MUSIC: Kurt Atterberg
CHOREOGRAPHY: Ninette de Valois
SETTING: William Chappell
COSTUMES: William Chappell
COMPANY: Sadler's Wells Ballet
PREMIÈRE: London, 1933

815 THE WISE VIRGINS, *Ballet in One Scene*
BOOK: Frederick Ashton
MUSIC: Johann Sebastian Bach; orch. William Turner Walton
CHOREOGRAPHY: Frederick Ashton
SETTING: Rex Whistler
COSTUMES: Rex Whistler
COMPANY: Sadler's Wells Ballet
PREMIÈRE: London, 1940

816 WITHIN THE QUOTA, *Ballet in One Act*
BOOK: Gerald Murphy
MUSIC: Cole Porter
CHOREOGRAPHY: Jean Borlin
SETTING: Gerald Murphy
COSTUMES: Gerald Murphy
COMPANY: Les Ballets Suédois
PREMIÈRE: Paris 1923

817 YANKEE CLIPPER, *Ballet-Voyage in One Act and Fifteen Scenes*

BOOK: Lincoln Kirstein
MUSIC: Paul Bowles; arr. Trude Rittmann
CHOREOGRAPHY: Eugene Loring
COSTUMES: Charles Rain
COMPANY: The American Ballet Caravan
PREMIÈRE: Saybrook, Connecticut, 1937

818 ZAPOROGS
BOOK: Harald Lander
MUSIC: Emil Reesen
CHOREOGRAPHY: Harald Lander
SETTING: Constantin Korovine
COMPANY: Royal Theatre
PREMIÈRE: Copenhagen, Denmark, 1934

819 ZÉPHYR ET FLORE
BOOK: Boris Kochno
MUSIC: Vladimir Dukelsky
CHOREOGRAPHY: Leonide Massine
SETTING: Georges Braque
COSTUMES: Georges Braque
COMPANY: Ballet Russe (Diaghilev)
PREMIÈRE: Barcelona, 1925

820 UNA BODA EN TUXPAN, *Mexican Ballet*
MUSIC: Blas Galindo
CHOREOGRAPHY: Waldeen
COSTUMES: Carlos Mérida
COMPANY: Ballet Waldeen
PREMIÈRE: México, D. F., 1945

821 CINCO DANZAS EN RITMO BULGARO
MUSIC: Béla Bartók
CHOREOGRAPHY: Waldeen
SETTING: Carlos Mérida
COSTUMES: Carlos Mérida
COMPANY: Ballet Waldeen
PREMIÈRE: México, D. F., 1945

822 CIRCO ORRIN
BOOK: Martin Luis Guzmán
MUSIC: Moisés Fernández de Lara
CHOREOGRAPHY: Gloria Campobello
SETTING: Carlos Mérida
COSTUMES: Carlos Mérida
COMPANY: Ballet of the City of México
PREMIÈRE: México, D. F., 1945

823 CLASE DE BALLET
BOOK: Nellie Campobello
MUSIC: Johann Strauss
CHOREOGRAPHY: Nellie Campobello
SETTING: Antonio Ruiz
COSTUMES: Antonio Ruiz
COMPANY: Ballet of the City of México
PREMIÈRE: México, D. F., 1945

824 ELENA LA TRAICIONERA, *Ballet-Corrida in Three Parts*
BOOK: Waldeen
MUSIC: Rodolfo Halffter
CHOREOGRAPHY: Waldeen
SETTING: Olga Costa
COSTUMES: Olga Costa
COMPANY: Ballet Waldeen
PREMIÈRE: México, D. F., 1945

825 EL ESPECTRO DE LA ROSA
BOOK: after Théophile Gautier
MUSIC: Carl-Maria von Weber
CHOREOGRAPHY: Nellie Campobello, after Fokine
SETTING: Carlos Orozco Romero, after Bakst
COSTUMES: Carlos Orozco Romero
COMPANY: Ballet of the City of México
PREMIÈRE: México, D. F., 1943

826 IXTEPEC
BOOK: Nellie Campobello
MUSIC: Eduardo Hernández Moncada
CHOREOGRAPHY: Nellie Campobello
SETTING: Carlos Mérida
COSTUMES: Carlos Mérida
COMPANY: Ballet of the City of México
PREMIÈRE: México, D. F., 1945

827 OBERTURA REPUBLICANA
BOOK: Martin Luis Guzmán
MUSIC: Carlos Chavez
CHOREOGRAPHY: Nellie Campobello
SETTING: José Clemente Orozco
COSTUMES: José Clemente Orozco
COMPANY: Ballet of the City of México
PREMIÈRE: México, D. F., 1945

828 PRESENCIA
BOOK: Martin Luis Guzmán
MUSIC: Antonio Vivaldi and Johann Sebastian Bach
CHOREOGRAPHY: Nellie Campobello
SETTING: José Clemente Orozco
COSTUMES: José Clemente Orozco
COMPANY: Ballet of the City of México
PREMIÈRE: México, D. F., 1945

829 LA SIESTA DE UN FAUNO
BOOK: after Stéphane Mallarmé
MUSIC: Claude Debussy
CHOREOGRAPHY: Nellie Campobello
SETTING: Julio Castellanos, after Bakst
COSTUMES: Julio Castellanos, after Bakst
COMPANY: Ballet of the City of México
PREMIÈRE: México, D. F., 1943

830 SILFIDES
  MUSIC: Frederic Chopin
  CHOREOGRAPHY: Gloria Campobello, after Fokine
  SETTING: Julio Castellanos
  COMPANY: Ballet of the City of México
  PREMIÈRE: México, D. F., 1943

831 EL SOMBRERO DE TRES PICOS
  BOOK: Martinez Sierra, after Alarcón
  MUSIC: Manuel de Falla
  CHOREOGRAPHY: Enrique Velezzi, after Massine
  SETTING: Roberto Montenegro
  COSTUMES: Roberto Montenegro
  COMPANY: Ballet of the City of México
  PREMIÈRE: México, D. F., 1945

832 SONATAS ESPAÑOLAS
  MUSIC: Antonio Soler
  CHOREOGRAPHY: Waldeen
  SETTING: Julio de Diego
  COSTUMES: Julio de Diego
  COMPANY: Ballet Waldeen
  PREMIÈRE: México, D. F., 1945

833 VESPERTINA
  MUSIC: Wolfgang Amadeus Mozart
  CHOREOGRAPHY: Nellie Campobello
  SETTING: Antonio Ruiz
  COSTUMES: Antonio Ruiz
  COMPANY: Ballet of the City of México
  PREMIÈRE: México, D. F., 1945

DESIGNERS

The figures following the names refer to the numbers of the
alphabetically arranged titles in the Ballet Index.

Abell, Kjeld, 413, 803
Agnini, Armando, 50
Agombar, Elizabeth, 79, 206, 410, 578, 585
Allegri, O., 241, 321
Allen, Nancy, 523
Andreù, Mariano, 244, 416, 731
Anisfeld, Boris, 388, 604, 681, 682, 706, 747
Annenkov, George, 141, 160, 800
Arendt, Benno von, 722
Armistead, Horace, 173
Armstrong, John, 88, 275
Aronson, Boris, 351, 591, 647, 724
Aud, Jon, 99
Ayrton, Michael, 297

Bakst, Léon, 33, 44, 76, 119, 154, 220, 237, 238, 293,
    294, 389, 404, 446, 466, 486, 506, 532, 534, 549, 571,
    691, 692, 733, 764, 825, 829
Balla, 303
Ballard, Lucinda, 337, 420, 580, 638, 667, 742, 743, 751
Banting, John, 600, 628
Barbier, Georges, 10
Baronov, Michel, 529
Basaldua, Hector, 7, 34, 42, 52, 93, 96, 175, 362, 371,
    384, 457, 530, 616, 625, 784, 792
Bauchant, André, 28
Beaton, Cecil, 31, 310, 568
Beaumont, Étienne de, 72, 73, 325, 381, 516, 696
Bell, Vanessa, 367, 601
Benois, Alexandre, 20, 51, 81, 94, 95, 105, 120, 294,
    332, 348, 466, 514, 524, 569, 575, 586, 614, 746,
    748, 797
Benois, Nadia, 114, 222, 232, 387, 436, 444, 574, 713,
    723, 739
Benois, Nicholas, 75
Bérard, Christian, 193, 254, 291, 315, 499, 708, 755
Berlandina, Jeanne, 205
Berman, Eugene, 104, 166, 207, 234, 235, 336, 377,
    392, 493, 519, 672
Berners, Gerald Hugh, 812
Bianco, Castelo, 167
Bianco, Enrico, 152, 247, 284
Bilibine, Ivan, 294, 536, 666
Bilinsky, B., 272, 615
Boberman, 22, 489, 553
Bobyshov, M. P., 109

Bockman, George, 250, 408, 603
Boden, Pamela, 577
Bolm, Adolph, 62
Bonnard, Pierre, 405
Bony, Paul, 613
Boquet, Pamela, 198
Borlin, Jean, 231
Borowski, Waclaw, 130, 138, 168, 729
Botton, Jean de, 786
Bouchêne, Dimitri, 39, 145, 253, 621
Braque, Georges, 276, 685, 748, 819
Brassai, 654
Brayer, Yves, 18, 409
Breinin, Raymond, 794
Brianchon, Maurice, 23, 754
Briggs, Hedley, 124, 246, 411, 665
Broggi, Achille, 78
Bufano, Benjamino, 172
Burra, Edward, 66, 492, 660
Butler, Horatio, 268

Cadmus, Paul, 306
Calligan, Edward, 181
Campobello, Nellie, 3
Canessi, Frederico, 243
Caramba, 488, 711
Carl, Joseph, 230, 441
Cassandre, A.-M., 41, 136, 494, 520
Castellanos, Julio, 3, 243, 829, 830
Chagall, Marc, 5, 309
Champs, P. T., 153, 281, 725, 806
Chanel, Gabrielle, 776
Chaney, Stewart, 29, 439, 805
Chappell, William, 13, 67, 70, 117, 123, 128, 186, 274,
    334, 367, 393, 400, 418, 432, 437, 442, 457, 468, 482,
    507, 542, 559, 562, 573, 584, 622, 645, 648, 655, 697,
    760, 814
Chiang-Yee, 86
Chirico, Georges de, 19, 49, 55, 399, 630
Colin, Paul, 113, 261, 539, 695
Collomb, 434, 606
Colt, Alvin, 132, 350, 538, 561, 689, 718, 765, 810
Conde, Mario, 48
Corot, 753
Costa, Olga, 824
Couteau, Lucien, 599
Cristofanetti, Francesco, 636

105

107

108

COMPOSERS

Adam, Adolphe, 192, 332-339, 423
Albeniz, Isaac, 209, 375
Alfvén, Hugo, 521
Antheil, George, 777
Arensky, 155, 541
Asafiev, B. V., 144, 316, 453, 617
Atterberg, Kurt, 807, 814
Aubert, Daniel, 655
Auric, Georges, 169, 276, 381, 471, 560, 635
Austin, Frederick, 338, 750

Bach, Johann Sebastian, 2, 16, 50, 153, 166, 172, 205, 253, 272, 514, 636, 801, 815, 828
Balakirev, Mily, 388, 764
Baron, Maurice, 476, 609, 752
Baron, Paul, 327
Bartók, Béla, 607, 608, 616, 821
Bate, Stanley, 114, 577
Bax, Arnold, 472, 789
Bayer, Joseph, 280, 281, 292, 633
Beecham, Adrian, 444, 713
Beecham, Thomas, 238, 341, 542
Beethoven, Ludwig van, 9, 152, 161, 196, 497, 537, 563, 625, 626, 628, 708, 799, 800
Behrens, Fritz, 634
Bellini, Vincenzo, 667
Bennett, Russell, 805
Bennett, Tom, 765
Berkeley, Lennox, 218, 418
Berlioz, Hector, 733, 755
Berners, Gerard Hugh, 203, 318, 456, 787, 812
Bernstein, Leonard, 282
Bizet, Georges, 22, 356, 406
Bliss, Arthur, 135, 492, 507
Bloch, Ernest, 232
Boccherini, Luigi, 696
Borodine, Alexander, 91, 102, 211, 212, 541, 568, 610-612
Boss, Albert, 763
Boutnikoff, Ivan, 107, 459, 591
Bowles, Paul, 116, 561, 701, 817
Boyce, William, 629, 760
Bradford, Hugh, 393
Brahms, Johannes, 107, 141, 476
Brant, Henry, 151, 351, 650
Britten, Benjamin, 386, 408, 714, 751

Byrd, William, 256
Byrns, Harold, 346, 347

Campbell, David, 287
Caplet, André, 92
Carabella, Ezio, 809
Carpenter, John Alden, 87, 427, 717
Carter, Elliot Jr., 598
Casadesus, Robert, 762
Casella, Alfredo, 399, 400
Castillo, 209
Castro, Juan José, 475, 530
Chabrier, Emmanuel, 67, 193, 252, 314, 317, 398
Chausson, Ernest, 395
Chavez, Carlos, 374, 527, 827
Chopin, Frederic, 137-140, 164, 168, 173, 230, 286, 473, 529, 656, 746-753, 830
Christensen, Bernhard, 803
Cimarosa, Domenico, 116, 146, 391
Clifford, Julian, 13, 790
Cohen, Frederic, 63, 180, 229, 248, 249, 329, 352, 412, 495, 618, 621, 673, 707, 735, 738, 775
Cohn, Arthur, 647
Coleridge-Taylor, 79
Colman, John, 60
Copland, Aaron, 83, 365, 663, 769
Corelli, Arcangelo, 313
Costa, Mario, 368
Couperin, François, 302, 359
Creatore, G., 744
Crichton, Ronald, 300
Cutter, Murray, 725
Czerny, Carl, 204

Dahl, Viking, 462
Dargomijsky, Alexander, 213, 214
Debussy, Claude, 33, 34, 92, 93, 225, 258, 291, 404, 405, 491, 493, 518, 519, 630, 688, 829
Delannoy, Marcel, 147, 266
Delibes, Léo, 178-188, 754, 779
Delius, Frederick, 517, 672
Demuth, Norman, 596
Dent, 161
Desormières, Roger, 73, 516
D'Indy, Vincent, 389
Dohnányi, Erno von, 369, 756

Donath, J., 447
Dorati, Antal, 90, 278, 348, 349, 363, 568, 592, 636, 667, 672
Dowland, John, 559
Drigo, Riccardo, 10, 36, 489
Dukas, Paul, 571-574
Dukelsky, Vladimir, 396, 397, 819
Dvorak, Antonin, 298, 718

Egk, Werner, 409
Eichheim, Henry, 661
Elgar, Edward, 13, 263, 523
Enesco, Georges, 678
Erlanger, Frédéric d', 127, 149
Espert, 209
Evans, Edwin, 504, 623

Falla, Manuel de, 14, 15, 17, 18, 201, 209, 726, 782-784, 831
Farnaby, Giles, 256
Fauré, Gabriel, 300, 398, 477, 566, 582
Ferroud, Octave, 403
Field, John, 206
Foss, Lukas, 331
Françaix, Jean, 595, 664, 665, 696
Franck, César, 619, 786
Frescobaldi, Girolamo, 198
Fuentes, Eduardo Sánchez de, 240
Fuerst, Eugene, 337

Gabowitz, Martin, 550
Galdino, Blas, 820
Ganz, Rudolph, 454
Garcia-Lorca, Federico, 110
Gaubert, Philippe, 6, 136
Gerhard, Robert, 311, 522, 548
Gershwin, George, 12, 508, 658, 659
Ginastera, Alberto E., 268
Glazounov, Alexander, 10, 119, 155, 231, 242, 294, 541, 644, 697, 724, 761
Gliere, Reinhold, 646, 647
Glinka, Michael, 155, 294, 301, 416, 515
Gluck, Christoph Willibald, 244, 442, 543-545, 757
Godard, Benjamin, 599
Godard, Paul, 650
Goldschmidt, Berthold, 145
Goossens, Eugene, 773
Gordon, Gavin, 359, 407, 641, 648, 694
Gottschalk, L. M., 68
Gough, John, 500
Gould, Morton, 8, 385
Gounod, Charles, 157
Granados, Enrique, 346, 347, 592
Grétry, André, 128, 215, 299, 622
Grieg, Edvard, 541, 790

Grofé, Ferde, 111
Grovlez, Gabriel, 613
Guarino, Carmine, 59
Guion, David, 68

Hahn, Reynaldo, 237
Halffter, Rodolfo, 824
Handel, George Frederic, 4, 16, 238, 341, 542, 585
Haquinius, Algot, 531
Hawes, Joseph, 715
Haydn, Joseph, 623, 642
Haynes, Owen, 140
Herscher, Jeanne Clément, 289
Hertel, Johann Wilhelm, 304, 305
Hill, M. Wood, 594
Hindemith, Paul, 126, 228, 684, 781
Holbrook, Joseph, 43
Holst, Gustav, 70, 271, 597
Honegger, Arthur, 19, 20, 32, 113, 436, 467, 514, 700, 716
Hubay, Jenö, 199, 699
Hue, Georges, 710
Hughes, Spike, 367

Ibert, Jacques, 345
Inghelbrecht, D. E., 255, 375
Irving, Ernest, 209, 274, 790

Jacobson, Maurice, 224
Jasienski, Bruno, 57
Jaubert, Maurice, 417
Jaumeton-Epstein, Miriam, 312
Jolivet, André, 355
Joio, Norman Dello, 250, 538, 603
Jooss, Kurt, 438

Kalnins, Jànis, 676
Kenessey, Jenö, 452, 570
Kingsley, Herbert, 269, 435, 763
Koechlin, Charles, 267, 599
Kondracki, Michal, 443
Konstantinov, Constantin, 602
Konstantinoff, Fedor, 445
Korchmarev, Klementia, 423
Kordály, Zoltán, 428
Kósa, George, 415, 788
Kosma, Pierre, 654
Krein, Alexander, 440
Kroshner, M. E., 509
Kurpinski, Karol, 511, 813
Kurtz, Efrem, 458

Lalo, Édouard, 390, 737
Lambert, Constant, 31, 88, 162, 219, 373, 468, 600, 601, 629, 655, 660, 669

Roussel, Albert, 1, 273, 295-297
Rozycki, Ludomir, 26
Rubinstein, Anton, 423, 609

Sabeta, Victor de, 488
Saint-Saens, Charles Camille, 122, 167, 171, 668
Salzedo, Leonard, 324
Satie, Erik, 58, 197, 370, 394, 481, 482, 551, 552, 555, 649
Sauguet, Henri, 134, 290, 315, 494, 520
Sauveplane, Henry, 539
Scarlatti, Domenico, 293, 358, 468
Schiuma, Armando, 384
Schmid, Adolf, 173
Schmitt, Florent, 273, 540, 583, 772
Schoenberg, Arnold, 593
Schubert, Franz, 77, 81, 82, 226, 267, 371, 429, 454, 553, 645, 793, 811
Schumann, Robert, 119, 120, 129, 270, 288, 549
Schuman, William, 794
Scott, Raymond, 638
Scriabine, Alexander, 498, 627
Sévérac, Déodat de, 501
Sheinfield, David, 74
Shostakovich, Dimitri, 109, 342, 677
Sibelius, Jan, 170, 437, 690
Sijanec, Drago M., 16
Smetack, Vaclav, 35
Smetana, Bedrich, 69
Soler, Antonio, 832
Spendiarov, Alexander, 706
Stefani, 511
Steinberg, Maximilien, 485, 486
Still, William Grant, 354
Strauss, Johann, 71-73, 283, 348, 349, 412, 722, 806, 808, 823
Strauss, Richard, 104, 105, 239, 274, 302, 413, 414, 446, 693, 768
Strawinsky, Igor, 27-30, 51-54, 64, 76, 118, 131, 159, 207, 303, 308, 309, 402, 451, 513, 532, 533, 575, 586-590, 631, 632, 652, 653, 675, 680, 736
Swift, Kay, 8
Szelenyi, I., 25
Szyfer, J. E., 377, 378
Szymanowsky, Karol, 360, 361, 463

Tailleferre, Germaine, 465, 467
Tansman, Alexander, 382, 774
Tartini, Giuseppe, 328
Tchaikowsky, Peter, 5, 21, 44, 45, 61, 76, 123-125, 294, 319, 322, 357, 430-434, 466, 499, 524, 525,
Tcherepnine, Alexandre, 227, 321, 505, 780
Tcherepnine, Nicolas, 119, 189, 241, 344, 469, 506, 536, 549, 569, 666
Thomas, Henri, 353
Thomson, Virgil, 306
Toch, Ernst, 758
Tommasini, Vincenzo, 234, 235, 293
Toye, Geoffrey, 246, 364
Turina, Joaquin, 112, 209
Turner, James O., 410, 578

Villa-Lobos, Hector, 792
Vitolins, Janis, 380
Vittadini, F., 535
Vivaldi, Antonio, 16, 828
Voormolen, Alexander, 236

Wagner, Richard, 47, 48, 459, 802
Waldman, Frederic, 108
Walton, William Turner, 275, 310, 637, 712, 815
Warlock, Peter, 117
Weber, Carl-Maria von, 387, 733, 734, 805, 825
Weill, Kurt, 24, 419, 420, 639, 702
Weinberger, Jaromir, 689
Weiner, L., 200
Wellesz, Egon, 579
Wieniawski, Henri, 363
Wilckens, Frederick, 662
Wilder, Alec, 421
Williams, Vaughan, 143, 411
Wolf, Hugo, 705
Wolpe, Stefan, 464
Woytowicz, Boleslaw, 643

Zaylich, Piotr, 511, 813
Zlatin, Mois, 808

CHOREOGRAPHERS

Anderson, Elizabeth, 513
Andes, Angelo, 209
Argentina, 15, 110, 592
Ashton, Frederick, 31, 53, 117, 148, 203, 219, 234, 235, 275, 310, 313, 318, 359, 367, 373, 418, 437, 442, 468, 470, 479, 482, 503, 504, 517, 559, 562, 573, 584, 600, 601, 637, 645, 648, 655, 660, 712, 760, 773, 796, 811, 812, 815
Aveline, Albert, 233, 296
Aveline, Georges, 353

Balanchine, George, 8, 28-30, 38, 39, 41, 54, 55, 61, 64, 65, 71, 104, 105, 118, 126, 134, 165, 166, 169, 193, 207, 238, 252, 267, 268, 277, 284, 290, 307, 394, 413, 456, 460, 499, 543, 560, 650, 669, 675, 702-704, 730, 777, 787, 799, 810
Baratov, 611
Barona, Aida, 271, 627
Bercher, Louis de, 175, 362
Bolender, Todd, 159
Bolm, Adolph, 9, 14, 27, 37, 58, 62, 87, 143, 172, 190, 205, 257, 289, 308, 309, 317, 422, 427, 450, 463, 474, 537, 555, 580, 587, 588, 661, 682, 774
Borlin, Jean, 92, 194, 217, 231, 255, 372, 375, 399, 405, 462, 465, 467, 521, 531, 649, 674, 695, 716, 770, 771, 807, 816
Brada, Ede, 121
Brada, Ressö, 428, 699
Bradley, Buddy, 367
Brunelleschi, Elsa, 311
Burger, Albert, 781
Burian, E. F., 57

Campobello, Gloria, 3, 563, 793, 822, 830
Campobello, Nellie, 323, 527, 823, 825-829, 833
Caton, Edward, 299, 698
Chabukiani, Alexander, 440
Charrat, Janine, 402
Chasles, 583
Christensen, Lew, 132, 259, 306, 408, 561, 598
Christensen, William, 50, 69, 115, 139, 156, 634, 678, 759, 786
Cieplinsky, Jan, 7, 93, 174, 200, 208, 361, 415, 461, 607, 616, 788
Clustine, Ivan, 10, 178, 241, 292, 321, 572, 666
Cobos, Antonia, 502

Coralli, Jean, 333, 334, 336-338
Coudy, Douglas, 314, 726

Dauberval, 305
Dolin, Anton, 116, 337, 391, 638, 656, 658, 667, 742, 743
Dollar, William, 2, 173, 421, 439, 765, 801
Dolotine, J., 164
Doone, Rupert, 258

Eglevsky, André, 701
Egorova, Lubov, 312

Falla, Manuel de, 201
Federova, A., 524
Fenonjois, Roger, 635
Fernandez, José, 347
Fokine, Vera, 752
Fokine, Michael, 90, 95, 119, 120, 149, 155, 189, 212, 220, 237, 244, 253, 254, 265, 294, 322, 366, 379, 388, 416, 430, 446, 480, 485, 486, 506, 532, 533, 541, 544, 547, 549, 569, 571, 586, 604, 679, 681, 691, 692, 700, 706, 733, 746-753, 764, 825, 830
Fornaroli, Cia, 78, 84, 368
Franca, Celia, 112, 487
French, Leslie, 274

Galafres, Elsa von, 369, 756
Georgi, Yvonne, 184, 236, 590, 662
Gluck-Sandor, 269
Goleizovsky, Kasian, 791
Gore, Walter, 70, 114, 170, 554, 714, 798
Graff, Kurt, 74, 715
Grant, Pauline, 288
Gregory, Tony, 218

Harangozó, Gyula, 199, 452, 570, 670
Hawkins, Erick, 490, 709
Helpmann, Robert, 86, 162, 357, 492
Hoetzel, Elsa, 781
Holm, Hanya, 343
Howard, Andrée, 4, 122, 171, 197, 226, 297, 300, 324, 436, 484, 501, 546, 642, 790
Hyde, Leila, 688

Inglesby, Mona, 13, 260, 274, 596

Sergueff, Nicholas, 123, 124, 181, 185, 186, 188, 334, 338, 431-433, 723
Shabelevski, Yurek, 529
Slawinsky, Taddie, 142
Sokolova, Lydia, 444, 713
Sokolow, Anna, 651
Sorel, Felicia, 594
Staats, Léo, 295, 389, 710
Staff, Frank, 204, 263, 574, 581, 697, 728
Stone, Bentley, 11, 320, 356, 567
Strawbridge, Edwin, 557

Taras, John, 350
Tcherkas, Constantin, 302, 424, 448, 483
Terpis, Max, 488
Theilade, Nini, 518, 519
Toye, Wendy, 43, 441
Tudor, Antony, 198, 222, 223, 232, 239, 326-328, 346, 395, 419, 420, 457, 593, 597, 672, 739, 769, 794
Turner, Harold, 298, 472, 705

Valois, Ninette de, 66, 67, 88, 125, 128, 135, 195, 246, 301, 341, 364, 390, 393, 400, 407, 411, 507, 523, 542, 545, 622, 623, 628, 629, 641, 665, 694, 814
Varkovitsky, V. A., 144
Velezzi, Enrique, 831
Verchinina, Nina, 636
Vilzak, Anatol, 744
Vynonen, V. I., 342

Waldeen, 191, 820, 821, 824, 832
Wallmann, Margarete, 42, 85, 384, 530, 784
Wilson, Frank, 717
Wojcikowski, Leon, 17, 426, 602

Yermolayev, Alexei N., 509

Zakharov, Rostislaw, 150, 316, 453
Zaylich, Piotr, 387, 511, 813
Zullig, Hans, 103
Zverev, Nicholas, 36, 182, 183, 251, 610, 644, 720, 749

PLATES

I. PICASSO : LE TRICORNE

1. BAKST : LA BELLE AU BOIS DORMANT

2. ALEXANDRE BENOIS : GISELLE

3. GONTCHAROVA : BOGATYRI

4. GONTCHAROVA : LA LITURGIE

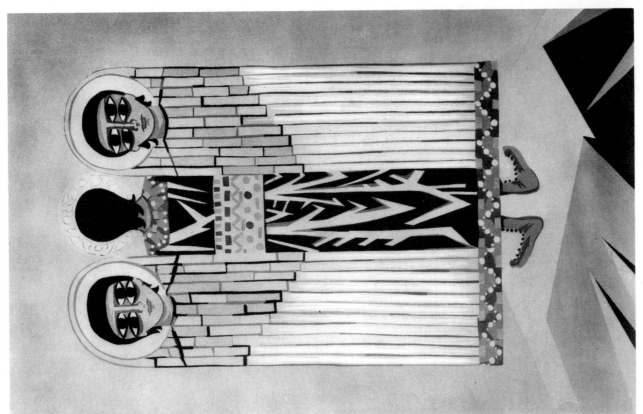

5. GONTCHAROVA : LA LITURGIE

6. GONTCHAROVA : LA LITURGIE

7. LARIONOW : LE RENARD

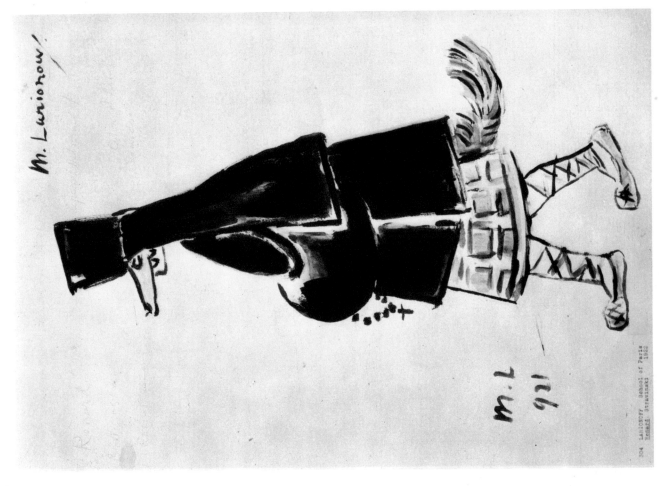

9. LARIONOW : LE RENARD

8. LARIONOW : LE RENARD

IO.   SOUDEIKINE : PAGANINI

11. SOUDEIKINE : LES NOCES

12. SOUDEIKINE : LES NOCES

13. DOBUJINSKY : RUSSIAN SOLDIER

15. DOBUJINSKY : MADEMOISELLE ANGOT

14. DOBUJINSKY : RUSSIAN SOLDIER

16.   DOBUJINSKY : BALLET IMPERIAL

Boris Aronson

17. ARONSON : SNOWMAIDEN

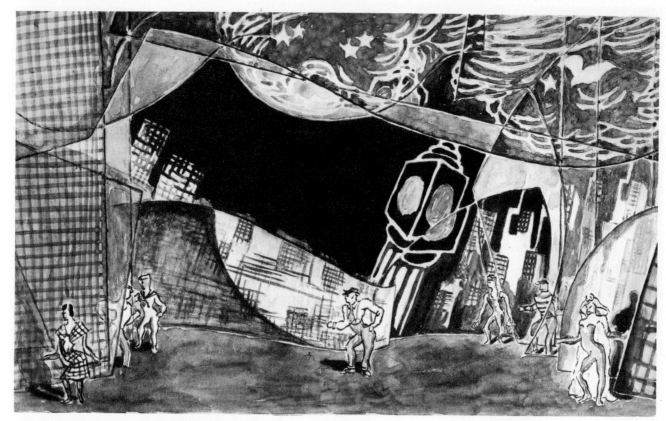

18. ARONSON: THE GREAT AMERICAN GOOF

19. ARONSON: THE RED POPPY

20. REMISOFF : GOLD STANDARD

21. REMISOFF : AN AMERICAN IN PARIS

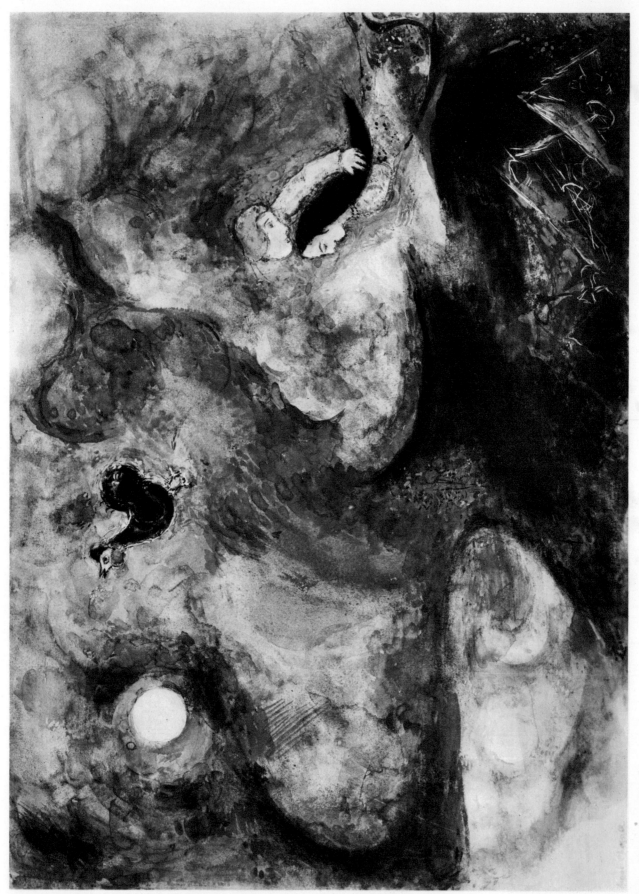

22. CHAGALL : ALEKO

II. BRAQUE : LES FÂCHEUX

24. CHAGALL : ALEKO

25. CHAGALL : ALEKO

27. CHAGALL: ALEKO

26. CHAGALL: ALEKO

29. CHAGALL : FIREBIRD

28. CHAGALL : FIREBIRD

30. CHAGALL : FIREBIRD

31. CHAGALL : FIREBIRD

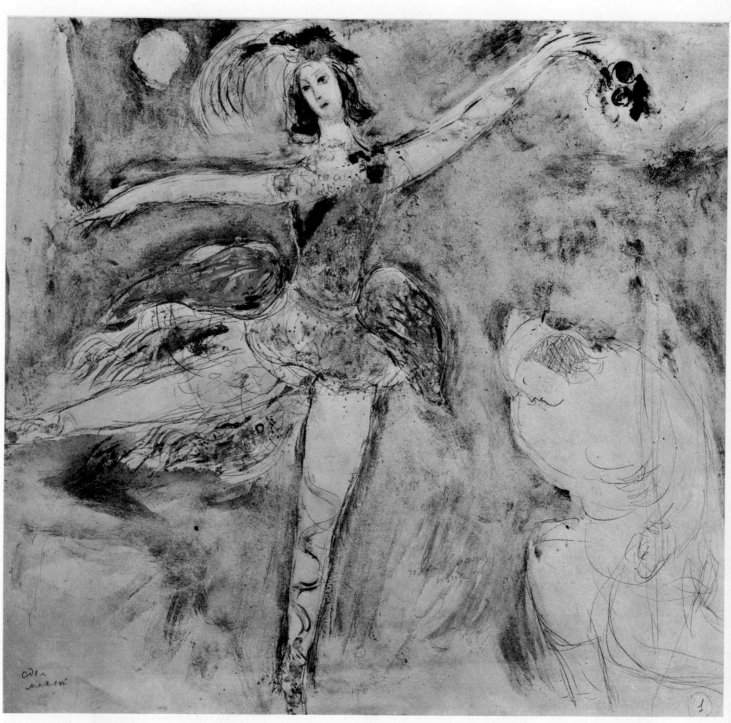

32. CHAGALL : FIREBIRD

33. PICASSO : LE TRICORNE

34. PICASSO: CUADRO FLAMENCO

35. PICASSO : CUADRO FLAMENCO

36. PICASSO : TRAIN BLEU

37. PICASSO : PARADE

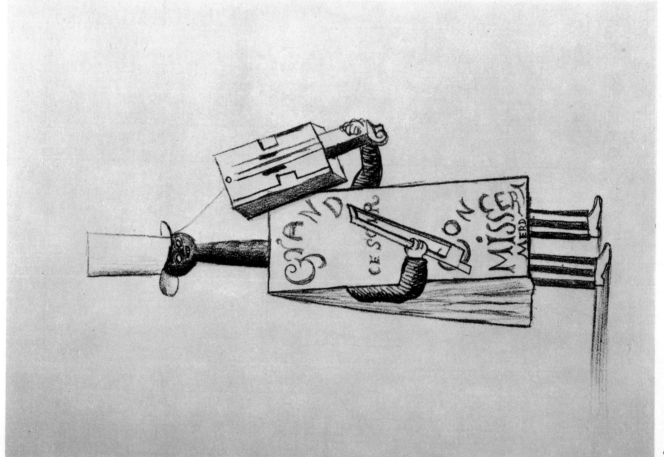

40. PICASSO : LE TRICORNE

III. DALI : LABYRINTH

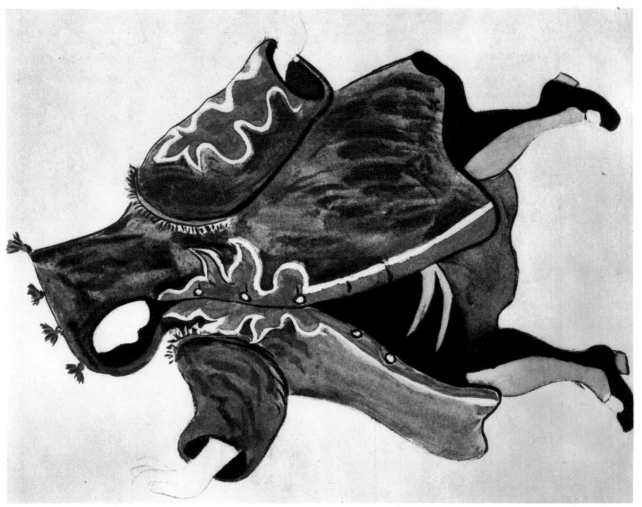

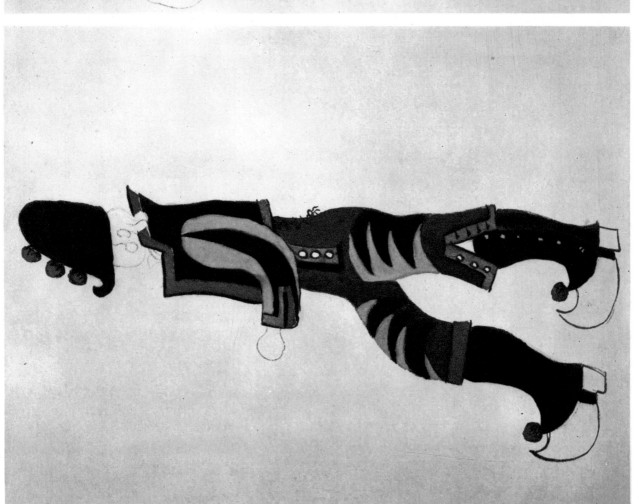

45. PICASSO : MERCURE

46. PICASSO : MERCURE

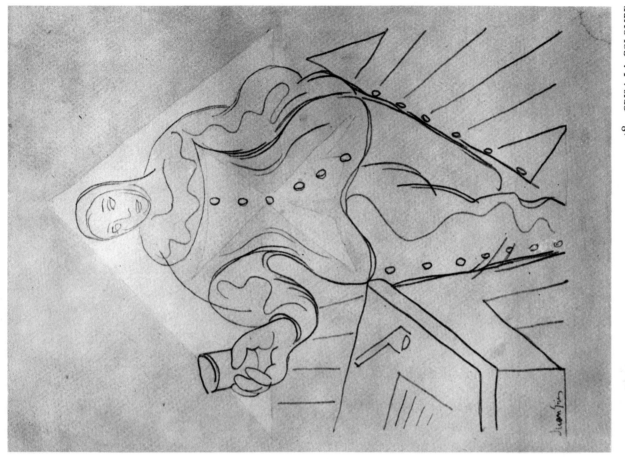

49. PRUNA : LES MATELOTS

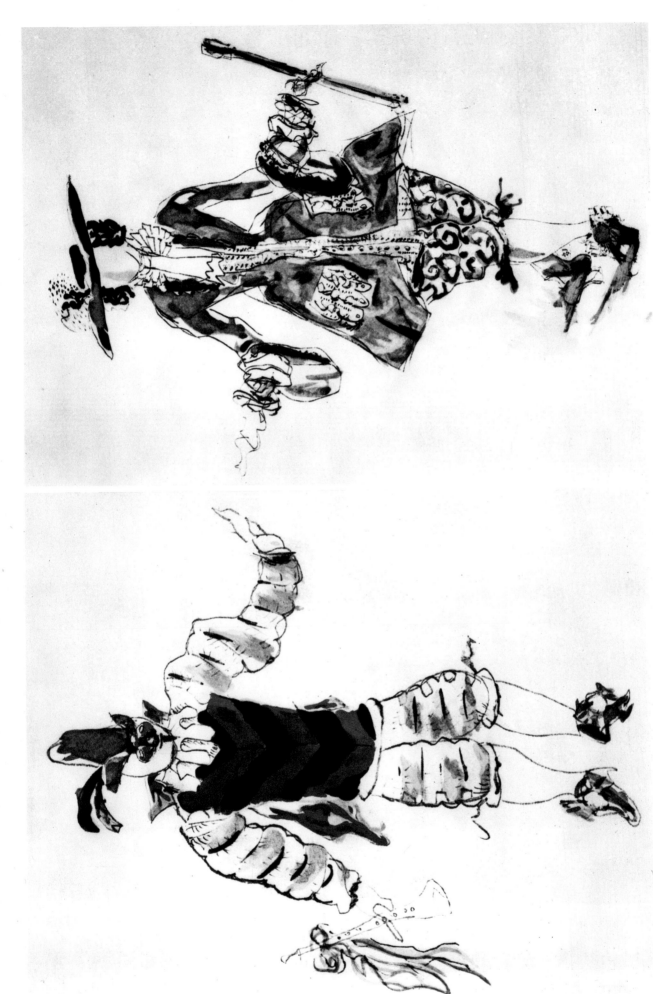

53. BRAQUE : LES FÂCHEUX

54. BRAQUE : LES FÂCHEUX

55. BRAQUE : LES FÂCHEUX

56. MATISSE : LE CHANT DU ROSSIGNOL

57. DERAIN : FASTES

58. DERAIN : FASTES

59. DERAIN : LA BOUTIQUE FANTASQUE

61. BÉRARD : SYMPHONIE FANTASTIQUE

63. BÉRARD : SYMPHONIE FANTASTIQUE

62. BÉRARD : SYMPHONIE FANTASTIQUE

65. BÉRARD : COSTUME FOR HARLEQUIN

64. BÉRARD : SYMPHONIE FANTASTIQUE

66. BÉRARD : LES ELFES   67. BÉRARD : LES ELFES

IV.　BÉRARD : THE SEVENTH SYMPHONY

68. LAURENCIN : LES BICHES

70. LAURENCIN : LES BICHES

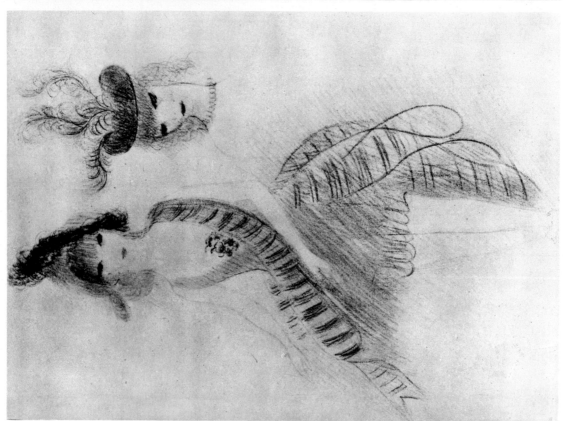

69. LAURENCIN : LES BICHES

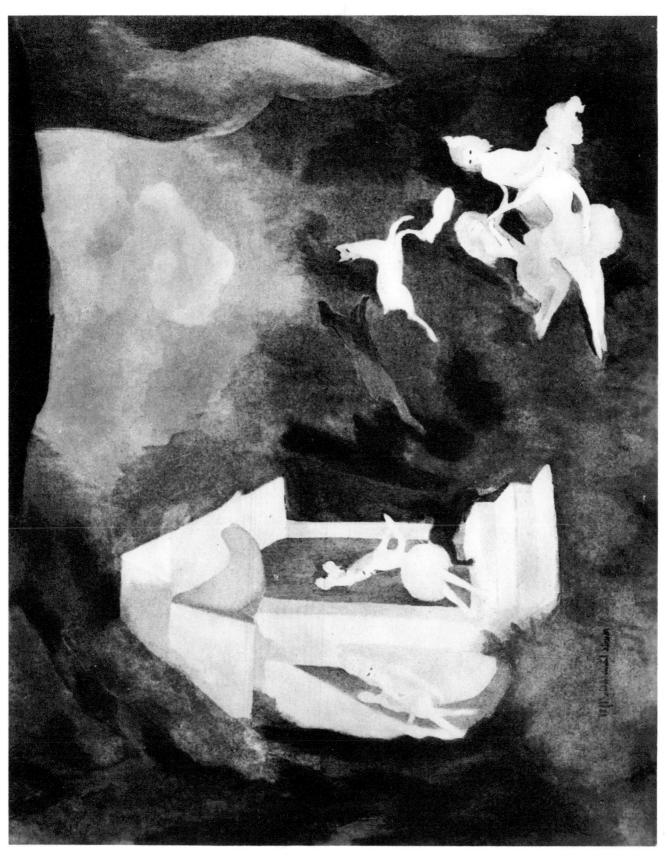

71. LAURENCIN : LES BICHES

73. VERTÈS . BLUEBEARD

72. VERTÈS : BLUEBEARD

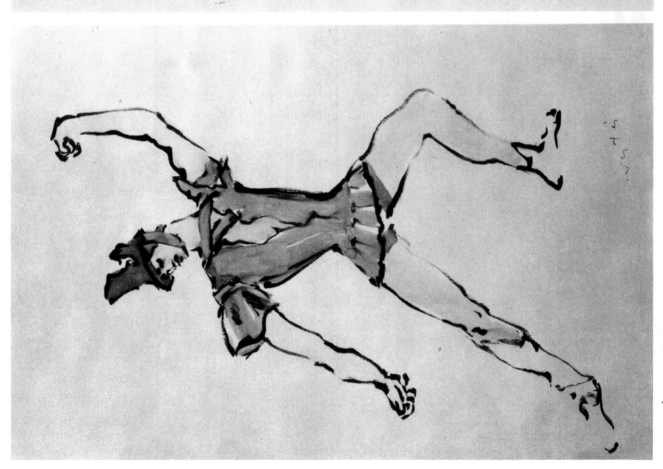

75. VERTÈS : BRAHMS VARIATIONS

74. VERTÈS : BRAHMS VARIATIONS

76. VERTÈS : BLUEBEARD

77. BAUCHANT : APOLLON MUSAGÈTE

78. BAUCHANT: APOLLON MUSAGÈTE

79. DE CHIRICO : LE BAL

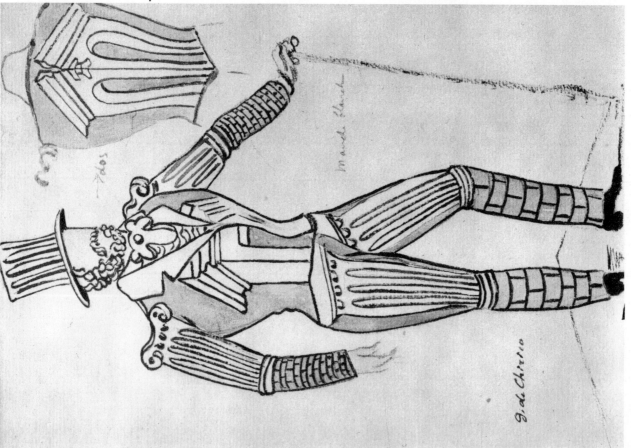

81. DE CHIRICO : LE BAL

80. DE CHIRICO : LE BAL

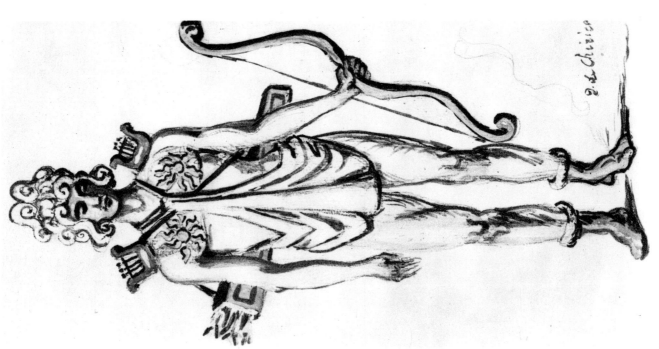

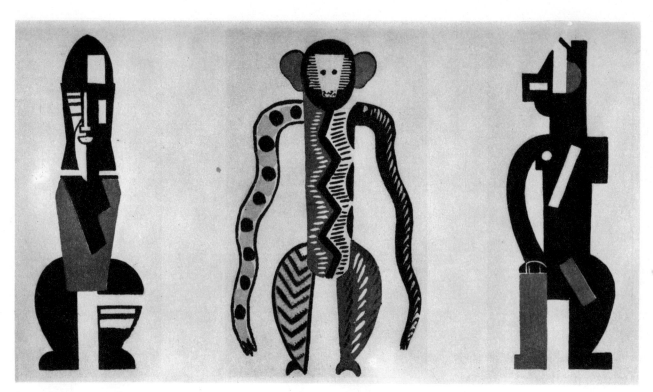

84. LÉGER : LA CRÉATION DU MONDE

85. LÉGER : LA CRÉATION DU MONDE

86. LÉGER : LA CRÉATION DU MONDE

87. LÉGER : LA CRÉATION DU MONDE

88. MASSON : LES PRÉSAGES

89. BERMAN : DEVIL'S HOLIDAY

90.　BERMAN : DEVIL'S HOLIDAY

V.   TCHELITCHEW : THE CAVE OF SLEEP

91. BERMAN : ICARE

93. BERMAN : LE BOURGEOIS GENTILHOMME

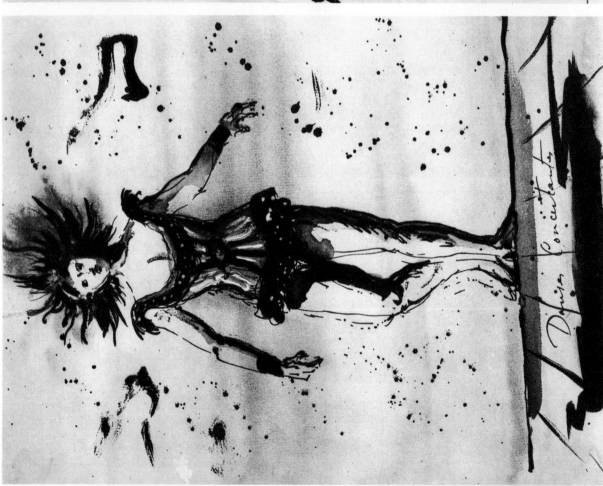

92. BERMAN : DANSES CONCERTANTES

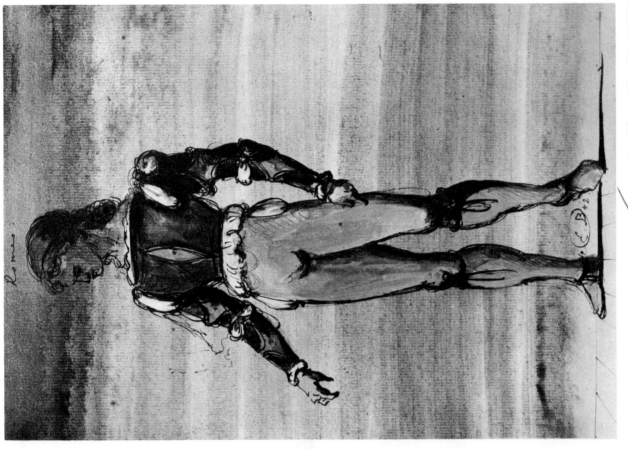

95. BERMAN: ROMEO AND JULIET

94. BERMAN: ROMEO AND JULIET

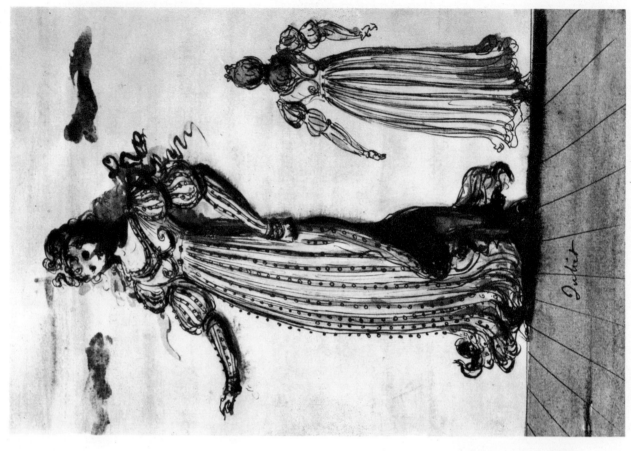

97. BERMAN : ROMEO AND JULIET

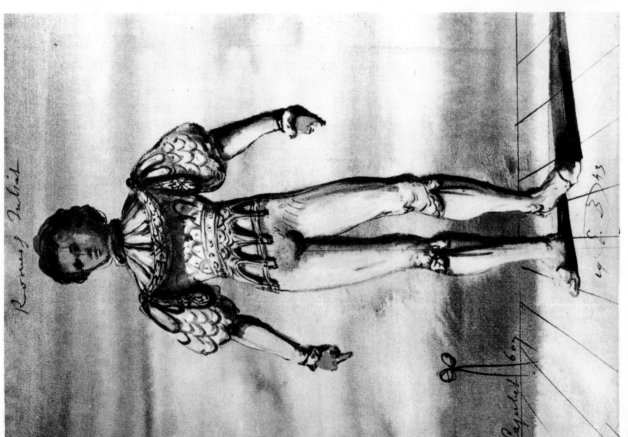

96. BERMAN : ROMEO AND JULIET

98.   TCHELITCHEW : THE CAVE OF SLEEP

101. TCHELITCHEW : CONCERTO

102. TCHELITCHEW : ORPHEUS

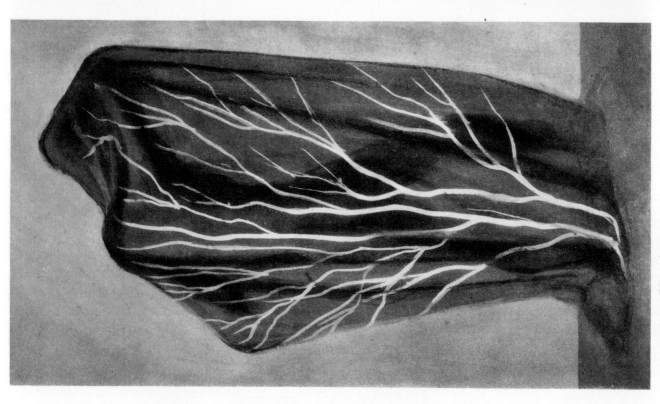

105. TCHELITCHEW : APOLLON MUSAGÈTE

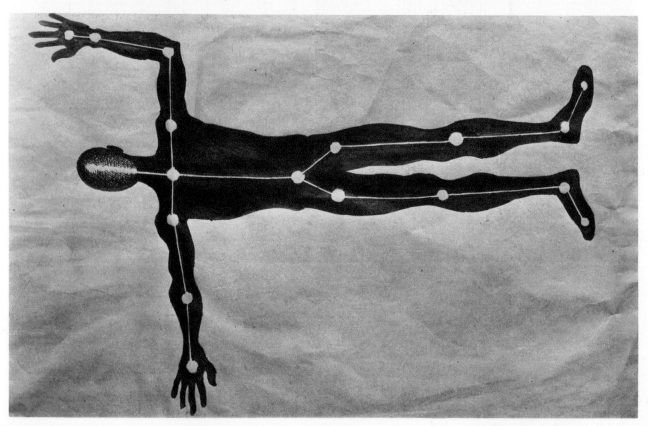

107. TCHELITCHEW : ODE

108. CASSANDRE : LE CHEVALIER ET LA DAMOISELLE

109. CASSANDRE : LE CHEVALIER ET LA DAMOISELLE

110. CASSANDRE : AUBADE

111. COLIN : SCULPTURE NÈGRE

113. PORTINARI : IARA

112. LURÇAT : JARDIN PUBLIC

114. BASALDUA : LE TRICORNE

115. BASALDUA : LE TRICORNE

VI. BERMAN : DANSES CONCERTANTES

116. BASALDUA : LA BOÎTE À JOUJOUX

117. BASALDUA : ALLELUIA

118. MÉRIDA : CINCO DANCAS EN RITMO BULGARO   119. MÉRIDA : CINCO DANCAS EN RITMO BULGARO

120. MÉRIDA : CINCO DANCAS EN RITMO BULGARO

121. MÉRIDA : CIRCO ORRIN

122. MÉRIDA : CIRCO ORRIN

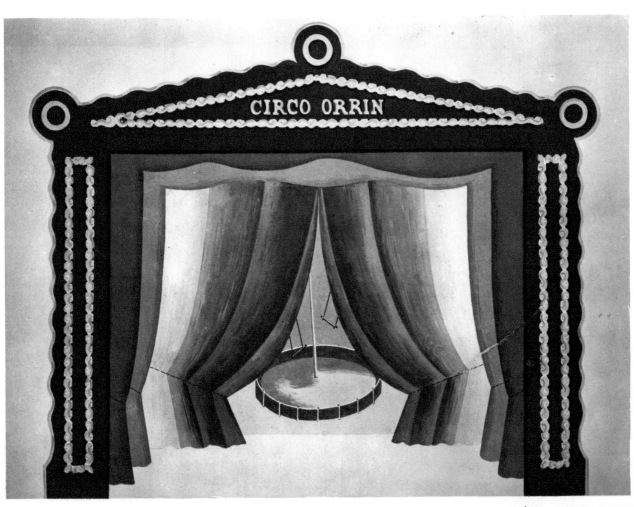

123. MÉRIDA : CIRCO ORRIN

124. RIVERA : H.P.

125. RIVERA : H.P.

126. RIVERA : H.P.

127. OROZCO : PAUSA

128. OROZCO : UMBRAL

129. OROZCO : PAUSA

130. OROZCO : UMBRAL

131. DE DIEGO : SONATAS ESPAÑOLAS

132. DE DIEGO : SONATAS ESPAÑOLAS

133. DE DIEGO : SONATAS ESPAÑOLAS

134. JUNYER: LA NUIT DE LA ST. JEAN

135. JUNYER: THE CUCKOLD'S FAIR

139. DALI : MAD TRISTAN

140. DALI: ROMEO AND JULIET

141. DALI: ROMEO AND JULIET

142. DALI : CAFÉ DE CHINITAS

143. DALI : CAFÉ DE CHINITAS

144. DALI: SENTIMENTAL COLLOQUY

145. DALI: SENTIMENTAL COLLOQUY

146. DALI: SENTIMENTAL COLLOQUY

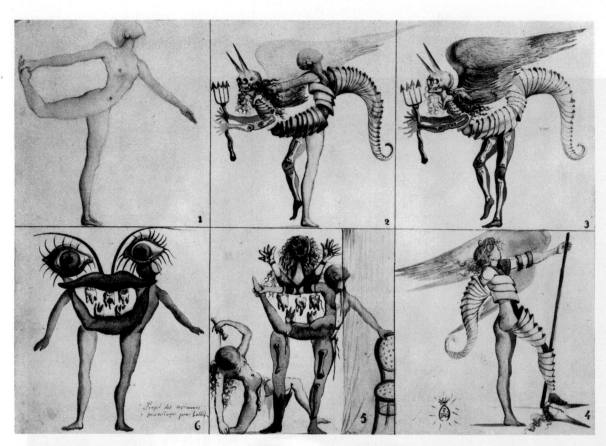

147. DALI : MYSTERIA

148. DALI : MYSTERIA

VII. DE CHIRICO : LA JARRE

149. DALI : MYSTERIA

150. SCHLEMMER: THE TRIADIC BALLET

151. HEYTHUM: BAL DES MANNEQUINS

154. AYRTON : LE FESTIN DE L'ARAIGNÉE

155. AYRTON : LE FESTIN DE L'ARAIGNÉE

157. HECKROTH : PANDORA

156. HECKROTH : PANDORA

159. HECKROTH : A SPRING TALE

158. HECKROTH : A SPRING TALE

160. HURRY : HAMLET

164. HURRY : LE LAC DES CYGNES

163. HURRY : LE LAC DES CYGNES

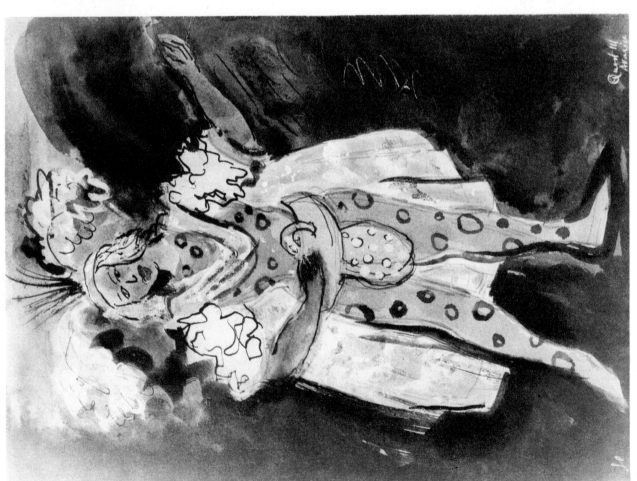

167. PIPER: THE QUEST

168. PIPER: THE QUEST

169. FURSE : THE PROSPECT BEFORE US

170. FURSE : THE PROSPECT BEFORE US

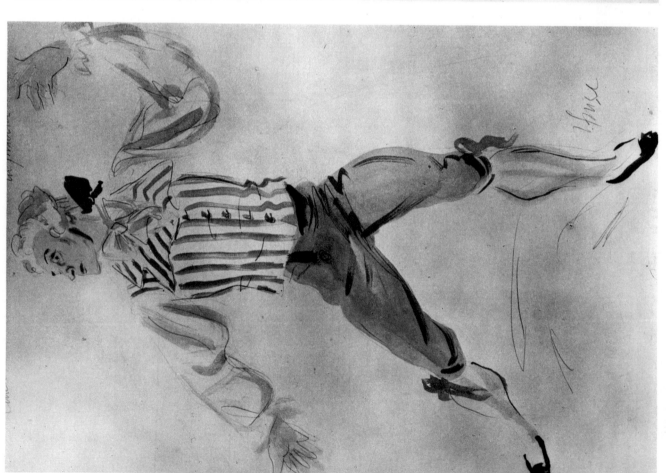

175. BURRA : MIRACLE IN THE GORBALS

176. BURRA : MIRACLE IN THE GORBALS

VIII. CHAGALL : FIREBIRD

177. WILSON : UN-SONGE

178. WHISTLER : THE RAKE'S PROGRESS

180. NASH : THE TRUTH ABOUT THE RUSSIAN DANCERS

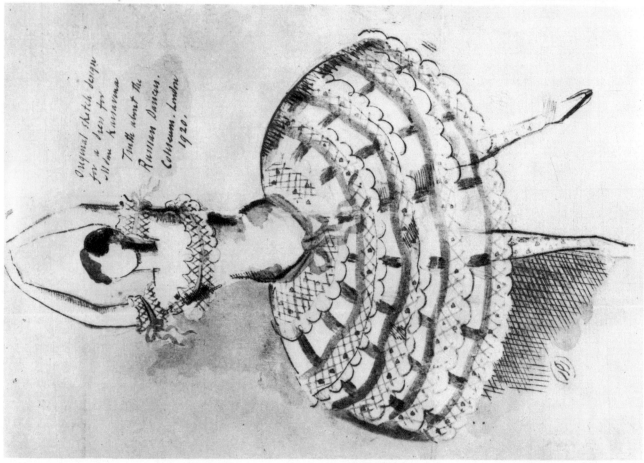

179. NASH : THE TRUTH ABOUT THE RUSSIAN DANCERS

182. NADIA BENOIS: LADY INTO FOX

181. NADIA BENOIS: LADY INTO FOX

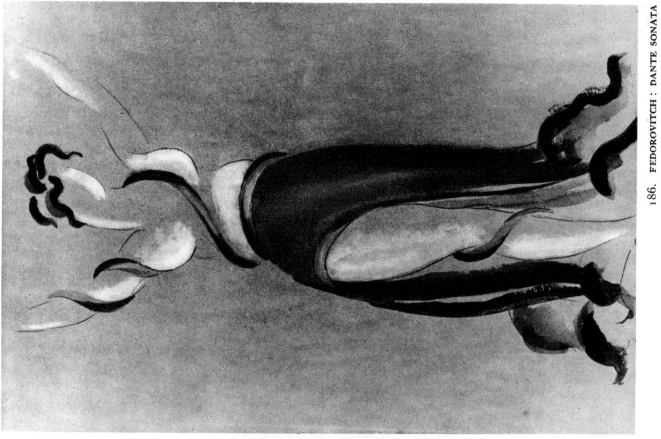

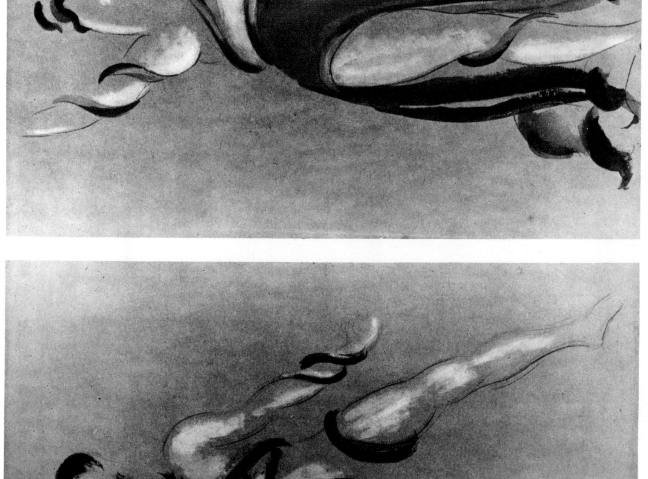

187. JONES : SKYSCRAPERS

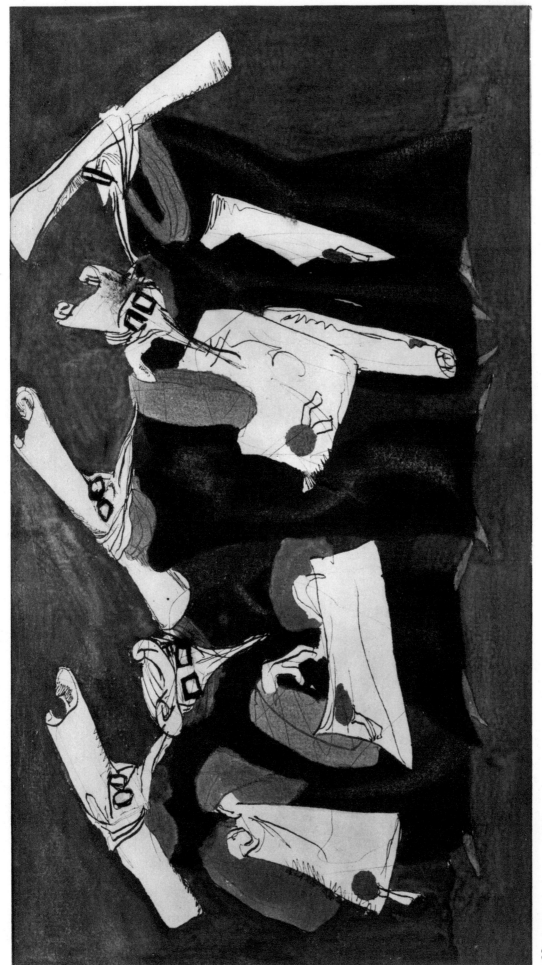

188. JONES : TIL EULENSPIEGEL

189. BREININ : UNDERTOW

190. BREININ : UNDERTOW

191. MIELZINER : PILLAR OF FIRE

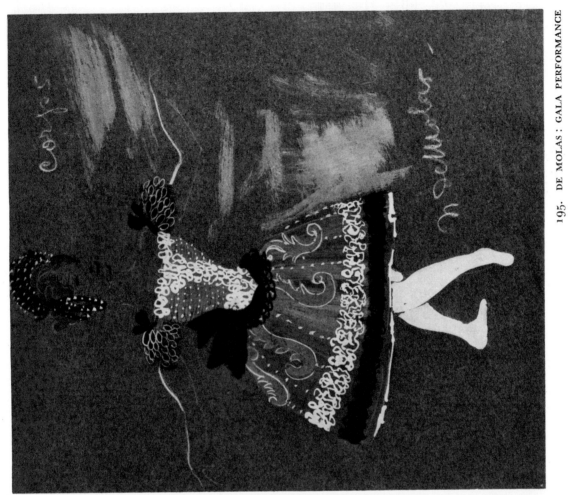

195. DE MOLAS : GALA PERFORMANCE

194. DE MOLAS : GALA PERFORMANCE

196.   DE MOLAS : CAPRICCIOSO

197. DE MOLAS : BLACK RITUAL

198. SMITH : FANCY FREE

199. SMITH : SARATOGA

200. SMITH : RODEO

201. SMITH : RODEO

202. SMITH : RODEO